BIOGRAPHY OF AN IDEA

The Story of Mutual Fire and Casualty Insurance

THE FATHER OF INSURANCE IN AMERICA

Benjamin Franklin was the motivating force in founding the Philadelphia Contributionship for the Insurance of Houses from Loss by Fire, the first successful insurance company established in America. Founded in 1752, this mutual company is today among the country's strongest insurance institutions. Original of the above likeness is in the collection of the Mutual Assurance Company for Insuring Houses from Loss by Fire, the second oldest insurance company in America.

BIOGRAPHY OF AN IDEA

The Story of Mutual Fire and Casualty Insurance

by

JOHN BAINBRIDGE

Garden City, New York
DOUBLEDAY & COMPANY, INC.
1952

Library of Congress Catalog Card Number: 52–5748

PRINTED IN THE UNITED STATES
AT
THE COUNTRY LIFE PRESS, GARDEN CITY, N.Y.

FIRST EDITION

To
CRAIG B. HAZLEWOOD

Acknowledgments

The author wishes to acknowledge with appreciation the work of Mrs. Barbara Kerr, Mrs. Marshall Holleb and Mr. Richard Purviance, who assisted in gathering material for this book.

He also wishes to thank the scores of mutual companies that lent their early records and documents and provided an abundance of other useful information.

Finally, he wishes to thank Mrs. Eleanor Hauser for her secretarial assistance in preparing the manuscript.

Contents

Illustrations

BIOGRAPHY OF AN IDEA

The Story of Mutual Fire and Casualty Insurance

CHAPTER I

A Triumph of Human Thought

ALL human history, as H. G. Wells has observed, is in essence the history of ideas. Since the beginning of civilization, ideas have ruled the world. Every nation has brought forth tyrants and benefactors. Their names are written with a bold flourish on the pages of history. Yet in the long perspective of time they are seen to have been but instruments for translating ideas into action. The nations that have prospered most and lasted longest are those that have produced the greatest number of the greatest ideas. To the Western world, the greatest ideas have always been those that contribute most to man's freedom and security. One of the most notable and practical of these is the idea of insurance, an idea that has been described as "the victory of human thought over the rude violence of life."

Though the roots of the insurance idea are buried deep in the past, it has reached its fullest flowering in modern times. In its technical development and world-wide expansion, insurance has made more progress in the last hundred years than in the previous thousand. Its rise as a social force has paralleled the rise of capitalism and the extension of the democratic system. In important measure it has made both possible. Insurance is indispensable to a free economy and a free society because it not only protects the values produced by men and women who work for themselves but fosters in them the confidence to produce more. What oxygen is to the air, insurance is to the economic and social life of our time.

Insurance being part and parcel of the democratic system, it is not surprising that the idea has been more widely adopted in this country than in any other. The American predilection for insurance amounts to a national trait. This is strikingly demonstrated by the fact that more than eighty million Americans own life insurance policies. Altogether these policies add up to $214 billion of insurance, 70 per cent of all the life insurance in force in the world.

On their purchases of insurance of all kinds the people and business enterprises of the United States spent $13.5 billion in 1949. That is a little more than one quarter of the amount that Americans spent that year on food, and nearly three quarters as much as they spent on shoes and clothing. Insurance is plainly one of the staples of American life.

In size and scope insurance ranks as one of the country's big businesses. Two hundred years ago there was one American insurance company; today there are 4,480. The insurance business gives employment to 652,000 persons; settled in one place, they would make a city bigger than Minneapolis or a state with a population greater than Montana's. More people are employed in the insurance business than in the steel industry.

The combined assets of all American insurance companies have now reached the staggering total of $72 billion. The total budget of the federal government in 1949 was, comparatively, a mere $40 billion. The income of all American insurance companies in 1949 came to $16.5 billion. That is nearly twice the 1949 income of American railroads, and only $1.5 billion under the amount the federal government collected that year in personal income taxes.

Useful as these figures are in picturing the broad design of American insurance, they cannot convey what insurance means to the individual policyholder. The basic function of insurance is to provide security, and that is a concept that neither figures nor words can adequately describe. However, one impressive indication of the performance of American insurance companies is the money they annually disburse to their policyholders in benefits and in payments to make good individual losses. In 1949, these benefits and payments amounted to $6.7 billion—an average of $18 million every day of the year.

If the free and wide acceptance of an idea is proof of its merit, insurance is one of America's most valued institutions. It is also, paradoxically, one of the least understood. To the vast majority of Americans, insurance is almost as mysterious as love. Recent polls have shown that more than 90 per cent of the people who own insurance policies neither read nor fully understand them; 55 per cent do not know one kind of company from another; and 35 per cent forget even the name of the company that insures them. No self-respecting citizen would willingly admit that he doesn't have a fair grasp of the automobile business, the railroads, banks, and other leading enterprises that affect his existence. But toward insurance, which impinges on nearly every aspect of his daily life, he inclines to the peculiar position that ignorance is bliss.

This attitude, though curious, is in some measure understandable. People acquire their knowledge and form their opinion of a business mainly through their personal contact with it. Nearly everybody considers himself well informed on public utilities because of his direct, daily contact with the services they provide, and he is reminded by his monthly bills of what he has bought. His contact with the insurance company, on the other hand, is customarily no oftener than once or twice a year, and even then it is frequently indirect, the business being handled through an agent. Furthermore, aside from his policy, put away in a drawer or file, the purchaser of insurance has no concrete evidence of what he has bought. Insurance is an intangible. It appeals to none of the five senses. A person who buys insurance buys a promise, and a promise, however secure and binding, is not easy to visualize.

Another distinctive and sometimes confusing characteristic of insurance is the fact that it produces no raw materials, fabricates no goods, and, in fact, fits into none of the four conventional divisions of economics—Production, Exchange, Distribution, or Consumption. Insurance, which economists prefer to call risk and risk-bearing, is in theory a separate, fifth division of the science of economics. In practice, however, insurance affects every phase of our economic existence because it protects wealth in every step of its creation from producer to consumer. There is no substitute for insurance.

However complicated some of its aspects may be, insurance is essentially a simple proposition. As Calvin Coolidge once remarked, "Insurance is part charity and part business, but all common sense." Basically, insurance is a plan by which the many make good the losses of the few. It scatters the effects of the hazards which beset human affairs so widely among the whole community that no member is heavily burdened. It is in essence a modern refinement of the age-old custom of passing the hat to relieve distress. Nowadays, of course, the hat is passed before the untoward event occurs, and as a result it is no longer necessary for a member of the community who suffers economic misfortune to rely on impulsive, erratic charity. Insurance makes recompense certain and equitable. It is the principle, an insurance executive has said, "which unites the fundamental law of practical economy—that he best serves humanity who best serves himself—with the counsel of St. Paul: 'Bear ye one another's burdens.'"

The practice of insurance involves the gathering of small, regular sums from the many to form a pool. The contributors agree that a loss to one will be treated as a loss to all. When losses occur, sums are drawn from the pool in line with this agreement. The machinery used to administer the pool is known as an insurance company.

There are several kinds of insurance companies. The two that most people have heard about are called mutual companies and stock companies. These two are most widely known because together they do 97 per cent of all the insurance business in this country. As the polls have shown, many people have trouble distinguishing between the two, probably because they have a number of major features in common.

In the first place, both mutual and stock companies engage in the four principal branches of insurance: fire, casualty, life, and marine. Second, both are subject to the general corporation and insurance laws of the states in which they operate. Third, they are both founded on the principle of mutuality. "The nature of all insurance is essentially mutual," a former New York commissioner of insurance has said, "because whether the carrier is of the so-called mutual or the stock-company type, the fundamental principle is that the many contribute small amounts and set up a common fund to pay the losses of the few. Insurance, whether stock or mutual, is the American version of the co-operative way of doing things."

Though mutuality is the heart of all insurance, the word "mutual," when applied to an insurance company, designates a kind of company that is essentially different from any other.

A mutual insurance company is owned and operated by its policyholders. It is run for their exclusive benefit. They *are* the company. There are no stockholders. Each policyholder is entitled to a voice in the affairs of the company. Together they elect its board of directors. They, in turn, elect the officers who serve as the active managers of the business. From its policyholders, in return for agreeing to secure them against loss, the company collects sums of money called premiums. Out of this fund and from income derived from investments the company pays the losses sustained by its policyholders and the expenses of running the business; it also sets up the reserves required by law or by good judgment for the safe operation of the company. What is left over is returned to the policyholders in the form of dividends. A mutual company sells insurance at cost.

The characteristics of mutual companies become clearer when compared with those of stock companies, the other major type of insurance organization. A stock insurance company is owned and controlled by the people and firms who have invested money in it. It is run for the purpose of giving its stockholders a return on their investment. The stockholders, who need not be policyholders in the company, elect the directors, and they select the officers to manage it. In a stock insurance company, as in a mutual company, the funds collected as premiums and those derived from investments are used to pay losses and expenses and to set up the reserves required for the safe operation of the enterprise. What remains from these funds is distributed by a stock company in the form of dividends to its stockholders rather than to its policyholders. A stock company sells insurance at cost—plus a profit to the owners of the business.

Mutual insurance, it is generally agreed, is insurance in its purest form. It is also the oldest form known to America. A mutual insurance company was doing business in this country twenty-four years before the signing of the Declaration of Independence. The first successful company was founded in Philadelphia in 1752. The prime mover in its establishment was Benjamin Franklin. That company, bearing the wonderfully descriptive name, the Philadelphia Contributionship for the Insurance of Houses from Loss by Fire, is doing business today, two centuries later.

During the two hundred years that have passed since the founding of the pioneer company, mutual insurance has flourished like the nation itself. An American institution that antedates even the Constitution, mutual insurance has developed rapidly and soundly through the years to keep pace with the changing needs of an expanding nation. Two hundred years ago, mutual insurance provided protection against fire and nothing else. Today it provides protection against fire and practically everything else. It renders its myriad services through companies that write life and marine insurance and those that write fire and casualty insurance.

This book tells the story of mutual fire insurance and mutual casualty insurance. They are, respectively, the oldest and the youngest branches of mutual insurance in America, but their story is essentially one. The lifeblood of each is the mutual idea. A biography of that idea, like the biography of a man, can perhaps best throw light on its subject by looking first at its interesting ancestors.

CHAPTER II

Heritage of an Idea

FIRE insurance is a direct descendant of marine insurance, whose ancestry can, in turn, be traced to antiquity. Compared to marine insurance, which was being practiced by the Phoenicians and the Greeks around 1000 B.C., fire insurance is a youthful institution. It was born in England two hundred and eighty-five years ago. Its birth was one of the few happy results of the Great Fire of London in 1666.

On Sunday night, September 2, 1666, the King's baker, who is known to history as "one Faryner," left a pile of fagots carelessly by the open oven in his house on Pudding Lane. By Monday morning, the Great Fire of London was under way. It blazed for five days, eventually spreading over an area of 436 acres. One of the few eyewitness accounts of the holocaust was left by Samuel Pepys, a public official who had already begun keeping his famous diary. "Having stayed, and in an hour's time seen the fire rage every way," Pepys recorded, "and nobody, to my sight, endeavouring to quench it, but to remove their goods and leave all to the fire. I to Whitehall." After an audience with the King, Pepys returned with instructions for the Lord Mayor. He was given authority by the King to tear down any buildings, the removal of which might arrest the spread of the flames. Nothing effective was done, and the fire raged on. Before burning itself out, it had laid waste 13,200 houses, 89 churches, including St. Paul's Cathedral, the Custom House, the Royal Exchange, and dozens of other public buildings. Only six people perished in the flames, but hundreds died from shock and exposure. The heart of London, where three quarters of the city's buildings had stood, was reduced to ashes. According to *Stow's Survey*, the total property loss was well over £10,689,000.

The last embers of the fire had scarcely flickered out before fire insurance had sprung into existence. It was the brain child of an eccentric London doctor named Nicholas Barbon. His father, a moderately well-to-do leather merchant and an ardent lay preacher who was known as Praise-God Barbon, conferred upon his son the full baptismal name of "If-Christ-had-not-died-thou-hadst-been-damned Nicholas Barbon." This was later conveniently shortened by some of his distrusting contemporaries to "Damned Nicholas Barbon."

Although trained as a doctor and elected an honorary fellow of the College of Physicians, Barbon seems never to have devoted much time to medicine. "He was a man, I suppose, better known as a builder than a physician," Daniel Defoe wrote of him. Both before and after the fire Barbon was involved in building houses, in the manner that would today be described as speculative. Where his money came from or how he managed his financial affairs nobody was ever sure. Personally and professionally, Barbon was always something of a mystery man. He gave evidence of believing that three can keep a secret if two are dead. In his building operations he was frequently in financial straits, but what he lacked in capital he made up in self-confidence, and he had a showy and engaging manner that helped him carry off daring ventures. He comported himself with considerable dignity and made a habit, one of his contemporaries remarked, of being "as finely and richly dressed as a lord of the bedchamber on his birthday." He favored good living and rich eating. "The belly must not be starved to clothe the back-part," he sometimes remarked while feasting. There is little doubt that Barbon took good care of himself both fore and aft.

Within a year after the Great Fire, when Barbon was twenty-seven, he set up an "office for insuring houses and buildings." At that time he was building houses on a rather extensive scale, and his insurance system probably consisted in inducing each of those to whom he sold a property to pay something extra in return for Barbon's promise to rebuild the house in case of fire. Fortune evidently favored this enterprise, for he branched out to offer a similar proposition to the owners of houses other than those he had built. Barbon operated his insurance scheme as a one-man show for thirteen years. During this time he was an individual underwriter. His system was much the same as the one then in use in marine underwriting, but whereas marine underwriters customarily distributed the risk, Barbon took it all. Since his office was in his hat and he was operating on a strictly *caveat emptor* basis, there are no existing records showing the manner in which he conducted his business. From what is known of his character, it can safely be assumed that his charge for insurance was all the traffic would bear and that the equitable settlement of his losses was problematical.

Deciding, in 1680, to abandon his one-man venture, Barbon formed with several other men a new insurance project, which they called the Fire Office. They took space in a newspaper to advertise its service. "There is a new office to be kept at the backside of the Royal Exchange, London, and will be opened on Thursday next," the advertisement said. "They do undertake for a very reasonable rate to secure the houses in London and the suburbs thereof from fire, and if burnt down to build them again at the cost of the office, for which end is provided a considerable bank of money and a fund of free land, to such value as will secure those that agree with the Office. There being now in print a particular thereof, we need not give you any further account."

The Fire Office was the first stock company organized to write fire insurance. It was capitalized at about $200,000. Barbon and his associates expected that interest on this fund would not only pay all the company's losses by fire but leave them a good margin of profit. The company insured houses to a stated amount for a fixed premium. For reasons best known to the promoters, the premiums were based on the rental value of a property; this was assumed to be 10 per cent of its actual value. On brick houses the premium was 2½ per cent of the yearly rental, and on frame houses it was 5 per cent. Aside from considering the construction feature, the Fire Office gave little thought to discrimination among risks; the object was to gather in all the risks they could and hope for a generally satisfactory financial result. After three years the company had some 4,000 houses insured; it had taken $90,000 in premiums and paid claims amounting to $35,000. Since the wily Barbon was in charge of paying claims, they may not have been allowed to become excessive. His house, it has been recorded, was not infrequently "crowded like a court with suitors for money," who were lightly dismissed by the high-handed doctor as "litigious knaves."

During its first four years the Fire Office had the field virtually to itself. Its monopoly was challenged but once. That effort was made by the City of London, which set aside municipal funds and property to establish an insurance scheme patterned after that of Barbon and his colleagues. From 1681 to 1683 the office sponsored by the government wrote insurance on houses within the city. The venture was not successful and was shortly abandoned by court order, which questioned the legal right of the city to engage in the business. Thus ended the first experiment in state insurance.

Within a year after the failure of the governmental enterprise, the Fire Office was obliged to take account of a more formidable competitor. It called itself the Friendly Society and issued circulars telling of "a new way or method for securing houses from any considerable loss by fire by way of subscription and mutual contribution." People who insured according to this new way were required, first, to pay an annual premium, the size of which depended on the amount of insurance taken and whether the house insured was brick or frame; second, to deposit in advance with the Society a sum equaling five annual premiums; and third, to agree to contribute toward the settlement of each fire loss of the Society up to an amount not exceeding $7.50 on each $500 of insurance carried. The Friendly Society, though it used the word "mutual" in its literature, was not a mutual company. The policyholders were obligated to share each other's losses, but they had no voice in the management of the enterprise and no share in the profits. These went to the managers, or "undertakers" as they were called, who assured themselves of some return by making a charge of 35¢ on each $500 of insurance for "expenses."

The Friendly Society, like the Fire Office, took all the business it could get, accepting bad risks as well as good in the hope that the average would work in their favor. A little more than a year after its founding, the Society had 1,265 houses insured. Barbon and his associates, taking alarm, promptly went into action and attempted to stifle their competitor, using methods that have changed little in the subsequent two and a half centuries. They circulated broadsides alleging that in the Friendly Society the "deposit money is not repaid to the members according to agreement" and proclaiming that there could be "no insurance unless there is a fund settled that is both certain and able to make good the loss." The Friendly Society replied that "the fund in the Fire Office is neither greater nor the insurance cheaper than in the Friendly Society."

Propaganda failing, Barbon and the Fire Office officials decided to see what they could do through governmental channels. They appealed to the Crown for an order compelling the Friendly Society to cease writing insurance. All the Fire Office asked was the exclusive privilege of conducting a fire insurance business for thirty-one years. After several hearings had been held, it was announced that "His Majesty in Council, having fully considered what was alleged by them, and it appearing to the Board that the way of insuring houses by the Friendly Society is of more benefit and satisfaction to the public than by the Fire Office, His Majesty is graciously pleased to declare his pleasure that Letters Patent be granted to the Friendly Society." In other words, the Fire Office was ordered to close up shop.

This was indeed a blow to Barbon, but being a man who "could endure all manner of affronts and be as tame as a lamb," he smoothly talked himself out of his predicament. The Crown subsequently granted Letters Patent to the Fire Office "in order to preserve it from ruin," and a compromise scheme was devised by which Barbon's company and the Friendly Society were allowed to write insurance during alternate periods of three months each. This unwieldy measure was in effect for six years.

At the end of that time, Barbon's company, which had changed its name to the Phenix Office, embarked on a pseudomutual scheme of insurance. The details of its demise, like so many other things connected with the peculiar doctor who originally promoted it, are shrouded in mystery. The best authorities believe that it went to the wall during the period of the so-called South Sea Bubble, one of history's most fantastic speculative enterprises, and was swept away in the panic that occurred when the bubble burst in 1720. The details of Barbon's departure are well known. He died insolvent at the age of fifty-eight, and in his will instructed his executor not to pay any of his debts.

The first purely mutual fire insurance company was established in 1696. Its founders, of whom there were about a hundred, were largely master builders of London. They were moved by the desire to secure safer and cheaper insurance. Being builders, they no doubt had firsthand information about Barbon's buccaneering ventures and were not favorably impressed. Furthermore, they resented the fact that the Friendly Society posed as a mutual concern, requiring its policyholders to contribute to losses while denying them any participation in profits. The projectors of the first mutual were explicit on this point in their original announcement, which stated plainly that "the offices of insurance from loss by fire are for the private interest of the particular undertakers, who have made great advantage to themselves exclusive of all others concerned therein." As a remedy, the announcement concluded, and "to the end that all persons who are desirous to insure from loss by fire may be accommodated upon more equal and advantageous terms, this office is erected, wherein all are equal sharers, in profits as well as loss, in proportion to their insurance in the same."

Though the founders of the first mutual were devoted to economy, they turned spendthrift in selecting the name of their organization, which they called Contributors for Insuring Houses, Chambers or Rooms from Loss by Fire by Amicable Contributionship. It soon became known, however, as the Amicable Contributionship or, more widely, as the Hand-in-Hand. The latter derived from the emblem adopted by the organization—a hand clasping a hand—which was symbolic of its intent. Before commencing operations, the organizers of the Hand-in-Hand got together and drew up an elaborate charter, which they called a Deed of Settlement. This carefully worked out document, consisting of thirty "clauses" or bylaws, laid down in detail the rules by which the company was to be run.

In accordance with its Deed of Settlement, the Hand-in-Hand was managed by a group of twenty directors, who were elected by the policyholders. At the outset, the directors made it clear that the company would offer pickings for nobody, including themselves. A resolution passed at their first meeting forbade paying fees to directors. Not only did the directors serve without pay, they were fined a shilling for absence from any of the directors' meetings, which were held once a week. To keep expenses down, the directors put off for three years acquiring an office for the company; they met meanwhile and kept their books in the home of one or another of the directors. At length a room was engaged as an office for a yearly rental of five pounds sterling. The books of the company, as required by the Deed of Settlement, were always open to inspection by the policyholders. General meetings of all policyholders were held once a year for discussion of the company's affairs and election of directors. Members of the Hand-in-Hand, according to their Minute Book, even promulgated rules to guide their conduct at the general meetings. "No more than one to speak at a time," one of the rules declares. Another provides, "Every man after he has spoke his sentiment to sit down."

Insurance in the Hand-in-Hand cost less than half of what it did in either of the two other existing companies. Because the company was run to benefit only its members, the premiums were kept as low as possible. They were set at ten cents for each hundred dollars of insurance on brick buildings and double that on frame structures. Each policy was written for a term of seven years. Upon taking out a policy, a member was required to deposit with the company a sum roughly equivalent to seven years' premiums. The fund of money accumulated from these premium deposits was put out at interest. (Clause 12 of the Deed of Settlement forbade the directors to "lend or let any sum or sums of money" to any policyholder.) It was the hope of the founders—and one that was largely fulfilled—that income from investment of the premium deposits would pay most of the company's losses and expenses. Upon the termination of a policy, the member's deposit, after his share of losses and expenses had been deducted, was returned to him. If the company's operations provided profits, these were distributed annually among the policyholders. To add stability to the plan, each policyholder was liable to an assessment, in proportion to the amount of his insurance, if extra funds were required to pay losses. The Hand-in-Hand never levied an assessment.

In contrast to the promoters of previous insurance schemes, the organizers of the Hand-in-Hand had no interest in making their business mushroom. Since the company was not organized for profit, the quantity of policyholders was not nearly so important as their quality. The company accordingly did not solicit business, and the directors did not issue a policy to everyone who applied. Their aim was to insure only those who would try to protect their property from fire and, by holding down the losses, benefit themselves as well as every other member of the company.

Adhering to this principle of selectivity, the Hand-in-Hand grew slowly and conservatively during its formative years. In 1699, three years after its founding, it had issued 321 policies. The following year, despite paying losses totaling $2,600, the company paid a dividend amounting to 10¢ on each $100 of insurance, and the directors proudly announced that "members may expect another dividend in a little time."

As soon as the mutual idea of fire insurance had proved itself in practice, there was no holding it back. By 1732, the number of houses insured in the Hand-in-Hand had reached 45,873, and the company's total insurance in force amounted to £11,612,000. The Hand-in-Hand continued to prosper and led a useful, independent existence for more than two centuries, after which, in 1905, it was absorbed by the Commercial Union Assurance Company, Ltd., of London.

Like all sound ideas, the one pioneered by the Hand-in-Hand cast its influence far beyond the place in which it arose. Reports of its success, as well as accounts of the other experiments in fire insurance that had been made in England, were carried by travelers across the seas to the Colonies in America. When Benjamin Franklin and the other original projectors of fire insurance in the New World sought a model upon which to build their venture in the field, they chose the sturdiest and most successful—the Hand-in-Hand.

CHAPTER III

The Philadelphia Story—1

SOME EVENTS AT THE WIDOW PRATT'S

AS BEFITS the father of American insurance, Benjamin Franklin was, above all, a practical man. He worshiped wisdom, but he had no time for purely speculative reasoning. "The great uncertainty I found in metaphysical readings disgusted me," he wrote in his *Autobiography*, "and I quitted that kind of reading and study for others more satisfactory." Though Franklin was greatly admired by the profoundest philosophers of his time, he was never content to be a mere thinker. He was a tireless doer. "I have always believed," he wrote at the age of eighty-two, "that one man of tolerable abilities may work great changes and accomplish great affairs among mankind, if he first forms a good plan . . . and makes the execution of the same plan his sole study and business." No man of his century accomplished greater affairs among mankind than Franklin did, and very few since have been as truly eager as he was for the public good.

Practical ideas for social improvement appealed to Franklin even as a boy. His favorite reading during his early years (he read at five and taught himself to write at seven) were Daniel Defoe's *Essay on Projects* and Cotton Mather's *Essays to Do Good*. These two works, especially the first, were practical, down-to-earth dissertations on how to bring about civic improvements, such as the building of roads, the establishment of mutual-benefit societies for seamen and their widows, and the organization of insurance companies.

After two years of formal schooling Franklin, at the age of twelve, became an apprentice in his brother's newspaper and printing shop in Boston. When he was sixteen, he contributed to the paper a series of articles written in the form of letters to the editor and signed with the pseudonym, Silence Dogood, who was supposedly the thoughtful widow of a country parson. In his Dogood articles, Franklin not only entertained his readers but also, as a result of his voracious reading, gave them advice and practical suggestions for improving their lot through mutual undertakings. Concluding one of his articles, Franklin remarked, "I am humbly of the opinion that the country is ripe for many such friendly societies, whereby every man might help another, without any disservice to himself."

Chafing under the rough treatment meted out by his overbearing brother, Franklin left Boston when he was seventeen and made his way to Philadelphia. He obtained work there in the printing establishment run by Samuel Keimer. One of Franklin's first jobs was to set the type for a book written by Francis Rawle that bore the extremely provocative title, *Ways and Means for the Inhabitants of Delaware to Become Rich.* This was the first American book to mention the subject of insurance. It was Rawle's suggestion that the Loan-Office of Pennsylvania go into the business of insuring ships and cargoes and that its losses be paid out of the money collected as interest on the province's paper currency. The idea might be described as novel.

In 1724, Franklin went to England, where he worked for

nearly two years as a journeyman printer. Possessing an extraordinarily inquisitive mind, he no doubt learned during his stay abroad of the fire insurance schemes then in operation. By the time he returned to the Colonies, many of his ideas for civic betterment had matured, and he was ready to start putting them into practice.

Philadelphia provided fertile ground. When Franklin took up permanent residence there, the city had no firemen, police, paving, street lighting, or municipal sanitary services. The young printer took upon himself the task of correcting these as well as other shortcomings. He was then twenty.

In the next twenty-five years, owing to his manifold public-spirited activities, Franklin became the city's first citizen. He became the proprietor and editor of the *Pennsylvania Gazette,* a newspaper which had the largest circulation of any in America. He wrote and published *Poor Richard's Almanack,* which contained his witty and worldly-wise sayings (e.g., "Keep your eyes wide open before marriage; half shut afterwards") and was the most popular periodical in the Colonies. He founded the Library Company of Philadelphia, the first circulating library in America. He established the American Philosophical Society. He founded the Junto, a society of enterprising young men of Philadelphia who banded together for mutual help and public benefit. He organized an academy, which developed into the University of Pennsylvania. He was elected a member of the City Council as well as a member of the Pennsylvania Assembly, to which he was re-elected for fourteen terms. He raised the money to build Philadelphia's first hospital. He married, engaged in a prodigious amount of reading and correspondence, and in his spare time taught himself French, Italian, Spanish, and Latin.

Franklin had done all this by the time he was forty-five. His greatest triumphs still lay ahead of him.

Of all Franklin's contributions to the public welfare, none was more valuable than his constant crusade against fires. Because he despised waste in any form, he launched a broad attack on fire, the greatest perpetrator of waste. His approach was typically sound and practical. He began by urging the citizens of Philadelphia to take steps to safeguard their property against fire. Thus, years before founding the country's first successful mutual insurance company, he was already expressing what was to be its basic principle—prevention of loss.

At the time Franklin began crusading against fires, Philadelphia was a city of about seven hundred dwellings. It had been spared any great fires, by good fortune rather than by good management. Those that did break out were bound to be destructive because of the absence of an organized fire-fighting force and the fact that equipment for extinguishing fires was most primitive. Aside from one battered engine which had been imported from England in 1719 at a cost of $250, the only fire-fighting appliances in use were leather buckets, wooden ladders, and iron hooks attached to the end of long wooden poles. The hooks, most ancient devices, were used for pulling down walls and sections of burning buildings. When a fire broke out, every able-bodied male in town became a fireman. Filled with fervor and good intentions, the amateur smoke-eaters, buckets in hand, rushed to the scene, but their efforts provided, as one of the residents recorded, "but slight hindrance to the flames."

In the spring of 1730, Philadelphia was threatened by a general conflagration when a fire, breaking out on Fishbourne's wharf, destroyed a number of stores and several fine houses, at a combined loss of about $25,000.[1] The city, alerted anew to the ever-present danger, authorized the purchase of three additional engines, 400 buckets, 20 ladders, and 25 hooks. This equipment was placed at various strategic spots around the city, such as in the Baptist Meeting Yard and in the courthouse. To pay for the apparatus, the city fathers levied a series of fines for a number of minor public offenses. One of these was for smoking on the streets. (There was no penalty for smoking indoors.) Anyone caught puffing on the streets, either by day or by night, was subject to a fine of twenty-five cents. The hazard created by burning tobacco, which, together with matches, is still today the number-one cause of fires, was apparently recognized even in colonial times.

In spite of the additional fire-fighting equipment, Franklin continued to be gravely concerned about the great potential danger, and talked anxiously to his friends of the destruction that might be wreaked by "a lusty blaze." He decided to wake up the town through the columns of his newspaper.

There accordingly appeared in the *Gazette* of February 4, 1735, a highly readable letter, presumably written by an old citizen but actually composed by Franklin, on the prevention and control of fires. The letter advised Philadelphians to be careful about carrying burning coals from one room to another or up and down stairs "unless in a warming pan and shut." Otherwise, Franklin said, "scraps of fire may fall into chinks and make no appearance until midnight; when your stairs being in flames, you may be forced (as I once was) to leap out of your windows and hazard your necks to avoid being over-roasted." He went on to suggest the passage of a

[1]In the interest of clarity, the English monetary units in use in the American Colonies have been converted into their approximate dollar equivalents.

law forbidding "too shallow hearths" and the dangerous practice of putting wooden moldings on each side of the fireplace. He said that fires might be prevented "if chimneys were frequently and more carefully cleaned," and proposed that chimney sweeps be licensed by the mayor. And he further proposed that if a fire broke out in a chimney within fifteen days after it had been cleaned, the sweep who did the job should be fined. "An ounce of prevention," Franklin declared, "is worth a pound of cure."

He was equally persuasive on the matter of putting fires out. He said the city had enough engines but no proper force for handling them. He suggested that the people of Philadelphia might well consider the "example of a city in a neighboring province. There is, I am well informed, a club or society of active men belonging to each fire engine, whose business is to attend all fires whenever they may happen. Besides becoming proficient from practice, these men hold quarterly meetings to talk over how they can improve their methods. Since the establishment of the Society," Franklin said, "it seems there has been no extraordinary fire in that place; and I wish there had never been any here." It had pleased God, Franklin concluded, "that in the fires we have hitherto had, all the bad circumstances have never happened together, such as dry season, high wind, and little or low water; which perhaps tends to make us secure in our own minds; but if a fire with those circumstances, which God forbid, should happen, we should afterwards be careful enough."

The citizens of Philadelphia read this letter and were aroused. It was, Franklin modestly remarked, "spoken of as a useful piece." More than that, it resulted in the formation of Philadelphia's first fire-fighting organization.

Called the Union Fire Company, the pioneer organization

was founded by Franklin and four of his friends. The company limited its membership to thirty men. Each equipped himself at his own expense with six leather buckets, one hook, and four stout linen bags, which he carried to every fire. The linen bags were used to carry portable goods and furnishings from burning buildings and to protect salvaged property from theft. (Looting at fires had become nearly as familiar as smoke.) A member was fined fifty cents for not attending a fire unless "a suitable and satisfactory reason is given to the company," and he was also liable to a fine of twice that amount for failure to keep his fire-fighting equipment in good condition.

The Union Fire Company was a great advance over previous organizations of a similar kind. The first fire brigade of modern times was organized in London in 1680 by the enterprising Dr. Barbon, who hired a group of men to fight fires that broke out in buildings insured by the Fire Office. Insurance companies that were organized later also adopted the practice of maintaining, as one of them advertised, "a company of men versed and experienced in extinguishing and preventing of fire." Upon alarm of fire, these "watermen in livery" rushed to the scene, and if the buildings ablaze were insured, the fire brigade in the employ of the company carrying the insurance went to work. The other brigades, acting under their employers' orders, didn't lift a bucket. If the householder in trouble had no insurance, all the watermen departed, leaving the luckless owner to cogitate on the value of insurance while trying singlehandedly to put out the flames.

By contrast, the Union Fire Company was a purely voluntary association, unhampered by selfish considerations. "Since this Association is intended for a general benefit," the constitution drawn up by the members read, "we do further agree that when a fire breaks out in any part of the city, though none of our houses be in apparent danger, we will, nevertheless, retire hither with our buckets, bags and fire hooks and give our utmost assistance to such of our fellow citizens as may stand in need of it as if they belonged to the company." This honorable precept was followed by the company throughout its career, which lasted for eighty-four years.

Members of the company met once a month and, after dining, spent what Franklin described as "a social evening together, in discussing and communicating such ideas as occurred to us on the subject of fires." Interest in the company spread and, according to the founder, "many more desiring to be admitted than we thought convenient for one company, they were advised to form another, which was accordingly done; and this went on, one new company being formed after another, till they became so numerous as to include most of the inhabitants who were men of property." The names taken by some of the other companies—the Fellowship, the Hand-in-Hand, the Heart-in-Hand, and the Friendship—were expressive of their purpose, and they numbered among their members lawyers, clergymen, physicians, and other eminent Philadelphians of the day. Within a few years after Franklin had shown their practical value, half a dozen volunteer fire companies were earnestly functioning in the city. As a result of their collective zeal, Philadelphia became, so far as fires were concerned, the safest city in America.

But Franklin was not content to stop there. He never wearied of urging prevention. When a fire developed from boiling oil to be used for painting, he wrote an account of the affair in the *Gazette*. "Boiling oil," he cautioned, "is a wild, ungovernable thing; such business should never be done indoors. After a fire near Christ Church, he remarked in his newspaper that "axes were observed to be of great use; for when holes were made in the shingling, the water from engines and buckets readily entered and did ten times the service it could otherwise have done."

Four years after organizing the Union Fire Company, Franklin made another notable contribution to fire prevention by inventing a new kind of stove that was safer than anything then available. The inventor named it the Pennsylvanian Fire-Place, but it was commonly called the Franklin Stove. Besides saving fuel, the new stove contained the flames; crackling embers did not shoot out from it, as they did from the old-fashioned fireplaces. The governor offered Franklin a patent on the stove, but he declined. "As we enjoy great advantages from the inventions of others," he said, "we should be glad of the opportunity to serve others by any invention of ours, and this we should do freely and generously."

Guided by his sense of the practical, Franklin was pursuing his attack on fire with nice logic. Having started by crusading for prevention of fires, he proceeded to set up a volunteer fire company to control those that did occur, and then went on to invent a heating device that reduced one important cause of fires. However, it became obvious to Franklin that the taking of precaution could not prevent the occurrence of fires and that once property had been damaged or destroyed there was need for some assurance that the property owner would be indemnified for his loss. Having come to the realization that fire, like death and taxes, cannot be abolished, Franklin was ready to take the next logical step: to form an insurance company that would make up the loss caused by fire.

FIRE FIGHTING IN ENGLAND IN 1762

This caricature, engraved by the famous satirical artist, William Hogarth, shows eighteenth-century methods of fighting fire in considerable and amusing detail. Note the engine with the hand-in-hand emblem of the Union Office and the men carrying leather buckets of water to fill it. Also the three gentlemen in the Temple Coffee House, who seem to be misdirecting their efforts.

TWO EARLY FIREMEN AND THEIR PRIZE POSSESSION

Volunteer firemen, like the nattily attired members of the Hibernia Company in the upper picture, were very proud of their societies and their fire-fighting equipment. Gathering at their firehouses on Sunday mornings, they spent hours polishing the brass fittings on the engines, scouring the lamps, and sharpening the axes. Rivalry among the various companies to be the first to reach the fire was intense and often led to fist fights.

This idea occurred to Franklin not later than 1750, and out of it eventually developed the first successful insurance company in America. An attempt to furnish fire insurance had been made in Charleston, South Carolina, in 1735, when a Friendly Society, operating under a royal charter, came into existence. In 1741, Charleston suffered a disastrous fire, and as a consequence the Friendly Society went out of business, six years after it had started.

At the time of the Charleston conflagration, Philadelphia had already become the leading city in the Colonies, and it continued to grow by leaps and bounds. It outranked Boston in volume of commerce and level of culture, and it was also the political nerve center of the country. By colonial standards, the city was huge and rich. In 1750, the year Franklin introduced fire insurance to the city, its population numbered more than seven thousand taxable citizens. According to a census gathered personally by Franklin and nine of his public-spirited friends, the city boasted 2,076 dwellings. There were about a thousand additional buildings, such as sheds and stables. And there was not a single penny of insurance on anything.

Franklin used the Union Fire Company as the nucleus of an organization to meet this need. He first broached the idea of forming an insurance company to the members of the company at their meeting held on the evening of February 26, 1750. According to the minutes of that meeting, the members agreed to raise a thousand dollars for "a fund for an Insurance Office to make up the damage that may arise by fire among this Company." In other words, all the members chipped in equal shares to build up a fund, out of which each would be indemnified if his dwelling were damaged by fire. At the same meeting the members voted to put half of the money from the fund out at interest. Franklin and two other members—Hugh Roberts and Philip Syng—were appointed a committee to be responsible for investing the money. They subsequently loaned the sum to a merchant named James Coates. The simple transaction has the distinction of being the first known investment by an American insurance company.

After the Union Fire Company's insurance scheme had been in operation for more than a year, the members voted favorably on "a proposal from Benjamin Franklin" to look into the advisability of extending its benefits to other citizens. They accordingly appointed a committee consisting of Franklin and Philip Syng to call a meeting to discuss the matter with representatives of the other fire companies, of which there were then six, with a combined membership of 225. Committees named by the other fire companies met with Franklin and Syng at the Standard Tavern on September 7, 1751. There it was decided to form an insurance organization for the benefit not only of the members of the various fire companies but of all the citizens of Philadelphia.

When plans for the new company had been drawn up, it was brought to the attention of the public through a small notice printed in Franklin's newspaper. The notice, placed inconspicuously between an advertisement for goods lately imported from England and on sale at Daniel Benezet's Store and another calling attention to the ironmongery and tobacco sold by Hugh Roberts, appeared on February 18, 1752. It read in full:

> All persons inclined to subscribe to the articles of insurance of houses from loss by fire, in or near this city, are desired to appear at the Court-House, where attendance will be given, to take their subscriptions, every seventh day of the week, in the afternoon, until the 13th of April next, being the day ap-

pointed by the said articles for electing twelve directors and a treasurer.

The "said articles" were embodied in a document that set forth in detail the terms and conditions upon which those who decided to take part in the new company would insure each other's houses "upon the most equal terms and apart from all views of separate gain or interest." This document was called the Articles of Association or the Deed of Settlement. Who was responsible for drawing it up is not certain, but it is evident that whoever did prepare it had access to the Deed of Settlement of the Amicable Contributionship of London. The similarities between the two are many and unmistakable.

Every Philadelphian who wished to insure in the new company was required to visit the courthouse and sign the Deed of Settlement, which was engrossed on a strip of parchment fifteen feet in length. The first signer was James Hamilton, the lieutenant governor of the province. Though he had taken no part in originating the company, his signature was proof that the government approved the project. The first private name was that of Benjamin Franklin—"private in the unofficial sense," an officer of the company later remarked, "but publicly known in the Colonies and thereafter to be universally known among men." Next to sign was Philip Syng, Franklin's close associate in the Union Fire Company, after which the quill was passed to the hands of other subscribers. The list of charter members includes, besides Franklin, two other men—John Morton and Robert Morris—who were destined twenty-four years later to sign the Declaration of Independence.

The first meeting of the subscribers was held, according to the company's charter, on March 25, 1752, at the courthouse.

The members proceeded to elect twelve directors and a treasurer. Heading the list of directors was Benjamin Franklin. The other members of the original board were also men of character and of standing in Philadelphia. They consisted of Philip Syng, a silversmith who afterward served for ten years as treasurer of the City of Philadelphia; four prominent merchants—William Coleman, Joseph Morris, Jonathan Zane, and William Griffits; two master craftsmen in carpentry—Samuel Rhodes and Joseph Fox, who was also a member of the Pennsylvania Assembly; two importers and marine underwriters—Amos Strettel and John Mifflin, who was also a city alderman; Hugh Roberts, owner of an ironworks and a member of the Assembly; and Israel Pemberton, Jr., a wealthy Quaker and political leader. It was a representative and balanced board and included, as a director of the company remarked one hundred years later, "names of some of the most respected citizens of Philadelphia, whose descendants are still among us, and are personally esteemed and honored."

As their first treasurer, the subscribers elected a public-spirited, thirty-year-old Quaker merchant who bore the sound American name of John Smith. A son-in-law of James Logan, one of the wealthiest and most eminent Quakers of the city, Smith was well-to-do in his own right, occupying a handsome brick residence in the quarter of the city where the most affluent families lived. In the course of his business, which involved large importations of goods, Smith had become well acquainted with the practice of marine insurance and did considerable underwriting himself. He was well qualified for the post of treasurer, who, in the early days of the company, was the main executive officer.

Before adjourning, the subscribers settled on a name for

their company. They decided to call it the Philadelphia Contributionship for the Insurance of Houses from Loss by Fire, a name that was, at least, not ambiguous.

The directors held their first meeting on May 11, 1752. Since the company had no quarters of its own, the directors convened at the Royal Standard Tavern, an establishment colloquially known as "The Widow Pratt's," after the proprietress. Eleven of the twelve directors were present, the absentee being John Mifflin. It was perhaps his absence that moved the board to agree that each director should "pay a forfeiture of one shilling for not meeting precisely at the hour appointed, and two shillings for total absence." To William Coleman was delegated the task of preparing "a proper method of keeping the Books & Accounts of the Company." As clerk, the directors decided to hire a successful shipper and marine underwriter named Joseph Saunders, who had business associations with John Smith, the treasurer. It was agreed to pay Saunders $200 a year for his services and the rental of a room in his house as the company's office.

The final item of business at the first meeting was the selection of a design for the company's "badge" or "fire-mark." Fire-marks, now valued only by collectors, were essential in the early days to all fire insurance companies. They were plaques usually made of lead or wood on which was devised the company's emblem and as a rule its name. They were supplied for a fee by the insurance company to each policyholder, who was required to affix the mark in a prominent place on the exterior of his house. Fire-marks originated in England; their purpose was to identify the houses insured by the various companies so that their paid fire brigades would know which dwellings were supposed to be protected. The situation was somewhat different in Philadelphia, whose volunteer fire companies were pledged to respond to every fire regardless of whether they had any personal interest at stake. Though Franklin and the other directors of the Contributionship had the highest regard for the character of the volunteer fire companies, they also had the highest regard for human nature. They accordingly decided not only to identify with fire-marks the property they insured but also, before long, they found it expedient to make financial contributions to the various fire companies and from time to time to reward one or another of them with a special cash donation for "meritorious services," such as putting out a fire in a house bearing the Contributionship's mark.

To Philip Syng, the silversmith, was entrusted the working up of the design of the Contributionship's mark, which the directors decided was to be of four hands crossed and clasped in the form commonly referred to as "Jacob's Chair." The Contributionship's mark was an adaptation of the one used by the first mutual fire company in England. Because of this and other similarities, the Philadelphia company, like its ancestor, was to become familiarly known as the Hand-in-Hand. Having completed their business, the directors "adjourned to the 16th inst. to meet at Widow Pratt's at 4 o'clock in the afternoon."

In choosing a tavern as their meeting place, the directors set a precedent that was followed by their successors until 1836, when the company erected its own office building. During the eighty-four years in which they held their meetings at the Widow Pratt's or at another of Philadelphia's famous taverns, such as Ben Davis's Golden Fleece or The Sign of the George, the directors forgathered in the late afternoon and, after transacting their business in a private room, they dined well and heartily and spent a social evening together. These occasions were not lacking in warmth and good cheer. An itemized bill from one of the early meetings, at which eleven directors were present, shows that they consumed food costing $8.35, washed down with punch, toddy, Madeira, and porter costing $11.18. Commenting nearly two centuries later on the robust appetites of the founders, an officer of the Contributionship remarked dryly, "In this emasculate age, it is interesting to note one more example of the rugged virility of the men who founded our country and so many of its enduring institutions."

By their fourth meeting the directors had completed most of their organizational chores. A bookkeeping system had been devised, ledgers purchased, a cubbyhole of office space engaged, and from the famous metalworking firm of Pass & Stow, which recast the Liberty Bell, a supply of one hundred fire-marks had been secured. Only one thing now was lacking, and that was taken care of at the fourth meeting, when the directors resolved that "Benjamin Franklin is desired to get a sufficient number of policies printed."

Franklin handled this assignment with dispatch, and the Contributionship wrote its first policy on June 26, 1752. Policy No. 1 was issued to the company's treasurer, John Smith. Written in the amount of $2,500, it covered his three-story dwelling house "on the East side of King Street between Mulberry and Sassafras." On July 4—a date that would before long assume lasting significance—Policies 19 and 20 were written on two houses owned by Benjamin Franklin. Mutual fire insurance had become a reality in America.

CHAPTER IV

The Philadelphia Story—2

IN THE INTERESTS OF SHADE AND INSURANCE

FOR thirty-two years after its founding, the Philadelphia Contributionship was the only fire insurance company in America. During this period, from 1752 to 1784, the country had expanded from a thin strip of some million and a half colonial settlers perched on the rim of the civilized world to an independent nation with a population approaching four million. With the need increased, it seems at first glance odd that fire insurance did not also expand.

There were good reasons, the principal one being that those were the times that tried men's souls. During the years of the Revolution—and for several years before—Americans had little time to concern themselves with anything beyond their common struggle for independence. With the war won, they embarked on their great political experiments—independence, republicanism, and federal union—and were plunged again into a period of grave and recurrent crises. The first effort toward federal government, the Articles of Confederation, proved unworkable. Most of the four and a half million dollars of paper money issued to finance the war depreciated to zero. There was a currency famine, followed by economic depression and wide unrest. With only half a million dollars being paid annually into the federal government, the country teetered on the edge of bankruptcy. While Europe looked on with an I-told-you-so attitude, the new nation rescued itself by supplanting the Articles of Confederation, which failed to give adequate powers to the central government, with the federal Constitution, the unique contribution of the United States to the science of government. The Constitution was not ratified until 1788. By that time mutual fire insurance was in its thirty-sixth year, but it was still confined to Philadelphia.

The physical conditions under which the American people then lived did not favor the spread of the insurance idea. Except in southern New England and along the coastal area of the Middle Atlantic States, most of them lived in isolated circumstances, in clearings cut out of the woodland. Only six cities—Philadelphia, New York, Boston, Charleston, Baltimore, and Salem—had a population of eight thousand or more; and all of their inhabitants together did not exceed 3 per cent of the total population. The principal occupation of nine tenths of the people was agriculture, but the cultivated area of the country was insignificant compared with that covered by forest. After an extensive journey through the thirteen states, a contemporary French traveler remarked, "Compared with France, the entire country is one vast wood." The difficulties of communication were enormous. What few roads existed were little more than wide tracks through the forest, and many of those were so full of rocks, holes, and stumps that a wheeled vehicle could not be drawn over them. It took twenty-nine days for news of the signing of the Declaration of Independence to reach Charleston, South Carolina, from Philadelphia—a distance of 650 miles.

The fact that mutual fire insurance did not quickly proliferate was actually advantageous, for time was thus provided in which the mutual idea could be put into practice in America and be tried, tested, and perfected. Two improvements on the methods of the early English companies were made immediately by the Philadelphia Contributionship.

First was the practice of inspecting every building before issuing insurance on it and, if necessary, requiring changes to bring the property up to a high standard. The inspecting—or, to use the original term, surveying—was done in the early days of the Contributionship by two of its directors, Samuel Rhodes and Joseph Fox. Being master craftsmen in carpentry, they had a keen eye for judging construction and sensing where it was hazardous. It was not unusual for them to note on their surveys that a prospective policyholder had been "ordered to make a way out at the top" of his house before insurance would be written on it. This alteration was required to provide a way for firemen to reach the roof and get at the flames. Another applicant was required "to fix the rails on the roof." Since the rails enabled the firemen to steady themselves while working on the roof, the purpose again was prevention.

The system of inspection instituted by the Contributionship was a great step forward. It was the rude beginning of the science of rating risks. The Contributionship did not avoid hazardous risks—it selected those that had an interest in preventing loss. Thus was laid down the principle of selectivity, which became an integral part of mutual insurance. Selectivity brought less losses and, in turn, lower rates. Over the centuries the result was a reduction in costs for the benefit of all buyers of insurance.

The second valuable improvement made by the Contributionship was originating the practice of setting the rate, or cost, of insurance in accordance with the quality of the risk.

Unlike the English companies, the Contributionship did not simply establish a certain rate for brick buildings and another for frame buildings and then apply one of these two rates to all structures regardless of differences among them. On the contrary, the Contributionship determined the rate on each building it insured by taking into consideration the construction, occupancy, and general character of the risk.

How this system operated is well illustrated by Franklin's first two policies, which covered houses that he owned and rented. Policy No. 19 was written on Franklin's house "on the South side of High Street, where Daniel Swan dwells." This house was insured for "£200 @ 35 per cent," the company's terminology for a rate of thirty-five shillings per hundred pounds of value. For every $1,000 of insurance on this house Franklin was charged $17.50. On Policy No. 20, however, the rate was higher. This policy, covering the house on High Street, "where Edon Hadock dwells," was written for "£150 @ 50 per cent." This means that for each $1,000 worth of insurance on the second house Franklin was charged $25, or $7.50 per $1,000 more than on the first.

What accounted for this difference in rate? The explanation can be found in a notation made by Rhodes and Fox on the report of their survey of the house covered by Policy No. 20. On the side of this report they wrote, "A Painter's Shop." It is clear that combustibles were stored on the premises and, since the inflammable quality of paint was well known to the directors, they obviously decided that this building should bear the highest rate, which was 50 per cent. The lowest was 17 per cent.

Following the English pattern, the Contributionship in its early years wrote all policies for a term of seven years. After a house had been surveyed, the owner was required to make a deposit to a common fund. The amount of the deposit was based on the amount of insurance taken and on the rate determined by the directors. For example, Franklin's deposit on his two policies was $36.25. A separate account was then opened on the books of the company for each insured, or contributor, in the manner of a savings bank. His deposit was charged its proportion of the expenses and losses of the company, and credited with any interest earned. If at the end of seven years a balance remained in his account, a contributor was permitted either to withdraw this sum or to apply it on a new policy running for another seven years.

By the time of the first annual meeting, in 1753, the Contributionship had issued a total of 143 policies. It had $108,360 insurance in force, and deposits amounting to $1,261.93. The company had come through the year without a single loss.

At the meeting Franklin was re-elected a director and served for another year. After his second term he ceased to hold office because of the press of official business which required his absence from Philadelphia for long periods. He had been named Deputy Postmaster General of America and, applying himself with his usual vigor, made extended trips to inspect post offices throughout the country. (When he was named to the job, the Post Office had a deficit of $3,390; eleven years later it had a surplus of $10,350.) Other official missions kept him from home for weeks at a time.

In addition, though he had already become the world's foremost investigator of electricity, he was still adding to his tremendous discoveries. With his famous kite experiment he had discovered the identity of lightning and electricity—"the most brilliant discovery of the century." Putting his newfound knowledge to practical use, he went on to invent the lightning rod. Characteristically, he refused to patent the invention; instead he explained in *Poor Richard's Almanack* how anyone could construct the newly discovered device that protects men's "habitations and other buildings from mischief by thunder and lightning." Franklin, the philosopher Kant said, was a new Prometheus who had stolen fire from heaven. Yale and Harvard conferred honorary degrees on him. The Royal Society in London elected him a member and awarded him their Copley Medal. King Louis XV of France sent him a letter congratulating him on his scientific discoveries. "I think," Franklin wrote at this time in a letter to a friend, "I have never been more hurried in business than at present."

Despite his manifold public activities, Franklin retained an active interest in the Contributionship and in fire prevention. In 1763, he took out his third policy with the company and, four years later, he insured a new nine-room house "where his family dwells" by Policy No. 1148. In subsequent years, while serving his country in Europe, he wrote several letters bearing on fire prevention to Samuel Rhodes, who had continued as a director. "It appears to me of great importance to build our dwelling houses, if we can, in a manner more secure from danger by fire," one of Franklin's letters from abroad begins. "We scarcely ever hear of fire in Paris. When I was there, I took particular notice of the construction of their houses, and I did not see how one of them could well be burnt." He went on to explain his ideas on fireproof construction. As late as 1785, when he was seventy-nine and returning for the last time to Europe, the subject of fire prevention was still occupying his attention. During the long sea voyage Franklin, hale and hearty and bubbling as ever with new ideas, wrote two treatises on a familiar topic. They were titled, "The Causes and Cures of Smoky Chimneys" and

"Description of a New Stove for Burning Pitcoal and Consuming All Its Smoke."

During the 1750s, while its founder was receiving worldwide acclaim, the Contributionship was getting established in Philadelphia, but progress was slow. The condition of the company at the end of its tenth year actually was less favorable then it had been at the close of the first. True, the number of policies had increased during the ten-year period from 143 to 801; but the insurance in force had dropped from $108,000 to $68,000, and the deposits had decreased from $1,260 to $982. There had been a falling off during the first decade of nearly two fifths, and new business was not coming in. Something was wrong.

The defect was lack of reserves. Under the initial scheme, the money in the deposit fund was handled for the profit or loss of the individual policyholder. No provision had been made for using the interest on the deposits for building up a reserve to give the company stability. A loss of a few thousand dollars could have swept away the entire deposit fund and broken up the company.

Recognizing the defect, the policyholders voted unanimously to eliminate it at their general meeting in 1763. They agreed, first, that thereafter the interest on the deposit money should be carried to a common account, out of which the losses should be paid; and, second, that the deposit money should not be drawn upon until the interest had been exhausted. Thus was enunciated for the first time in America the great principle of insurance—accumulation of safety reserves.

This principle, put into practice by the Contributionship, had a salutary effect. Eighteen years after it had been adopted, in 1781, the company had some two thousand policies on its books and insurance in force of approximately two million dollars. The basic structure of mutual insurance had now been built, tested, and perfected. The mutual idea was ready to advance.

It soon did. In 1781, when the Contributionship had reached the highroad to success, its members took a step which resulted three years later in the establishment of the second fire insurance company in America—also a mutual company.

Thanks to the poet, it is widely understood that only God can make a tree, but it is less well known that trees were the making of an insurance company. That is what happened in Philadelphia in the latter part of the eighteenth century. At their annual meeting in 1781, members of the Contributionship voted that the company would thereafter not insure any building, nor renew insurance on any building, that had trees near it. The sponsors of this movement held the opinion that trees were a fire hazard because their branches, extending over low shingled roofs, were liable to take fire in winter from chimney sparks and because they interfered in both winter and summer with the work of the firemen.

At least forty of the Contributionship's policyholders, anxious to be deprived neither of shade nor insurance, organized a committee to try to get the anti-tree ruling repealed. They offered to pay a higher premium for "the supposed risk," but their efforts were unavailing. In fact, to make its position unmistakably clear, the Contributionship wrote the anti-tree resolution into its bylaws at its annual meeting held in April 1784. This was the last straw. In August, the outnumbered tree lovers announced in the *Gazette* that plans had been drawn for a "New Society" for insuring houses, with or without trees near them. Their rather wistfully worded announcement implied that this step was being taken more in sorrow than in anger. Explaining that they had "no design or intention to prejudice the institution already established," the sponsors promised that if the Contributionship's arboreal by-laws were repealed by September 5, the plan for founding a new company would be called off. The fifth of September came and went. The Contributionship stood pat. Accordingly, on September 29, the subscribers to the new society, of whom there were sixty-one, held their first formal meeting and brought into existence the Mutual Assurance Company for Insuring Houses from Loss by Fire. Deciding upon the new company's fire-mark took no time at all. The design selected was a tree in full leaf. As a result, the company has always been commonly known as the Green Tree.

The thirteen trustees who were elected by the members to manage the Green Tree were all public-spirited men of high standing in Philadelphia. They included several merchants, a lumber dealer, a cordwainer, a retired importer, a goldsmith, and a jurist who later was appointed Chief Justice of Pennsylvania. The leading spirit in founding the company and for sixteen years its most prominent trustee was a merchant and importer named Mathew Clarkson, whose countinghouse served for many years as the company's office. Clarkson held many public offices and was subsequently elected mayor of Philadelphia. He was not without experience in fire insurance, since he had served for seven years as clerk of the Contributionship.

From its Deed of Settlement to its policy form, the Green Tree was patterned closely on the Contributionship. There was, of course, an important difference in the matter of insuring tree-shaded houses. This was covered in Article XXXII

Early Fire Marks

Upper left, the fire mark of the Hand-in-Hand Insurance Company, founded in England in 1696. Upper right, the Philadelphia Contributionship, 1752. Lower left, the Mutual Assurance Company, 1784. Lower right, the Baltimore Equitable Society, 1794. Fire marks were generally made of lead and mounted on wood. They were first used in England in order that private fire brigades maintained by insurance companies might identify property insured by their employers. Later, when volunteer fire companies were formed, the marks served to indicate to firemen that they would probably be rewarded if they saved an insured property.

Survey'd June ye 13th: 1752

At ye request of Benj: Franklin
his House in High=Street where Edon Hadock

and find
16 ft: 4 front 37½ feet deep 2 Storys high
Brick front
wooden Back & Partitions
Shingling ½ Worn in front back pt: new

No: 20

a Painters Shop

wooden Kitchen 9 ft: 3 by 16 feet one Story high

Jos: Fox

£150 @ 50/ pr Ct

£140 on the House
10 on ye Kitchen
150

Samuel Rhoad

A TYPICAL PHILADELPHIA CONTRIBUTIONSHIP SURVEY

Before the Philadelphia Contributionship issued insurance on a property, it was carefully inspected, or "surveyed," by two of the company's directors. The survey above, the company's twentieth, was on a house owned by Benjamin Franklin but occupied by Edon Hadock, who used it, as the survey notes, as "a Painter's Shop." Altogether, Franklin insured four houses in the Contributionship.

of the Deed of Settlement, which required that "all trees planted near houses shall be trimmed every fall in such manner as not to be higher than the eaves," and provided that the trustees were to fix the rate on tree-shaded buildings. It developed that the additional deposit required on these risks averaged one fourth of 1 per cent of the amount insured. The Green Tree's first policy, issued in December 1784 to Archibald McCall, included a charge of $8.75 for the one tree that stood in front of his house.

Though the Green Tree started out modestly, it soon prospered and, by the opening of the nineteenth century, it had accumulated a surplus of $25,400. In 1801, the Green Tree ceased writing seven-year policies and began writing what is known as perpetual insurance. Nine years later, the Contributionship adopted this innovation, and both companies have since written only this kind of insurance.

Perpetual insurance is not widely known except among insurance men and in the few communities where it is offered, but as practiced by the Green Tree and the Contributionship it has been enormously successful. To secure a perpetual policy on his house, the owner makes a cash deposit to the company of an amount that ranges as a rule from 2 to 3 per cent of the amount of insurance taken. If, for example, a policy is written for $10,000 at the minimum rate of 2 per cent, the policyholder pays the company $200. That is his first and last payment, provided the general conditions of the building insured remain unchanged. The policy may be canceled at any time; if it has been held for five years or longer, the policyholder's deposit is returned in full; if canceled before that, between 95 and 98 per cent of the deposit is returned. The payment of a partial loss does not reduce the policy. For example, if a $9,000 loss by fire occurs on the house insured for $10,000, the company pays the loss without requiring the payment of any additional deposit. If the loss is total, the company pays the loss and the policy is terminated, the deposit money being retained by the company. The great bulk of the income of both the Contributionship and the Green Tree is derived from their investments.

During the years following their adoption of perpetual insurance, both companies moved forward with great strides. Taking at length a less deplorable view of foliage, the Contributionship rescinded its anti-tree ruling in 1823. That year, the company had $3,700,000 of insurance in force and a surplus of $229,000. The Green Tree had accumulated a surplus of about the same size. Both companies continued to build up their surplus accounts so assiduously that they had more than doubled by 1850.

It was well that they had, for in the afternoon of July 9, 1850, a fire followed by an explosion in a warehouse on Water Street resulted in the worst conflagration that Philadelphia had suffered. Before the flames were brought under control by the local volunteer fire companies (Philadelphia had no paid fire department and wouldn't have for another twenty-one years), thirty persons were dead or missing, more than a hundred injured, and 354 buildings laid waste. The total property loss was estimated at $1.5 million; less than a third of the properties destroyed were insured. The Green Tree's losses totaled $65,000; the Contributionship's, $78,000. Steep as these losses were, both companies were able to absorb them with equability, thanks to the healthy condition of their surplus accounts.

In 1852, two years after suffering its greatest loss, the Contributionship celebrated its one hundredth anniversary. In an erudite address delivered at the centennial meeting of the policyholders, Mr. Horace Binney, who was associated with the company for forty-one years, during twenty-six of which he served as chairman of the board, reviewed the past and expressed hopes for the future. "We shall none of us be here at the next centennial meeting," he said in conclusion, "to speak of those who have gone before us in the administration of the company or to trace the influence of their operations upon the comfort of the inhabitants and the stability and improvement of the city. But I trust that those who may then be present will have as much reason to speak as favorably of us for our constancy in the maintenance of the great principle of 1763—the devotion of all that the company can gain to the payment of all that the members can lose—as I have had to speak of their wisdom and foresight in introducing the principle among us. I fervently hope that its operation may never be arrested or impaired, and that the company may continue and prosper for centuries to come, a great and perennial public blessing."

Were the venerable chairman present at the two-hundredth-anniversary meeting of the Contributionship in 1952, he would have reason to be well satisfied. Not only has the great principle of 1763 been maintained, it has been improved. The improvement has taken the form of allowing the policyholders to share in the profits of the company through dividends. Since 1895, the Contributionship has paid an annual dividend of 10 per cent on all policies which have been in force for ten years or longer. If a house had been insured in 1895 for $10,000 and a deposit of $200 made, the policyholder would have received a dividend of $20 in 1905, and the same amount each succeeding year; by 1952, he would have received a total of $960 in dividends, plus payments for any fire losses he may have had, and if he cared to cancel the policy, he could withdraw the $200 originally deposited.

Since 1912, the Green Tree has also paid annual dividends to its policyholders. Differing slightly from the Contributionship, the Green Tree pays 5 per cent on deposits on policies in force from five to nine years, and 10 per cent on policies in force for ten years or longer. By December 31, 1949, the Green Tree had returned a total of $1.3 million in dividends to its policyholders; as of the same date, the Contributionship had returned $3.6 million.

It was with considerable pride that Mr. Binney informed the members assembled for the centennial meeting in 1852 that their company then had insurance in force amounting to $8 million and a surplus of $695,000. He would be gratified to note that after its second hundred years the company now has $77 million insurance in force and a surplus of $14 million. And, since the Contributionship and the Green Tree have always been most cordially disposed toward each other (aside from that little trouble about the trees), Mr. Binney would also be pleased to see that the Green Tree now has $30 million insurance in force and a surplus of $13.4 million. He would take pleasure in the observation of a contemporary insurance executive who described these two pioneer mutual companies as being today "the strongest insurance institutions in the world and, considering the amount at risk, the strongest financial institutions of any kind, anywhere."

The atmosphere around the offices of both the Contributionship and the Green Tree, which are located a few doors from each other at, respectively, 212 and 240 South Fourth, is one of gentility, unhurriedness, and the quiet confidence that comes from scores of years of successful operation. Both companies conduct their business with small staffs; the Contributionship has eighteen employees; the Green Tree, eight. Neither company actively solicits business. In fact, becoming a policyholder in either is not unlike securing membership in an exclusive club. Coverage is limited to buildings of brick or stone "or other approved masonry construction," the occupancy of which is non-commercial and non-hazardous. The acceptable category includes residences and institutions such as churches, hospitals, and schools. Both companies give preference to residential risks located in Philadelphia and its suburbs and in the adjoining counties. The practice of accepting only the highest-caliber risks has resulted in very low losses; in 1948 the Contributionship's net losses amounted to $52,000, while the Green Tree's were only $21,000.

Tradition is properly respected by both of the pioneer companies, and each is proud of the long continuity in office of its officers and directors. Until recent times, the principal executive office in each company had been held by a member of the same family for more than a hundred years. The directors of the Contributionship, like the trustees of the Green Tree, continue to be drawn from among the outstanding citizens of Philadelphia. "It is not true that to be on the board of one of these companies you have to be descended from a signer of the Declaration of Independence," a Philadelphia insurance historian once observed, "but, of course, that helps."

The directors of both companies continue to observe the pleasant and civilized custom of holding their monthly meetings in the late afternoon and afterward taking dinner together in the tastefully furnished dining room with which each of their offices is supplied. Legend has it that while the trustees of the Green Tree were holding their regular meeting on December 14, 1799, news was received that George

Washington had died, and the chairman proposed a toast to the late, great patriot. Word of this gesture has been carried down by word of mouth through successive generations of the Green Tree's trustees. Ever since 1799, the concluding ceremony of their monthly dinners has been the drinking of a toast in memory of Washington.

Though the present directors of the Contributionship may not eat as heartily as Franklin and the other founding fathers did at the Widow Pratt's, they still dine very decently. A recent dinner, according to the printed menu distributed to each of the directors, consisted of Chincoteague oysters, clear mushroom soup, terrapin, Saratoga chips, brown-bread sandwiches, guinea hen, currant jelly, braised celery, Bermuda potatoes, French vanilla ice cream with strawberry sauce, fancy cakes, and coffee. On the back of this menu was printed a poem which had been written by one of the company's policyholders under his endorsement on a dividend check. The poem read:

Bless Franklin on this, his dear natal day
And this child of his brain who its policyholders pay.
He's a Hero of Peace, not a fierce battle slayer,
And more wonderful still—he's a dividend payer.

This tribute in doggerel would have amused Franklin, who had the rare faculty of being able to treat the weightiest matters without ever losing the twinkle in his eye.

If the illustrious founder of the Contributionship were to take his old place—Seat No. 1—at a meeting of the directors today, he would not only be completely at home but also justifiably proud. Through two centuries of war and peace, inflation and deflation, adversity and prosperity, the Contributionship has unremittingly hewed to the mutual idea, and so has prospered. Organized for the benefit of the policyholders, it has never wavered in placing the interests of the policyholders first, last, and all the time. The Contributionship has passed that most rigorous of tests—the test of time—and stands today as one of the strongest and soundest institutions ever formed. It has proved the wisdom of the mutual idea which, as Franklin said more than two hundred years ago, is an idea "whereby every man might help another, without any disservice to himself."

CHAPTER V

The Founding Fathers Approve

MY MOVEMENTS to the chair of government," wrote George Washington in 1789, shortly before his first inauguration as President of the United States, "will be accompanied by feelings not unlike those of a culprit, who is going to the place of his execution; so unwilling am I, in the evening of a life nearly consumed in public cares, to quit a peaceful abode for an ocean of difficulties, without that competency of political skill, abilities and inclination, which are necessary to manage the helm."

However wrong Washington's unduly modest appraisal of himself may have been, his estimate of the difficulties he faced was by no means exaggerated. Plans for the new republic were excellent; administrative machinery for carrying them out did not exist. The staff of the federal government consisted of a dozen clerks. The country was saddled with debt, there was no money in the treasury, and no funds were coming in because no agency had been formed for collecting taxes. There was not a single federal court in the land. The new government had yet to set up machinery to establish its authority over four million people living in a country two thousand miles long and still largely a wilderness. Sectional interests of the thirteen states, being widely

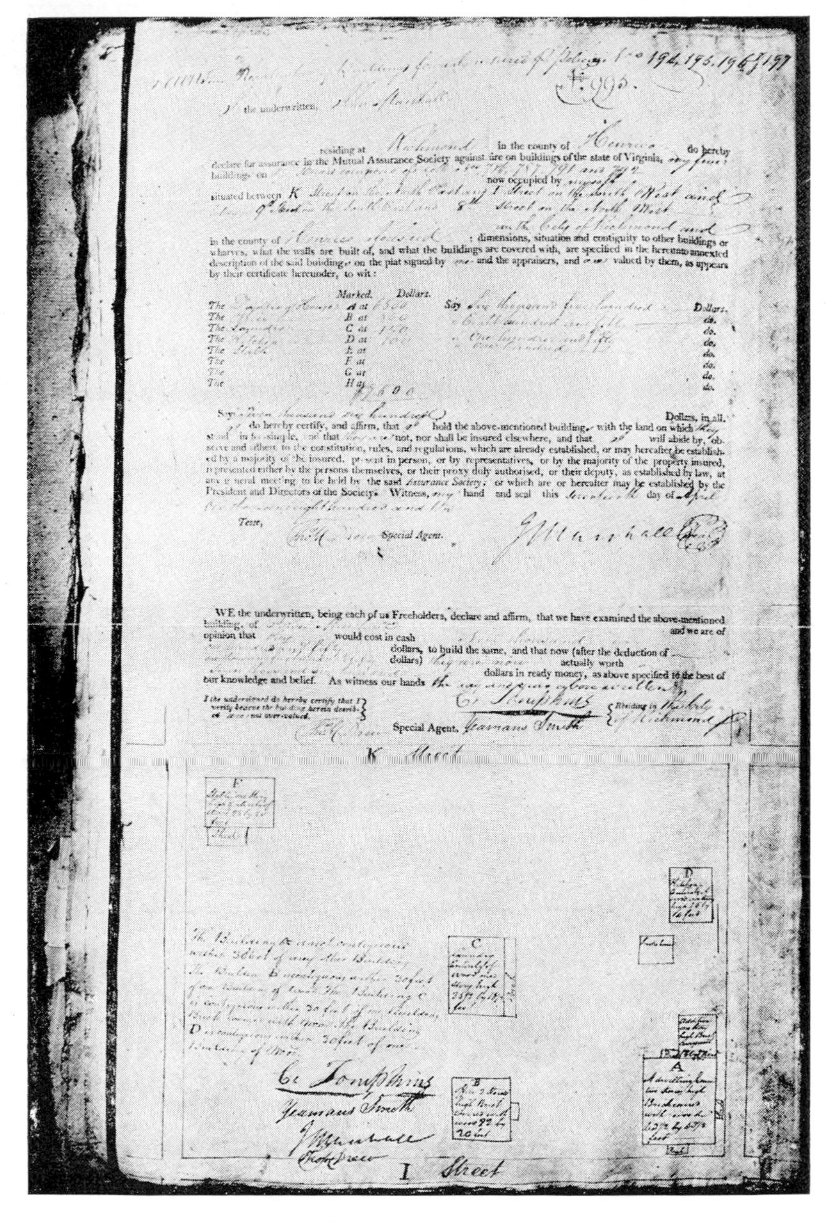

No. 194, 195, 196 & 197

No. 995.

I the underwritten, John Marshall

residing at Richmond in the county of Henrico do hereby declare for assurance in the Mutual Assurance Society against fire on buildings of the state of Virginia, my four buildings on

now occupied by myself

situated between K Street on the North East, I Street on the South West and

in the City of Richmond and

in the county of Henrico aforesaid; dimensions, situation and contiguity to other buildings or wharves, what the walls are built of, and what the buildings are covered with, are specified in the hereunto annexed description of the said buildings on the plat signed by me and the appraisers, and are valued by them, as appears by their certificate hereunder, to wit:

		Marked.	Dollars.		
The	Dwelling House	A at	6500	Say Six thousand five hundred	Dollars.
The		B at	500		do.
The		C at	150	One hundred and fifty	do.
The		D at	100	One hundred	do.
The	Stable	E at			do.
The		F at			do.
The		G at			do.
The		H at			do.
			7500		

Say Seven thousand five hundred Dollars, in all.

I do hereby certify, and affirm, that I hold the above-mentioned buildings with the land on which they stand in fee-simple, and that they are not, nor shall be insured elsewhere, and that I will abide by, observe and adhere to the constitution, rules, and regulations, which are already established, or may hereafter be established by a majority of the insured, present in person, or by representatives, or by the majority of the property insured, represented either by the persons themselves, or their proxy duly authorised, or their deputy, as established by law, at any general meeting to be held by the said *Assurance Society*, or which are or hereafter may be established by the President and Directors of the Society. Witness, my hand and seal this seventeenth day of April

Teste,

Special Agent. J Marshall (Seal)

WE the underwritten, being each of us Freeholders, declare and affirm, that we have examined the above-mentioned building, of and we are of opinion that they would cost in cash dollars, to build the same, and that now (after the deduction of dollars) they are now actually worth dollars in ready money, as above specified to the best of our knowledge and belief. As witness our hands the day and year above written.

I the underwritten do hereby certify that I verily believe the building herein described are not over-valued.

C. Tompkins

Special Agent. Yeamans Smith — Residing in the City of Richmond

K Street

F

C

D

A

B

C. Tompkins

Yeamans Smith

J Marshall

I Street

John Marshall's Application for Insurance

John Marshall, famed Chief Justice of the United States, not only insured his property with the Mutual Assurance Society of Virginia but served, with Edmund Randolph, as the company's legal counsel. Above is a reproduction of Marshall's original application for insurance. Now a shrine, Marshall's home has been insured continuously by the Mutual Assurance Society since 1796.

Bettmann Archive

Answering a Night Alarm

What it meant to be a volunteer fireman was once described by a veteran fire-eater, who recalled: "Often I was out with my engine four nights a week, yet I was at work as usual in the morning. The charm of it all lay in the excitement of the running, in the victory over rivals, and in the daring feats in and about burning buildings. We would leave our business, our dinner, our anything, and rush for the engine. The night I was getting married there was a fire. I could see it, and I wanted to go immediately. But the next morning early, before breakfast, there was another fire, and I went to that. So you may judge how we liked it."

disparate,.contained the seeds of trouble. More trouble could be expected from England and Spain, both of whom continued to lay claim on territory of the United States. Repercussions of the French Revolution were to bring the United States into sharp conflict, verging on war, with France. To deal with these threats to its security, the United States, at the time Washington first took the oath of office, had an army of 672 officers and men, and no navy.

When nearly eight years later Washington delivered his Farewell Address, a government had been organized and was operating. Peace had been preserved. A federal judiciary was functioning, taxes were being collected, and the commercial life of the nation was expanding. There was still no manufacturing to speak of, but agriculture was flourishing; exports of tobacco and rice, mainstays of the economy of the Southern states, were larger than they had ever been. Commerce with the West Indies had been revived, and New England shipowners had opened a thriving trade in the Far East. The problems yet to be solved were momentous, but the accomplishments of Washington's two terms gave added reason to believe that America was proving itself, in the words of a French statesman, "the hope of the human race."

By the time Washington retired in 1797 to his beloved Mount Vernon, the mutual idea, introduced in Philadelphia forty-five years before, had crossed three state borders. Mutual fire insurance companies had been established in New York, Maryland, and Virginia, in that order.

When the first fire insurance company was founded in New York City, the settlement at the mouth of the Hudson River had a population of thirty-three thousand, a Chamber of Commerce, and a geographical site that was to make it the greatest city in the Union. Its first fire insurance company, organized in 1787, was called the Mutual Assurance Company of New York. Alexander Hamilton was one of its original directors, but he left two years later when, at the age of thirty-two, he was appointed by Washington to be the nation's first Secretary of the Treasury. Fortune did not smile as benignly on the first mutual insurance company in New York State as it had upon its Philadelphia predecessor; the Mutual Assurance Company was destined to cease existence in the early part of the nineteenth century. But the two other companies—the Baltimore Equitable Society and the Mutual Assurance Society of Virginia—both of which were founded during Washington's second term, are still doing business today.

Though both companies were organized in 1794, the Baltimore Equitable Society was the first by many months to begin doing business. It ranks today as the oldest existing business corporation chartered under the laws of Maryland. When the company was organized, Maryland had a population of 300,000; Baltimore, its leading city, had 14,000 inhabitants, and there was insurance for no one. There had been some bad fires. In one, a resident named Mr. Greenbury Dorsey, his four children, and a colored serving maid were burned to death before help could reach them. This disaster led to the formation of Baltimore's first volunteer fire company. In spite of their efforts and those of other companies that were subsequently formed, fire continued to wreak such serious property damage in Baltimore that a group of citizens at length got together to consider the problem. Following the genial custom of the day, they met at Stark's Tavern. "A number of respectable inhabitants of the town being assembled," the minutes of the first meeting read, "a motion was made that an Insurance Fire Company be established here, upon a plan similar to one in Philadelphia instituted by the late Dr. Franklin." The suggestion met with "general approbation," and those present accordingly resolved that as soon as twenty or more persons promised to subscribe to the new institution, an organization meeting would be called. The gentlemen who came together in Stark's Tavern tempered serious discussion with refreshments. Though they did themselves well, the mutual principle was early established, and their good cheer was not charged against the future earnings of the Society. The transaction was recorded: "Reckoning at Stark's—$2.00 . . . received of sundry members $2.25."

Appropriately, the organization meeting was held at the home of Joseph Townsend, who had been the leading spirit in advocating formation of a fire insurance company. A prosperous Quaker merchant, Townsend was a prominent figure in the city's civic and philanthropic affairs. Besides holding many other public offices, he was elected a Special Commissioner of Baltimore, a body charged with responsibility for maintaining the city's streets, water supply, and fire-fighting service.

It was fitting that Townsend was elected treasurer and secretary, the chief executive position of the newly formed fire insurance company. A lifetime of devoted service proved his fitness for the task. How soundly he built is indicated by the fact that in October 1950 the Baltimore Equitable Society issued a policy insuring the home of Joseph Townsend's great-great-great-granddaughter.

For more than a century and a half, the Baltimore Equitable Society, which writes perpetual insurance on buildings in Baltimore and its immediate suburbs, has faithfully adhered to the mutual idea, and is today one of the city's most venerable and respected institutions. It has earned its enviable reputation. One of the accomplishments of which it has reason to be proud is its record in the great Baltimore fire of 1904.

On a Sunday morning in February of that year, the Sabbath was broken by an alarm of fire. Starting in the basement of a wholesale dry-goods firm, the fire burned for thirty-six hours and destroyed 1,343 buildings before it was brought under control by the combined efforts of seventy-two fire companies, of which thirty-eight had sped to the city from out of town. The loss was more than $125 million. As a result of the conflagration, six local fire insurance companies were forced out of business. The Baltimore Equitable Society paid its claims, which numbered 445, in full. Altogether, it paid out $1,905,000, which was the largest single contribution of any insurance company toward the rebuilding of Baltimore's business district. Payment of the claim drained the company of approximately four fifths of its surplus. Left with about $500,000 in surplus, as well as an enhanced reputation for integrity, the Society resolutely set out to build up its resources again. Today, with $47 million of insurance in force and more than $3 million in surplus, the Baltimore Equitable Society is more favorably situated than at any time in its history.

Like the pioneer company in Maryland, the Mutual Assurance Society of Virginia was incorporated in 1794, but its first policy was not written until February 1796. The primary reason for this long interval was that the articles of incorporation required that a minimum of $3 million of insurance be subscribed before the company commenced business—a very stiff requirement for those times. However, this solid base was considered essential because the Virginia Society, unlike all the other early mutual companies, planned to operate throughout the state. With a population of three quarters of a million, Virginia was then the largest and wealthiest of the thirteen states. Not one of its handsome plantation houses or other beautiful buildings was protected by fire insurance.

The company founded to provide this protection was brought into existence largely through the efforts of a Richmond resident named William Frederick Ast. "Mr. Ast was a Prussian by birth," a Richmond historian has written, "a small, shriveled, wizen-faced man, who looked as if he were a descendant of the mother of vinegar; but although his aspect was sour, he was a man of considerable talent and was devoted to the institution of which he might be considered the founder." Ast was supported in this project by many of the most eminent citizens of the state, of whom 450 were charter subscribers. At their first meeting, they elected Ast to the post of principal agent, a position he held until his death twelve years later. The first president was a Richmond physician, Dr. William Foushee, who was, according to a record left by a contemporary, "a gentleman of fine personal appearance and deportment, and a favorite physician with the ladies, who said his visits were a restorative without the aid of medicine, so bland and kind were his manners and conversation. This calm and sunshine, which distinguished his medical career, could be changed to storm and thunder in his political one." At different periods of time, Dr. Foushee was mayor of Richmond, postmaster, and president of the James River Company, a corporation fathered by George Washington (who held a hundred shares in it) to improve the navigation of the James River. It was one of the most successful corporations of the day.

The Society's other officers and directors were men of corresponding eminence. One of the original directors was

Bushrod Washington, a nephew of the President and later a Justice of the United States Supreme Court. Bushrod Washington was executor of George Washington's estate and heir to Mount Vernon. In 1803, he insured Mount Vernon with the Mutual Assurance Society of Virginia, taking out two policies, one on the mansion and the other on the outbuildings. The total sum of the two policies was $16,960.

Few corporations have been represented by such distinguished counsel as the Mutual Assurance Society of Virginia in its early years. Its attorneys were Edmund Randolph, former governor of Virginia and later the first Attorney General of the United States, and John Marshall, one of the country's most esteemed lawyers, who later served for thirty-four years with unparalleled brilliance as Chief Justice of the United States Supreme Court. One of the early questions upon which they were called to render legal advice came up four months after the Society had issued its first policy. Many charter subscribers had been tardy in paying their premiums. The Society had had no losses, but the directors, at a meeting in 1796, pondered this question: If a charter subscriber who had paid his premium suffered a loss, would he be entitled to indemnity, even though all the other charter subscribers had not yet paid their premiums? They asked counsel for an opinion. "I feel no difficulty in answering the above question in the affirmative," John Marshall wrote. "On the principle of justice and convenience such ought to be the construction of the contract." In three additional, cogent paragraphs totaling two hundred and fifty words, Marshall amplified his opinion on the basis of justice and convenience. Edmund Randolph's opinion agreed in substance with Marshall's. The lawyers were paid eight dollars apiece for their services.

By their active participation in the Mutual Assurance Society of Virginia, by insuring their properties in it, and by encouraging others to do the same, many other founding fathers gave practical evidence of their belief in the mutual idea. In 1800, the year that he was elected the third President of the United States, Thomas Jefferson insured his home, Monticello, with the Society, taking $4,000 on the main house and $1,040 on the outbuildings. In the same year, James Monroe, who was then governor of Virginia and was destined to become our fifth President, insured the dwelling house on his plantation in Albemarle County. Prompted by heavy losses on country properties, the members of the Society voted in 1822 to cancel policies on such properties and to insure thereafter only structures in the cities and towns of Virginia. This ruling did not affect the insurance on John Marshall's home in Richmond, which was insured in the Society by Policy No. 72. Marshall's home, now a shrine maintained by the Association for the Preservation of Virginia Antiquities, has been insured continuously by the Mutual Assurance Society since April 8, 1796.

The Society enjoyed a steady, uninterrupted growth from the beginning. It nearly tripled the number of its policies within a year after issuing its first one. The president and the directors from Richmond and Norfolk voted to donate their first year's salaries, which were figured on 1 per cent of the premiums and totaled $287.19, for the purchase of a fire engine for Richmond. Total losses of the Society during its first three years amounted to only $1,500, but the following year it suffered a loss of $35,000 as the result of a bad fire in the city of Norfolk. After having destroyed several frame structures, the fire was finally checked by blowing up the adjacent houses, in which operation twenty-five casks of gunpowder were expended and, since no water supply was available, by playing one thousand gallons of vinegar on the flames.

The Civil War years were the most trying period in the Society's history. The main office in Richmond was kept open throughout the war, but many branch offices in other cities and towns, being in the hands of the Union forces, were obliged to close down. Premiums went unpaid and fires unreported. A footnote in the Society's financial statement of 1863 makes a rather understated reference to the troublesome situation. "In consequence of the occupancy by the enemy of many of the towns in which the Office has insurance," the note reads, "the amount of quotas [premiums] in arrear continues to be much larger than usual." In 1863 the Society patriotically bought $40,000 worth of Confederate 6 per cent convertible bonds, exchanged them in 1864 for $50,000 in 8 per cent bonds, and, subsequently judging them valueless, dropped them from its listed assets.

A considerable portion of the Society's securities were thus swept entirely away as a consequence of the war and many of its other investments greatly impaired in value. In addition, the company was presented at the close of hostilities with accumulated loss claims totaling more than $100,000. The end of the war nevertheless found the Society in good shape financially. "A fair view of the Society's assets and liabilities revealed the gratifying fact that after a full allowance for all its obligations and losses on investments, there was still left a surplus fund exceeding one hundred and twenty-six thousand dollars, whilst the foundation on which the superstructure rested remained firm and sound." So wrote Colonel John Buchanan Danforth, who was for thirty-eight years an officer of the Society, shortly after the war. "In a reasonable time," Colonel Danforth continued, "every just demand was fully met, inspiring public confidence in the stability and honorable dealing of the Society, and eliciting a prosperity that has flowed in a constant and steady stream ever since."

During the three quarters of a century since those words were written, the Society's stream of prosperity has continued to flow in ever-increasing volume. Its one hundred and fifty-fifth annual statement shows that the company now has more than $83 million of insurance in force and that its surplus exceeds $7 million. The foundation remains firm and sound. One of the factors contributing to its soundness is the practice, started at the beginning and still in effect, of carefully inspecting each property before issuing insurance on it. Many of the early applications for insurance contained detailed drawings of the location and construction of the dwellings insured. These records have frequently proved of historical value. For example, when Williamsburg was being restored, the architects in charge of the project often consulted the Society's old records and were thus able to determine not only the dimensions of the buildings but also their exterior appearance.

To sum up the Mutual Assurance Society of Virginia, one need search no farther than the observation of Colonel John Buchanan Danforth, made in 1879, that the Society "has pursued a long, useful, peaceful and honorable career, and been a great benefactor and protector to the cities and towns of old Virginia."

CHAPTER VI

The Flowering in New England

DURING the first thirty-five years of the nineteenth century, the mutual idea spread slowly but steadily, keeping pace with the expansion of the burgeoning new nation. In every direction the borders of settlement were being pushed constantly outward. President Jefferson, putting his constitutional scruples momentarily aside, negotiated the Louisiana Purchase from Napoleon in 1803, and thereby doubled the territory of the United States, at a cost of fifteen million dollars. Between 1800 and 1835, the population of the country nearly tripled, rising at the end of this era to approximately fourteen million, of whom somewhat less than 20 per cent were slaves. Though the flag had been carried to the Rockies, by the close of the first third of the century the settled frontier was only halfway across the continent. The farthest Western settlement was Independence, Kansas.

Under the presidential leadership of the so-called Virginia Dynasty—Jefferson, Madison, and Monroe, each of whom served two terms—the country passed through stirring times of war and peace. Provoked by Great Britain's maritime policy in her war with Napoleon as well as by her continuing practice of stirring up trouble with the Indians of the Northwest, the United States went to war in 1812, and two years later concluded what has since been called our Second War for Independence. Meanwhile, the rough-and-ready troops under frontiersman Andrew Jackson had defeated the Creek Indians in Alabama, thus breaking the Indian power east of the Mississippi and focusing attention on Jackson as presidential timber. Though the War of 1812 had been so bitterly opposed in the North that Massachusetts, Rhode Island, and Connecticut had threatened to secede in protest, the period following the conflict was so tranquil that it was known at the time as the era of good feeling.

While the frontier was being pierced by the adventurous, the settled area of the country was being brought into closer contact and commerce was being spurred by the development of inland navigation. The Erie Canal, opened in 1825, was the most stupendous engineering feat performed in America up to that time. Eight years in the building, 363 miles in length, and completed at a cost of seven million dollars, the first great canal in the Union opened a pathway from the Atlantic to the Great Lakes and performed a miracle in opening the Western wilderness to settlement, productivity, and trade. Water transport was further stimulated by the invention of the steamboat in 1807. A dozen years later, the steamship *Savannah* made the first trip across the Atlantic. Manufacturing was encouraged by the enactment in 1816 of the first protective tariff. The same year, a new United States Bank was chartered, and in Boston the first savings bank was established. Though the first third of the nineteenth century was in general a boom period, it suffered from intermittent setbacks, the worst of which was the Panic of 1819, when the price of cotton fell 50 per cent within twelve months and the cost of living soared so high that even United States senators were moved to complain. One of them went so far as to resign his position, explaining that he could not support a family on his salary of nine hundred dollars a year. At the end of this era, an American named J. D. Phillips patented a device that was to prove of the greatest convenience and, to insurance men, of the greatest concern. The novelty that Phillips thought up was the phosphorous friction match.

By 1835 the Union had expanded to comprise twenty-four states. In thirteen of these, one or more mutual fire insurance companies, which are still in existence, were already doing business. With one exception, all these companies were on or near the Eastern seaboard. Two were founded in New Jersey, and three were added in Pennsylvania, bringing the total number of mutual fire insurance companies in that state to five. The mutual idea was most widely adopted during this period in New England. In Massachusetts fourteen companies were founded, two sprang up in Connecticut, and one each was established in Maine, New Hampshire, Vermont, and Rhode Island. Toward the end of this period, the mutual idea penetrated as far west as Ohio, where the Cincinnati Equitable Insurance Company was founded in 1826.

Since there were no newspapers or other periodicals of national circulation when these companies were formed, the idea upon which they were founded was spread mainly by word of mouth. The Cincinnati Equitable provides an illustration of the way the mutual idea circulated during the early part of the century. The leading spirit in founding this company was a man named John Jolley, who was also one of its incorporators and its first secretary. He, like most of the other original incorporators, had emigrated to Cincinnati, then a city of sixteen thousand, from Maryland. There they had become acquainted with the operation of the Baltimore Equitable Society. It was therefore natural that they should have patterned the Cincinnati Equitable, which has the distinction of being the oldest fire insurance company in Ohio, after the old Baltimore company.

In other sections of the country, the mutual idea filtered from one community to another and from state to state in much the same way. When in 1830 a group of prominent citizens in Easton, Pennsylvania, were preparing to set up a fire insurance company, they paid the expenses of one of their members to travel to the town of Morrisville for the purpose of gathering information on proper insurance procedures from the Bucks County Contributionship for Insuring Houses & Other Buildings from Loss by Fire, a mutual company that had already been in successful operation for twenty-one years. The Worcester Mutual Fire Insurance Company, which was founded in 1823 and is the oldest fire insurance company in Massachusetts, served as the direct model for at least two other New England companies. One of these is the Mutual Fire Assurance Company of Springfield, founded in 1827. At the second meeting of its directors, it was voted that the secretary should proceed "to examine the office of the Mutual Fire Insurance Company of Worcester and procure such information as may be necessary." The secretary came back with copies of the pioneer company's bylaws, application blanks, and policy forms, all of which were adopted verbatim. Word of the Worcester Mutual traveled all the way up the coast to Saco, Maine, where plans for establishing a mutual fire insurance company were set afoot in 1827. With true American enterprise, the incorporators of this company secured a charter, but, since they were not quite sure what to do next, they, too, consulted with the Worcester Mutual and eventually copied that company's forms and methods. This pattern of unselfishly helping one another is an indication of the kind of people who were propagating the mutual idea.

Another characteristic common to the founders of these early companies is that they were public-spirited, conscientious men who were leaders in their communities and respected by their neighbors. For example, the first chairman of the Providence Mutual Fire Insurance Company, which was founded in 1800 and is the oldest fire insurance company in Rhode Island, was David Howell, a brilliant lawyer and scholar, a member of the Board of Fellows of Brown University, and for twelve years United States district judge of Rhode Island. John Endicott, the first president of the Norfolk & Dedham Mutual Fire Insurance Company, was a member of the Constitutional Convention of 1820, commissioner of highways, and a state senator. Edward Augustus Newton, one of the incorporators of the Berkshire Mutual Fire Insurance Company, was president of the Agricultural National Bank and a trustee of Williams College. The first president of the Worcester Mutual was Levi Lincoln, later elected governor of Massachusetts. James Madison Porter, a lawyer and judge who served as chairman of the group that brought the Fire Insurance Company of Northampton County into existence, was also president of the Lehigh Valley Railroad and Secretary of War under President Tyler. Alvah Crocker, the man who contributed most to the founding of the Fitchburg Mutual Fire Insurance Company and served for twenty-three years as its leading director, was also a director or trustee of fifteen other institutions, including two banks and a railroad company, and in addition found time to serve in both houses of the State Legislature and as a representative in Congress.

The devotion that the founders felt toward their companies is proved by the long terms of service that they gave them.

The three men who incorporated the Barnstable County Mutual Fire Insurance Company never forsook it during their lifetimes; Zenas D. Bassett served as its president for thirty-two years, Amos Otis, Jr., as its secretary and treasurer for forty-two, and Ebenezer Bacon as a director for thirty-five. In its first hundred years, the Worcester Mutual had only seven secretaries and five treasurers. Nathaniel Wood, the first president of the Fitchburg Mutual, held office continuously for twenty-one years, while David Harding, the first secretary of the Hingham Mutual Fire Insurance Company, served in that post for forty-eight. The same pattern is repeated over and over again in the companies that have survived for a century or more. By their actions, the founders amply demonstrated their belief in the mutual idea.

Their allegiance was not prompted by what they could get out of it for themselves. The nominal sums they received for their services is proof of their disinterest in financial reward. What they were interested in was providing insurance at cost, and they were well aware that the way to do that was to keep down expenses, including the compensation of officers. The Hartford County Mutual Fire Insurance Company paid its president $30 a year. The directors of the Abington Mutual Fire Insurance Company were paid 50 cents per meeting, while the president received $1.00. After holding office for thirty-one years, the president of the Barnstable County Mutual was receiving an annual salary of $75. Double that amount was paid by the Mutual Fire Assurance Company of Springfield to its secretary and treasurer, but he was, in effect, the whole company. "This company," the Norfolk & Dedham wrote into its by-laws, "shall pay the secretary for his services 85 cents for each policy and each assignment and $1.00 per day at a directors' meeting, which shall be full compensation for writing applications and policies and all other instruments, likewise for fuel and office room." The company did, however, give the secretary a break by not requiring him also to furnish business stationery at his own expense.

Besides keeping the compensation of officers within most economical limits, the companies kept a close watch on other overhead items, such as office space. Many went along for several years without any regular office, the secretary keeping the books and records in his home, for which he was sometimes paid a portion of his fuel bill. The Abington Mutual engaged space in a corner of L. Faxon's Shoe Store at a rental of $17 a year, while the directors of Middlesex Mutual Assurance Company met for many years in the rear of John L. Smith's jewelry store, John L. being the first secretary of the company. David Harding, the first secretary of the Hingham Mutual, also donated space in a corner of his shop for the company's office. The annual meetings of the policyholders required more space, however, but these, too, were economically handled by being held, according to the early records, at rent-free places, such as the "School House near the Post Office" or the "School House on the Plain."

The charters of most of the companies ran for twenty-eight years, at the end of which they were renewable for a like period. Later they were extended for an indefinite length of time. As a rule, it was necessary for the early companies to postpone actually issuing policies until a certain amount of insurance had been subscribed. The amount varied, but it was usually between $50,000 and $70,000. This requirement proved in some instances to be a considerable barrier, especially in small communities, where a man owning a house valued at $3,000 was considered well off. More often than not, however, the amount subscribed exceeded the minimum requirement. The common rule among all the companies was not to insure more than three fourths of the value of any building. The majority wrote seven-year policies, although there were exceptions; the Hingham Mutual, for example, originally insured from one to seven years, and the Hartford County wrote from one to five.

At the time these companies were getting under way, the science of insurance was unknown. There were no rates and no table of experience upon which to base rates. The early pioneers, with nothing to go on but their own individual judgment and good sense, had to proceed by the method of trial and error. They were not practicing insurance—they were making it.

Because they were not interested in quick expansion for the sake of personal profit and because their primary aim was to fill a local need, the early companies at first insured only buildings within a severely restricted area. The Worcester Mutual, for example, confined its writings for many years to Worcester County, branching out later to include the whole state of Massachusetts. It was not until 1906, when the company was eighty-three years old, that it began insuring buildings outside the state. Even more conservative was the Hingham Mutual, which originally accepted insurance only on buildings located in the town of Hingham; within a year, however, it extended its operation to the county of Plymouth, and within five to the entire state of Massachusetts. The Providence Mutual also started out modestly by insuring only in the city of Providence and its immediate vicinity; it branched out slowly, for fifty years confining its business to Rhode Island and Massachusetts. By contrast, the Holyoke Mutual Fire Insurance Company from the beginning insured throughout the state, and by the time it was five years old was doing brisk business in three other nearby states. After a century or more of service, the great majority of the companies now operate widely outside the state in which they are located.

With few exceptions, the companies founded in the early part of the nineteenth century, particularly those in New England, adopted the agency system early in their careers. The Worcester Mutual, the pioneer Massachusetts company that led the way in establishing many mutual practices, had named forty agents within a year after commencing business. The directors of the Norfolk & Dedham voted "that each agent receive 25 cents for each written application for insurance he may file in the office." The Middlesex Mutual, somewhat more liberal, paid 37½ cents. The compensation ranged upward to 50 cents paid by the Fitchburg Mutual, while the Berkshire Mutual went clear up to $1.00. That was the top.

To make mutual insurance safe, the early companies required each policyholder not only to pay a cash premium but also to sign and deposit with the company a note for, as a rule, four times the amount of his premium. The premium notes were held with the other assets of the companies as a bulwark against any unforeseen disaster resulting in heavy claims. However, as the companies grew and accumulated large surplus accounts, the assessment provision became unnecessary, as proved by the fact that not one of the so-called New England dwelling-house mutuals has ever levied an assessment. (In fact, throughout the entire United States, no legal reserve mutual fire insurance company that acquired $400,000 in cash assets or $200,000 in cash surplus has ever failed or made an assessment.) With the need for the assessment provision removed and changes in the insurance laws permitting, the pioneer companies began dropping the assessment feature, with the result that their policies today are almost without exception non-assessable.

From the very beginning, all the early companies adhered religiously to the fundamental mutual principle of preventing loss through the careful selection and supervision of risks. Because they were more interested in safety than size and refused to take in all the risks that were offered, some of the companies were the butt of jokes to the effect that they would insure "nothing but stone wharves and railroad iron." Taking these mild witticisms in stride, the pioneers went on their way to make insurance history.

Since the insuring of dwellings was the primary object of the early companies, that class of risk made up by far the largest part of their business. Some companies, however, experimented with other kinds of risks. For example, the Worcester Mutual in its first few years insured sawmills, gristmills, taverns, and machine shops, but its experience was bad, and it later dropped these hazardous risks. The Norfolk & Dedham, on the other hand, made it clear from the beginning that it would not insure "any kind of cotton and woolen factories, or any building containing any engine or machinery operated by steam or water power." After ten years' experience, the policyholders of the Mutual Fire of Springfield voted to discontinue taking insurance on both taverns and churches. Though the Fitchburg Mutual also turned thumbs down on taverns, it was willing to insure churches, provided the buildings were brought up to the company's standard. In December 1855, the directors voted "to insure the meeting-house in Westminster, on condition that the pipe in the attic be cased and that it be faithfully examined once in each month." In 1871, it was voted "that the Calvinistic Congregational Society of Fitchburg be allowed to make improvements on their meeting-house without additional premium, if they remove the shavings daily and keep the house locked up." Though the Fitchburg Mutual turned down the application of one L. Warren to insure his pew in the Leicester meeting house, the Mutual Fire of Springfield acted favorably on a similar request by a policyholder named Jehiel Abbott. To the policy insuring his dwelling the company attached an endorsement that read, "In consideration of an additional premium of 24 cents and note for 96 cents, this policy is to cover ½ of pew No. 51 in the Westfield Meeting House for the sum of forty dollars."

Before issuing a policy on any property, it was inspected by an official of the company. According to an early manual issued by the Holyoke Mutual, the factors to be considered included "material of construction, roof covering, repair, exposures, including occupancy of exposures, the use made of the building, and the character and habits of the occupants and owner." An application containing this information, together usually with a plan of the building, was then placed before the directors. If a majority voted favorably, a policy was issued.

As a direct result of their careful selection of risks, the pioneer companies had phenomenally low losses. In its first year, the Worcester Mutual had none; the Abington Mutual had one, amounting to nine dollars. The Pawtucket Mutual went for three years and the Berkshire Mutual for three and a half before having a loss. During its first five years, the Hartford County had two losses, totaling twenty-two dollars. Neither the Bucks County Contributionship nor the Barnstable County Mutual was presented with a loss claim until they had been in business for more than seven years. Even more remarkable was the record of the Hingham Mutual and that of the Mutual Fire of Springfield, both of which were in their tenth year before they were called upon to pay their first loss.

Some of the early claims were frankly puzzling to the originators of mutual insurance. In April 1834, for example, the directors of the Norfolk & Dedham took under advisement a claim made by a policyholder named Horatio B. Alden, who, according to the company's records, asked indemnification for "damage by fire done to his house by lightning, altho nothing was burnt thereby." This seemed very curious to the directors: here was a man asking a fire insurance company to pay for damage by fire where there was no fire. The board pondered and finally requested their president, James Richardson, "to make inquiry what may have been the usage of insurance companies in cases similar . . . and if, in his opinion, said Alden has a legal claim, to settle with him." Summer came and went while President Richardson deliberated. In October, he made his decision. "Alden claim decided to be legitimate," the minutes of the October meeting read, "and voted that in all cases where losses may thus be sustained on buildings insured by this company, such loss will be paid, though no fire occur."

The majority of the companies made occasional cash donations to the local volunteer fire departments, enabling them to acquire additional apparatus and resplendent uniforms. The volunteer fire companies were rather exclusive social organizations, and as they increased, competition among them became keen, each company striving to be first to reach the fire and get water on it. This rivalry was, of course, considerably enhanced by the possibility of the successful company's receiving a gratuity for what was often called its "laudable exertions." However admirable the volunteers' zeal, it often had the unfortunate effect of embroiling them in fist fights and rioting, caused by their determination not to be beaten to the fire. These fights for priority not infrequently took precedence over fighting the flames. Having once arrived at the fire, the volunteers were apt to turn the occasion into a rather festive affair, since it was common for the doughty smoke-eaters to boost their morale, if not their efficiency, by the use of ardent spirits. Though many of the volunteer companies imposed heavy fines on members who tippled at a fire, the practice was not easily discouraged, as the following typical entries in the records of one of the companies indicate:

1814–January 29		Gin at the fire	$ .65
1814–May 1		Gin at the fire	$1.00
1815–October 25		Gin at the fire	$ .34
1815–December 13	½ Gal.	Gin at the fire	$ .62

Some of the business practices of the early insurance companies were also quaint. On April 6, 1841, the directors of the Norfolk & Dedham authorized their president, in the name of the company, to present a Mrs. Monroe with "a silk dress not exceeding ten dollars in cost, or make a present to her not exceeding that amount, in such other way as she may desire, as a gratuity for her having discovered the fire in the store connected with the dwelling house where Dr. Monroe resides." The prospect of receiving a silk dress apparently alerted the ladies to the advantages of keeping a sharp eye out for fires; the records show that a few months after Mrs. Monroe received her gown a similar gift was made to a Mrs. French for "having discovered a fire near her house and her exertions by which much of the property was saved."

As a result of economical management, careful selection of risks, and the high moral standard of their policyholders, the early companies were able from the beginning to live up to the mutual principle of providing insurance at cost. With no losses or very small ones, the companies found that they did not have to spend much of the money that the policyholders had paid in as premiums. So, since the companies were not being run for profit, the portion of the premiums not needed for losses or expenses was returned to the policyholders in the form of dividends, which were indeed sizable. They ran as high as 90 per cent in the Berkshire Mutual, 94 per cent in the Worcester Mutual, and up to 100 per cent in others, such as the Hingham Mutual. During its first seventeen years, the Barnstable County Mutual never paid a dividend of less than 100 per cent; in other words, the policyholders each year got back at least as much as they had paid in the previous year. Since the premium funds were invested and earning interest, some companies were able in years when losses were low to pay their policyholders dividends that were even larger than their premiums. At one time the Hingham Mutual returned to its policyholders in dividends $1.09 for every dollar they had paid as premiums, while the Barnstable County once paid a dividend of $1.11 for every dollar of premium.

The practice of returning all the savings to the policyholders was followed for many years, but as time passed and the directors learned more about insurance, they came to the realization that their companies would be endowed with greater stability if they possessed a cash fund on which to draw in case of necessity. The logical way to create this reserve, they concluded, was to retain a small part of each premium and place it in a surplus account for the protection of the policyholders. Also, as a result of their increased experience, the companies found that instead of charging high rates and paying high dividends, there were greater advantages to the policyholders in reducing the rates as well as the size of the dividends. Over the years, therefore, the early companies gradually built up a healthy surplus and at the same time established the remarkable record of paying a dividend every single year from the beginning to the present, a span that in many cases covers well over a hundred years.

The survival record of the mutual companies founded in the early part of the nineteenth century is equally impressive. Since more fire insurance companies, both mutual and stock, were established during this period in Massachusetts than in any other state, the experience in Massachusetts provides the best example. Up to the beginning of 1848, forty-one mutual fire insurance companies had been established; in the same period, thirty stock companies writing fire and fire and marine insurance were founded. Of the thirty stock companies, one was doing business seventy-five years later. Of the forty-one mutual companies, nineteen were doing business seventy-five years later. And of those nineteen, fifteen are still doing business today, more than a century after their founding.

As nineteenth-century Americans had learned the value of banding together for mutual protection against the ravages of fire, so the companies themselves discovered that advantages could be secured from their banding together. These efforts toward inter-company co-operation first took shape and were most successfully carried out among the mutual companies in New England. On March 22, 1853, the officers of six of the New England mutuals met at the American House in Boston to discuss and attempt to solve various common problems. This meeting, so far as is known, was the first gathering of representatives of insurance companies ever held in this country for the purpose of co-ordinating methods. After two additional meetings, this group arrived at a number of major decisions, such as the establishment of a minimum rate scale for the more common groups of risks, payment of uniform commissions to agents, limitation of the policy term to a period not exceeding five years, and an agreement for pooling information on premiums and losses for the purpose of establishing equitable rates. Though these principles seem commonplace today, they were the first pioneering steps toward the widespread co-operation which came to be a keystone of mutual insurance practice.

As time passed and the insurance business developed in scope and complexity, many mutual fire insurance officials in New England perceived the need for a more comprehensive association to promote their common interests. On September 10, 1879, there accordingly came into being the Massachusetts Mutual Fire Insurance Union, an organization of twenty-four Massachusetts mutual companies that had, among its first objectives, repeal of the statute limiting insurance in mutual companies to three fourths of the value of the property insured. In 1919, the members of the Union adopted a new constitution, making possible enlargement of its activities; at the same time its name was changed to the Mutual Fire Insurance Association of New England. The Association, or Union, as it is sometimes still referred to by old-timers, has been in existence now for seventy-three years. Working in harmony with other insurance organizations and through its membership in the National Fire Protection Association and in the United States Chamber of Commerce, the Association has made many notable contributions to the betterment of the insurance business in general and to the sound underwriting principles that have been responsible for the steady, sturdy growth of the New England mutuals.

Out of the Association have developed three important organizations. One is the Mutual Farm Underwriters, which inspects farms, provides measures for protecting rural properties from fire, and furnishes general advisory service on the underwriting of farm risks. The other two organizations are the Mutual Fire Underwriters Association of Massachusetts and the Mutual Insurance Underwriters of New England. These are essentially reinsurance organizations, the former composed of eleven companies, the latter of nineteen. Attached to every policy issued by each of the nineteen companies belonging to the Mutual Insurance Underwriters of New England is a "Certificate of Reinsurance," which provides that if the company issuing the policy should become unable to meet its obligations under the policy, the remaining eighteen companies agree to assume the liability. In other words, every policy is guaranteed by all the nineteen companies, each of whom assumes a stated percentage of the total liability, ranging from 1 per cent to 14 per cent. This system of reinsurance provides the individual policyholders with gilt-edged protection.

Of the twenty-four companies that comprise the Mutual Fire Insurance Association of New England, twenty have been in business for more than a century; the average age of the other four is seventy-four years. Besides having passed the test of time, these companies have achieved an impressive financial standing. As of December 31, 1949, their combined assets amounted to $64.6 million, while their combined surplus was $30 million. From their organization through December 31, 1947, they had returned to their policyholders dividends totaling $84.1 million. And they are continuing to return to their policyholders dividends—in effect, savings—amounting to 20 per cent or more of the annual premium. Considering the record, there is no cause for wonder that the mutual idea, adopted in the towns and hamlets on the Eastern seaboard more than a century ago, should continue to prosper.

CHAPTER VII

Three Men and an Idea—1

ZACHARIAH ALLEN

DESPISED by his enemies as a scheming dictator and revered by his friends as an incomparable champion of democracy, rough-hewn Andrew Jackson was midway in his second term as President in 1835 when there occurred in New England an event of the greatest importance in the history of mutual insurance. In the year 1835, a far-seeing textile manufacturer named Zachariah Allen established a mutual fire insurance company devoted exclusively to insuring factories. In so doing, he took the first step toward adapting the mutual idea to meet the needs of the business community and began the integration of mutual insurance into the commercial life of the nation. Out of Zachariah Allen's pioneering efforts developed a group of companies known as the Factory Mutuals, which revolutionized insurance in America and which today comprise one of the outstanding insurance organizations in the world.

Neither Zachariah Allen nor his spiritual ancestor, Benjamin Franklin, invented mutual insurance, but both developed the idea to fit the time and place in which they lived. In Franklin's day, there was little need for protecting manufacturing establishments. Generally speaking, they did not exist because manufacturing in America was largely forbidden during the colonial period by the British Acts of Trade. As William Pitt declared, Americans were not to be permitted "to manufacture a lock of wool or a horseshoe or a hobnail." Actually, hobnails, horseshoes, and other simple ironmongery were clandestinely manufactured in the Colonies, but not much else. When Franklin's Union Fire Company needed a few simple items such as leather buckets and wooden ladders, they had to be imported from the mother country.

By the time Americans had achieved their independence, the industrial revolution was under way in England. "We must now place the manufacturer side by side with the agriculturist," Thomas Jefferson said, but the transformation of the United States from an agrarian into an industrial nation was slow to develop. By 1810, for example, the annual production of pig iron in the United States amounted to a mere fifty-four thousand tons. This was increased by ten times in the next forty years, but Americans were still, in 1850, producing only half as much iron and steel as they were importing.

Though the development of heavy industry lagged, considerable progress was made in the manufacture of textiles. The textile industry was, in fact, the first major industry to become solidly established in this country. The largest impetus to its development was the War of 1812 and certain events that preceded it. In an effort to avoid war, Jefferson promulgated the Embargo Act, in force from 1807 to 1809, which forbade all exports from the United States as well as imports of many articles of British manufacture. The effects of this virtual embargo on shipping worked the greatest hardship on the seafaring states of New England and began forcing the transition of that area from a maritime to a manufacturing community. Before the embargo, there were fifteen cotton mills with eight thousand spindles in the United States. After the embargo had been lifted, there were eighty-seven cotton mills with eighty thousand spindles, 75 per cent of which were located in or near Providence, Rhode Island.

Spurred further during the war years, the textile industry received additional encouragement in the tariff of 1816, which imposed a 25 per cent duty on imported textiles. By 1840, the United States had twelve hundred cotton factories with two and a quarter million spindles, the great majority of which were located in New England. There, also, woolen manufacturing had begun to develop. In contrast to the cotton mills, which were relatively large-scale operations, most of the woolen mills were small, but by 1845, there were fifteen hundred of them turning out the simpler kinds of woolen goods, such as blankets and flannels. Zachariah Allen, who was to introduce mutual fire insurance into the new world of manufacturing, began his business career in 1822 as a manufacturer of woolens, but by the time he formed his first insurance company he had refitted his mill for the production of cotton goods, which was the predominant form of manufacturing in New England until well after the Civil War.

Though Zachariah Allen occupies a position in American insurance similar in some respects to that held by Benjamin Franklin, the background of the two pioneers was notably dissimilar. Franklin, a candlemaker's son with but two years of formal schooling, came up the hard way. Allen started with the advantages of wealth and education. The mutual idea appealed to both, as did their strong sense of social responsibility.

Born in Providence in 1795, Allen was the son of a wealthy shipowner and manufacturer who died when the boy was five. With his considerable inheritance and the encouragement of his mother, who provided him with a set of tools and gave him the run of the attic as a workshop, Allen was able at an early age to indulge his scientific and inventive bent. After receiving his primary education in private schools, he entered Brown University at the age of fourteen. There he discovered, as he mentioned in his diary, that some of the "young men entertained false and pernicious ideas, one of which was that the use of spiritous liquors is favorable to genius." (It is fair to assume that when Allen was appointed a trustee of Brown several years later some of the alleged inducements to genius were removed.) After graduating, he entered the law office of Senator James Burrill and was admitted to the bar two years later, at the age of twenty.

Allen, like Franklin, had an abiding interest in the prevention of fire. He had a very low opinion of the efficiency of the bucket brigades, which comprised the fire-fighting system of Providence. In 1821, while a member of the Town Council, he proposed that the city purchase "a forcing engine for the extinguishment of fires." As a result of his subsequent study and recommendation, Providence soon acquired a "Hydraulion" engine, which took thirty-six men to operate and was then the latest thing in fire-fighting equipment. Allen himself designed the engine's metallic suction pipe consisting of a number of folding joints. He was not satisfied with the hose then in use, so he devised a new kind by riveting linen hose with copper.

Possessing an inquiring mind, catholic tastes, and a love of travel, Allen, after his marriage in 1817, when he was twenty-two, embarked with his bride on an instructive if somewhat rugged honeymoon. The newlyweds decided to see America first, and accordingly set out for Washington, D.C., by stagecoach. It took them three weeks to reach the capital. From there they headed out to have a look at the newly opened territories in the Middle West, traveling on horseback and carrying with them only what would fit in their saddlebags. After his wedding trip, which lasted several months and included a journey down the Ohio River on a barge, Allen returned with his bride to Providence and tried his hand at politics, serving successively on the Town Council and as judge of probate. Then he went into the legislature but found that a couple of years as a representative was, as he remarked, "sufficient introduction to the chicanery of politics." In 1822, he entered the textile manufacturing business, and though that was his official business from then on, he retained, like Franklin, a spirited interest in a wide variety of civic and scientific matters and devoted an abundance of his time to promoting the public welfare.

Though privately schooled, Allen was a strong believer in public education. In 1840, after overcoming considerable opposition, he organized and put into operation two evening schools for adults in Providence. This was the first adult-education program founded in this country. He served for fifty-six years as a trustee of Brown University, which awarded him an honorary degree of Doctor of Laws. In addition, he was one of the founders and original trustees of many civic institutions, including the Providence Public Library, the Athenaeum, Butler Hospital, the Rhode Island Historical Society, and the Fireman's Relief Association, which provided assistance to families of firemen injured in the line of duty. While on a trip abroad with his family in

After the Fire in Salem, Massachusetts

is picture, one of the earliest successful aerial photographs ever taken, shows "Point District" of Salem after the Great Fire of June 25, 1914. The ruins of Naumkeag Mill, the city's largest single industry, are shown at the top of photograph. A storehouse of fire-resistive construction, in the center of the l buildings, stands practically undamaged. Fire broke out in a leather-nufacturing plant, and a gale sprang up to carry sparks and brands onto scores tinder-dry shingle roofs while half of the full-paid men in the fire department re at lunch. The first hydrant to which a hose was attached was out of order. thin half an hour, houses a quarter of a mile from the original blaze had ned to the ground. During the night a third of the city was ravaged and 000 people made homeless. Property loss was estimated at $13 million; the lyoke Mutual Fire Insurance Company, of Salem, alone paid $237,894 in ms.

ZACHARIAH ALLEN, 1795–1882

Founder of Factory Mutual Insurance, Zachariah Allen organized the Ma
facturers Mutual Fire Insurance Company and the Rhode Island Mutual
Insurance Company, both in Providence. He also suggested the formation of
Boston Manufacturers Mutual Fire Insurance Company. An outstanding lea
in mutual insurance, he was also a practical scientist of note.

1850, Allen was impressed by the waterworks of Rome and came home determined to secure a municipal water supply system for Providence. After much difficulty, he finally succeeded. At the dedication ceremony, he opened the valve that admitted the water to the system, and was referred to by the mayor on that occasion as the "Father of the Water Works of Providence."

Like Franklin, Allen had a natural curiosity about scientific phenomena and combined a native gift for inventiveness with a practical approach to scientific problems. He once took a trip to Niagara Falls with his family and, in addition to enjoying the scenery, made use of the opportunity to carry out the first systematic measurement of the flow of water over the Falls and of the power to be derived therefrom. He introduced an improved system for heating houses by the installation of hot-air furnaces in the basements and the transmission of heat through conducting pipes and registers to the floors above. He invented and patented an automatic cutoff valve for steam engines used in factories, and for this was awarded the Rumford Medal. He built the first reservoirs in the country to store water for providing power for manufacturing. This innovation enabled mills to operate during the summer months, when drought was apt to reduce the supply of water and thus curtail production. He also introduced a new system for dyeing cloth, which made it possible for a continuous line of cloth to be passed through the dye vats and washing apparatus and eliminated the labor, previously required, of repeatedly sewing the pieces together and tearing them apart before and after each operation.

Perhaps Allen's greatest scientific achievement was his improvements in the transmission of power. By discarding the massive shafts with cogwheels of rough, heavy castings of wood, which characterized the old system, and substituting light shafts with balanced, belt-driven pulleys traveling at high speed, Allen wrought a major change in the method of transmitting power. His method became known as "The American System of High-Speed Belting," and many representatives of foreign industry came over to examine it. Allen explained the principle in a volume titled *Transmission of Motive Power*. He was the author of several other highly regarded works, including *Philosophy of the Mechanics of Nature; Solar Light, Heat and Gravitation*, and *The Science of Mechanics*, which served as a textbook for two generations. In his spare time he designed, as a favor to his wife, the first greenhouse seen in the vicinity of Providence, and also undertook what is believed to be the first systematic attempt in this country to practice scientific forestry; on a ten-acre lot, he set out hundreds of oak, chestnut, and locust trees, which, when harvested forty years later, showed an annual profit of 6 per cent.

Like many men whose interests are varied and whose minds are keen, Zachariah Allen enjoyed a long life. He died at the age of eighty-six. How he accomplished all that he did may be accounted for, as he once explained, by the fact that he followed a strict regimen, had methodical habits, and took exercise daily. Of equal importance is the fact, as Allen remarked when he was eighty-four, that "I never knew a sick day in my life, although my mother said there was one morning when I did not get to school."

In addition to Zachariah Allen's notable accomplishments in many fields, he made lasting contributions to the field of insurance. His close interest in the subject began in 1822, when he built a textile mill in Providence, then a city of about twenty-one thousand people. Employing his scientific knowledge and his own considerable capital, Allen used exceptional care in the construction of his mill, which was sixty by forty feet, four stories high, had six hundred spindles, and employed about sixty workers. He spared no expense in selecting the best materials and methods of construction. He built the mill of stone, used extra-thick planking for floors, and laid the wooden shingles in mortar. He devised a heating system so that no stoves were placed among the machinery, and he shut off the picker room, a frequent starting point of fires, with a substantial fire wall. In addition, he fitted the mill with an unusual amount of fire-fighting apparatus, consisting of pumps, pipes, hydrants, and hose. When completed, the factory was as nearly fire-resistant as was then possible.

Since the mutual fire insurance companies in existence at that time did not insure factories, Allen insured his mill in a stock company, paying the then high but common rate of 2½ per cent, or $2.50 for each hundred dollars of insurance. There being no competition to force down the cost, Allen continued to pay this stiff premium for thirteen years, until 1835. Shortly before that, the economic pressures resulting from President Jackson's bitter fight with the Bank of the United States had caused Allen and other manufacturers to pay more than ordinary concern to their fixed expenses, including insurance. In 1832 Jackson vetoed the bill to recharter the Bank of the United States, which provided, through its main office and twenty-five branches, the backbone of the nation's commercial banking system. Without waiting for the expiration of the bank's charter, Jackson removed the government's deposits to the state banks, known to his opponents as "pet banks." The effects on the nation's economy were far-reaching; hard times and feverish speculation ensued. With prices tumbling, New England mills and factories began closing down or discharging workers by the hundreds. Not surprisingly in a period of financial panic, fire losses increased. As a consequence, the stock fire insurance companies (or "cash offices," as they were called, since their policies were delivered only for cash) advanced their rates, including those on Allen's mill, and thereby moved its owner to action.

His first step was to call on the president of the insurance company carrying the risk on his mill. Allen pointed out the extraordinary measures he had taken to protect his mill and on that basis applied for a reduction of his rate. As Allen recorded in his diary, the president replied, "I cannot go about to see all the mills we insure and attend to the business at the office. An average must be made. The good risks must pay for the poor."

Not satisfied with this brusque answer, Allen persuaded the president to present the matter to the company's board of directors at their next meeting. On the day they were to meet, Allen returned to the company's office, and at the conclusion of the meeting, two of the directors came out to inform their persistent policyholder of the company's decision. "Mr. Allen," one of the directors said, "although it seems unjust, the board has decided that a fire risk is a fire risk, and we can make no reduction."

"Gentlemen," Allen replied, "the day will come when you will regret what you admit to be unjust action on your part. Good day."

Angered by the refusal of the insurance company to recognize that one risk was better than another, Allen called together a number of his business friends and associates to consider, as he stated in a public notice, "the expediency of forming a Mutual Fire Insurance Company exclusively for insuring Mills." The men who attended the initial meeting called by Allen were mostly proprietors or operators of cotton mills, of which Rhode Island then had 116, with an invested capital of $6.5 million, and their insurance problem was therefore the same as Allen's. They decided to solve it by forming a mutual fire insurance company. A charter and by-laws were drawn up by a committee consisting of Allen and two other millowners, and the act incorporating the Manufacturers Mutual Fire Insurance Company was passed at the fall session of the legislature in 1835. The company was permitted by its charter to commence business "when the sum prescribed to be insured by the Associates shall amount to $1,000,000," and "to insure for a term not exceeding one year any manufactories or other buildings with their contents against loss or damage by fire."

The original directors, of whom there were thirteen, disdained not only superstition but also personal gain; they gave their services gratuitously. At their first meeting, held on November 9, 1835, a committee was appointed to solicit subscriptions for insurance. When the directors convened eight days later for their second meeting, they learned that insurance in the amount of $1,058,225 had been pledged. They thereupon elected a millowner named Amasa Mason as president; to fill the post of secretary, who was the real executive of the company, they elected John H. Ormsbee, who had had more than a decade of practical insurance experience as the Providence representative of the Aetna Insurance Company. Zachariah Allen, who preferred to be an organizer rather than an officeholder, was appointed a member of the three-man executive committee; its chief function was to fix the rate of premium. For an office the company engaged one small room at an annual rental of $87.48.

In the beginning, the Manufacturers Mutual limited the amount of insurance it would write on any one risk to $20,000, and it would insure no more than three quarters of the total value of any one property. The assured was required to pay a part of the premium in cash and to give notes for the remainder. The notes ran to ten times the amount of the cash payment. All these provisions were written into the company's charter. However, the important matter of fixing the rate of premium was placed in the hands of the executive committee. Allen and the two other members of this committee recommended that "75 per cent of the premiums established by the aforementioned standards of rules [i.e., the rates charged by stock companies] should be charged by them, reserving to themselves the right in any case to vary the premium according to their discretion as each case shall be presented." In other words, the Manufacturers Mutual started off by setting its basic rates at 25 per cent under those charged by stock companies, but each risk was to be judged on its own merits.

The company's first policy was issued on December 3, 1835, to Zachariah Allen, insuring his mill for $2,500. The premium was $15 for one year. At the end of the company's first year of business, it had 154 policies in force. There had been a few losses, none of them large. When the accounts were reckoned, it was found that total losses and expenses amounted to 49 per cent of the company's assets. The directors accordingly voted a dividend of 51 per cent. Actually, the record was more impressive than that figure indicates. Since the original premium had been set at 75 per cent of the stock company rate, the policyholders of the Manufacturers

Mutual had saved a total of 63½ per cent. Simply stated, they had reduced their cost of insurance to just about one third of what it had formerly been.

These agreeably low rates could be maintained, of course, only by insuring selected risks. Allen and his associates were interested in acquiring no other kind. Their company was not a promotion for making profit, and there were no stockholders expressing a lively hope for dividends. Subjected to no outside pressures and being moved only by the desire to provide sound insurance at low cost, they were in a position to adopt a conservative pattern of growth, and they did. The high standards of eligibility for which the Factory Mutuals were to become noted were established early. "Several risks have been discontinued for various causes and a number of applications for insurance have been declined," the minutes of an early directors' meeting read, "mostly because the assured do not keep them properly in that state of security against fire as is required by the rules and regulations of this institution."

To make sure that these rules and regulations were complied with, the directors of the Manufacturers Mutual started a system of inspecting the properties they insured. Before the company was a year old, they voted "to employ a suitable person at the expense of the Company to visit the manufacturing plants in this State and its vicinity . . . and to make report in writing of the situation and manner of conducting the establishments he may visit." Samuel Nightingale, who later became the second president of the company, was engaged as the first inspector. Thus, at the outset, was established the Factory Mutual practice, never dropped, of having an officer or representative make an initial inspection of each risk and continue to keep a close watch on all properties insured. It was the inspection service to which Zachariah Allen, in his memoirs, ascribed much of the success of the Factory Mutual System. "The improvement was effected," he wrote, "by instituting original examinations of every mill or building insured by a vigilant agent, personally; whose duty was to report a detailed description of each premise on a book kept specially for this purpose, and to revisit the premises every year on renewal of the insurance."

During the first couple of years, the policyholders of the Manufacturers Mutual consisted mainly of friends and acquaintances of the directors. Many millowners were frankly skeptical of the new system, despite its initial success. "So unpopular had become the system of mutual fire insurance of mills and machinery," Zachariah Allen remarked in his autobiography, "that the progress was at first very slow in acquiring public confidence. Gradually the advantages of the visits from the agents appointed to examine every mill began to be manifest. The manufacturers finding that the plans of their buildings and their means of extinguishing fires, employment of watch clocks and watchmen, and the cleanliness of their mills were all noted and recorded on the books of the Company, a sudden impulse was given to them all to have their fire insurance done at the lowest rate."

To take care of this sudden impulse, underwriting capacities had to be increased. Allen accordingly addressed himself to forming a second company to write fire insurance on factories. This step was the beginning of what was to develop into the Associated Factory Mutual Companies, or, as they became more commonly known, the Factory Mutual System. The second company to enter the System was named the Rhode Island Mutual Fire Insurance Company, which commenced business in 1848. Its board of directors was virtually the same as that of the Manufacturers Mutual. The kinship between the two companies was further emphasized by the fact that the new company began business in the Manufacturers' office. Zachariah Allen served as president of the Rhode Island Mutual from its founding until its first annual meeting, when, following his natural inclination to organize rather than to manage, he resigned and was replaced by another director of the Manufacturers.

When their underwriting capacity increased, the first two Factory Mutuals made steady progress. At the close of its first year, the Rhode Island voted a dividend of 80 per cent. Both companies were handicapped, however, by their size and the limitations of their charters. Though the Manufacturers began by limiting the insurance on any single risk to $20,000, it reduced the amount after two years to $15,000. The Rhode Island was similarly limited. Consequently, they were unable to provide complete insurance coverage on any plant.

Zachariah Allen was not satisfied with this state of affairs. The success of the two companies already doing business had convinced him that the mutual idea was sound. He wanted to extend it and thus abolish what he called the "evil" of penalizing first-class risks by making them pay for third-class risks. The remedy for this evil, he believed, was not to be found in enlarging the underwriting capacity of any one mutual company but by forming additional mutual companies in a number of localities. One large advantage of this system, he felt, was that the officers and directors of each company would have close acquaintance with the insurable properties in their respective localities, from the viewpoint of both the physical and moral hazard.

Since the textile industry had made great strides in Massachusetts, Allen believed that that locality offered a favorable opportunity for extending the mutual system of insuring factories. Toward the end of 1849, he accordingly wrote a letter to a Boston business acquaintance, James Read, in which he described the work of the Manufacturers Mutual and stated, "I take the liberty of respectfully urging upon the attention of the proprietors of the many well regulated cotton mills in the vicinity of Boston, the importance of proceeding forthwith to establish a mutual insurance company for taking risks on the first class of cotton mills." This letter led to the establishment, within a year, of the Boston Manufacturers Mutual Fire Insurance Company. To assure conformity with the principles of the Factory Mutuals already in operation, the secretary of the Rhode Island Mutual moved up to Boston to assume the office of secretary and treasurer of the new company.

With three companies doing business, the Factory Mutual System was now well established on a solid foundation. In 1851, Zachariah Allen, having served as a director of the Manufacturers Mutual for sixteen years, resigned that post and for nearly a quarter of a century thereafter devoted most of his time to the Rhode Island Mutual and to serving as elder statesman of the constantly expanding system.

Before his death in 1882, Allen had enjoyed the satisfaction of seeing his belief in the mutual idea handsomely proved. From a single company that started out in 1835 with $1,058,225 of insurance, the Factory Mutual System had grown by 1882 to an organization of seventeen companies with insurance in force of $268 million. Beginning with only an idea, the Factory Mutuals now occupied a dominant position in the insurance world. "It is seldom given to any man in his lifetime to view such incontrovertible proof of the soundness of his ideas," an executive of the Manufacturers Mutual, Zachariah Allen's pioneer venture, once wrote, "and he must have left this world with a pardonable glow of pride at the material benefits accruing to the manufacturing interests of the country as a result of his original work."

CHAPTER VIII

Three Men and an Idea—2

EDWARD ATKINSON

ALMOST coincidentally with the departure of Zachariah Allen there emerged in the Factory Mutual System another dominant and colorful personality, who is generally regarded as the second member of the System's "Big Three." This man was Edward Atkinson, for twenty-seven years the president of the Boston Manufacturers Mutual. Taking over the original work so well begun, Edward Atkinson provided the imaginative leadership that carried the Factory Mutuals into the twentieth century and on to new heights of success and prestige.

When Atkinson was elected president of the Boston Manufacturers in 1878, he became the chief executive of a company that was already the leader in its field. Founded in 1850 at the suggestion of Zachariah Allen, the Boston Manufacturers quickly assumed the ascendancy among the Factory Mutuals; leadership of the System soon shifted from Providence to Boston, and there it remained for the next fifty years. This development was the result of three important factors: the time, the place, and the men.

Between 1840 and 1860, the textile industry of New England experienced a tremendous growth. During this period, the number of spindles operating in New England cotton mills increased from two and a quarter million to four million. Proportionately, the increase was greater in the Massachusetts mills than in those of Rhode Island. With new mills being built and old ones enlarging, the Boston Manufacturers was offered a fertile field for business.

Of no less importance were the twin facts that Boston was the financial capital of the textile industry and that the mills in Massachusetts were much bigger than those in Rhode Island. The Rhode Island mills, working on the so-called Slater system, produced only the thread, the cloth itself being hand-woven on small looms in the homes of weavers. The Massachusetts mills, working on the Waltham system, did the entire manufacturing process—from the opening of the cotton bale to production of the finished cloth—under one roof. Whereas the average capitalization of the Rhode Island cotton mills was in the neighborhood of $45,000, those in Massachusetts were capitalized at around $500,000. Thus, the circumstances of place also worked in favor of the Boston Manufacturers, since the textile industry in Massachusetts involved big mills, large-scale operations, and heavy insurable values.

It is to the men of the Boston Manufacturers, who took advantage of the favorable conditions of time and place, that major credit for the company's success must be paid. The moving spirit in forming the company, James Read, was a prosperous commission merchant who had interests in cotton mills. One of ten children of a saddler, Read went to work at fourteen at a salary of less than a dollar a week. From his scant earnings he managed to buy a one-eighth share of a ticket in a lottery run by Harvard College to raise funds. His ticket won first prize, which paid $16,000. Read, who was then seventeen, used part of his winnings of $2,000 to pay off his father's debts and put the rest aside to start himself off in business a few years later. When at sixty-one Read turned his attention to founding the Boston Manufacturers, he had risen high in the commercial and financial circles of Boston, where he was respected not only for his business acumen but also for his flawless integrity.

Joined with Read as organizers of the company and members of its original board of directors were men of equal caliber who enjoyed social and business distinction in Boston. Seven were graduates of Harvard, one of Dartmouth; the others were, like Read, self-made men. Also like Read, several had close acquaintance with the practice of insurance through serving as directors of stock fire insurance companies, of which there were then more than a dozen in Boston. As president, William Amory brought to the new company his experience as a highly successful industrialist in addition to an engaging personality and an impeccable social position. A very proper Bostonian, whose family had been in the land of the cod and the bean for a hundred and thirty years, Amory was an officer in several of the largest textile mills in New England. He started out by placing $90,000 of insurance on three of his mills with the Boston Manufacturers, and within a few years had increased his insurance with the company to $823,000. Part of his devotion to the success of the company founded to provide insurance on cotton mills at cost may have stemmed from a friendly rivalry with his elder brother, Colonel Thomas Amory, president of a Boston stock insurance company. When asked if he insured cotton mills, Colonel Amory was fond of remarking, "We will insure them to burn up at a very low rate, but we will not insure them against loss by fire at *any* rate."

The Boston Manufacturers started out on a bigger scale than had either of the two Providence companies. The limit per risk, despite Zachariah Allen's advice to the contrary, was set by the organizers of the Boston Company at $40,000, or double the amount that Allen's first two companies originally accepted. In its organizational approach, the Boston Manufacturers also differed from the pioneer companies, which operated somewhat loosely through committees and whose officers worked only part-time. The Boston Manufacturers started out with a full-time paid secretary and treasurer, who was given a free hand as the officer in charge of underwriting. The first man to hold this post, John Hughes, had been one of the original directors of the Manufacturers Mutual and, before moving to Boston, secretary of the Rhode Island Mutual.

As an underwriter, Hughes proved to be bold but not always judicious. His first five years produced dramatic results. When he took office in 1850, the company had $1 million of insurance. In 1855 Hughes wrote $7 million of insurance—more than double the volume that had been written in any one year by any other Factory Mutual company. Total losses for the entire five-year period amounted to only $80,000, or about 31 cents per $100 of insurance. And the net cost of insurance to Boston's policyholders had been brought down to 40 cents per $100, compared to the rates ranging between $1.25 and $1.75 which were still being charged by the stock companies.

In his sixth year, however, Hughes ran into trouble. Losses that year totaled more than $100,000, revealing Hughes's vulnerability as an underwriter. He had, in some instances, accepted risks that did not come in the category of "the first class of cotton mills." Having suffered a serious illness the preceding year, Hughes resigned in 1857. Though his last year in office had been marred by losses that were large for the time, his six-year record was creditable. Policyholders had cut their net cost of insurance by 60 per cent.

Hughes's successor, Edward E. Manton, was destined to become the first czar of the Factory Mutual System. So completely did he dominate every aspect of its activities that the companies came to be known during his twenty-year tenure as the "Manton Mutuals." A Providence millowner and experienced underwriter, Manton had served as president of the Rhode Island Mutual before moving up to the Boston Manufacturers at the then big-time salary of $4,000 a year. Eight years later, when Manton was elevated to the presidency, his salary was raised to $6,000. He earned it.

Manton's first move was to examine all the risks on the company's books. He went out and inspected every mill personally. In his first year he traveled more than ten thousand miles—by train, stagecoach, and horse and buggy. He inspected each mill from basement to attic. Back in the office, he jotted down laconic pencil notes in the policy books. After looking over one mill, he noted: "Renew at same, if an additional force pump is added. If not, renew for $10,000 at 1¼." Another brought this comment: "Renew $10,000 only, at 1¼, if Picker [room] remains as now." Frequently he found that policies on mills insured by Hughes should not be renewed at all. On these he tersely noted the word "Drop." On one especially poor risk he wrote, with double emphasis, "Drop-discontinue." Within nine months Manton had pruned $960,000 of insurance from the books; that was about one seventh of the company's total insurance in force.

The pruning was timely. The year 1857 brought a severe panic, the effects of which were most harshly felt in the industrial East. A number of the biggest mills in New England went into receivership; commercial failures of all kinds were widespread. In such times, marked by bankruptcy, depreciated values, and the inclination of property owners to skimp on repairs and the replacement of equipment, both physical and moral hazards increase. On his inspection trips, which took more than half of his time, Manton accordingly watched with a keen eye for the danger signs. His rigid inspections brought results. In his first five years with the Boston Manufacturers, Manton had only one serious fire. During that time his losses were only 19 cents on each $100 at risk.

When Manton went to work for the Boston Manufacturers, there were six companies in the Factory Mutual System. The number steadily increased during his regime, three of the larger companies being the Arkwright Mutual, the Blackstone Mutual, and the What Cheer Mutual; the last took its name from the remark supposedly made by Roger Williams, the founder of Providence, when he first greeted the Indians. Altogether, eleven new Factory Mutual companies were formed during Manton's twenty-year association with the System, bringing the total to seventeen. Manton exercised a dominant influence over all of them. His leadership was so thoroughly respected and recognized by all the companies that he was given sole authority not only to pass on the eligibility of all risks but also to assign to each individual company the proportion it was to receive of each new risk accepted. In addition, he served as adjuster for all the companies. Thus were centralized in his hands for two decades all aspects of the enterprise.

During his first five years, Manton operated as a one-man show; his only help was one clerk. To take over part of the ever-increasing work of inspecting mills, Manton eventually hired a well-qualified assistant named William B. Whiting.

A self-made man with a mechanical bent, Whiting had worked his way up from bobbin boy in a cotton mill to master mechanic and finally to manager of a group of cotton mills. In addition to his years of practical experience, he was naturally studious, and he had a wide acquaintance with mill owners. Beginning as an inspector, he was successively promoted to secretary and vice-president. An indication of Whiting's early work can be seen from the amount of traveling he did. In 1863, his first full year as an inspector, Whiting put in 111 days on the road, covering a total of 6,500 miles. The same year, Manton put in 93 days in travel and covered 8,000 miles. Whiting gradually assumed a larger share of the inspection work; by 1867, he was responsible for two thirds of the 25,000 miles that he and Manton together traveled that year in the course of checking on the company's risks.

The effect on business of their apparently boundless energy was marked. In 1863, the annual volume of insurance written by the Boston Manufacturers passed $10 million—a figure no other Factory Mutual company had even approached. In 1869, the total insurance written passed $25 million, while the annual premium income had climbed to $220,000. All this was the work of two men, Manton and Whiting, with the aid of just one clerk.

Easily as important as the boosting of volume were the strides made in fire prevention. Within a month after going to work as inspector, Whiting began the practice of making brief notes on the cause of every fire suffered by a Factory Mutual policyholder. Gradually he enlarged this record to make it a complete history of each fire from origin to extinguishment, including causes, spread, and the performance of men and equipment in the emergency. By this action, a Factory Mutual executive has said, Whiting "laid the foundation for the first published experience table in the history of fire insurance in this country, if not in the world." If such statistics did exist in the general insurance field at that time, they were closely guarded trade secrets. However, in the general interest of fire prevention, Manton, beginning in 1865, made Whiting's careful summary and pertinent comment on each fire that had occurred in the preceding year an integral part of the company's annual report.

As a result of his skillful underwriting, Manton kept the cost of insurance to Factory Mutual policyholders at such an impressively low figure that the companies were besieged with applications for insurance. While continuing to insist on the highest standards of construction and fire-protective equipment, Manton enlarged the underwriting capacity of the Boston Manufacturers by raising the amount the company would accept on any one risk to $80,000; this practice was soon adopted by the other companies in the System. As the amount at risk was raised, the chances of large losses also naturally increased. In 1873, the destruction by fire of the Chicopee Manufacturing Company cost the System a total loss of $492,000. The following year, the System suffered another loss of about the same size when fire destroyed the Social Manufacturing Company. In spite of these stiff blows, the cost of Factory Mutual insurance rose only from about 30 to 36 cents per $100—still only about a quarter of the stock company cost.

Manton and Whiting had meanwhile increased their inspection service by hiring three full-time inspectors, one of whom was assigned to the specialized task of checking only on pumps and other fire apparatus. The old-timers, Manton and Whiting, continued to hit the road themselves, setting a fast pace for the new men. In 1876 the five men together traveled a total of 63,000 miles. Their traveling expenses never exceeded five cents per mile, including meals and lodging.

The year 1877 marked the twentieth anniversary of Manton's association with the Boston Manufacturers. He was then seventy-three. Seriously ill, he was forced to retire at the end of that year, and he died five weeks later. His record was remarkable. During his entire twenty years with the Boston Manufacturers, a period marked by a great war and two great depressions, Manton's losses averaged just a little over 21 cents on each $100 of insurance. When he departed, the company was 579 per cent larger in volume and 702 per cent greater in assets than it had been when he took over. So passed from the scene one of the outstanding men in the history of the Factory Mutuals, a man who, in the words of a New York stock company executive, was "one of the most capable underwriters who ever lived."

To succeed such a man is a challenging assignment. Edward Atkinson, who was chosen in 1878 by the directors of the Boston Manufacturers to take over the reins of leadership, proved more than equal to the task. Atkinson was fifty-one at the time of his election and, owing to his commercial and public activities, a figure of national prominence. He was a man of imposing appearance. Slightly above average height and broad-shouldered, he always wore a small black bow tie, black coat, and dark trousers. Over his black waistcoat was suspended a heavy gold watch chain to which was attached an antique Grecian coin. His hair and the full beard that he wore were snow-white. His clear eyes and steady gaze endowed him with a thoughtful aspect. Atkinson was a man of wide interests and pronounced individuality. "If he was considered by some to be egotistical," an insurance colleague once stated, choosing his words with care, "he was, at least, a man who, having perfect faith in himself and in his opinions, as all successful men must have, did not hesitate to express himself forcefully. He was an optimist in the true sense of the word, had great faith in human nature, and believed that no wrong would endure for any length of time. He was usually found on the unpopular side of an argument, but this fact neither discouraged him nor made him think less of the world. He had a wonderful capacity for work and was a firm believer in the necessity of work in all stages of life. Many important and far-reaching steps were taken by the Factory Mutuals under his leadership, and during his connection with the Companies, he dominated the Factory Mutual System as no other man had before."

Atkinson's background and experience differed in many respects from other leaders who had preceded him in the Factory Mutual System. He was the son of a well-to-do Boston merchant, the senior member of the firm of Atkinson & Rollins, whose ships sailed the seven seas, carrying Yankee goods. At the age of eleven young Edward Atkinson got his first taste of business, which he described years later: "My first business speculation was putting a dollar in the hands of John Storey, who went from my father's counting room out to Calcutta as supercargo. I commissioned him to buy me Indian bamboo arrows, of which he brought me home from India one hundred. . . . I kept a dozen for myself out of the hundred arrows that cost a cent apiece and sold the rest for ten cents each—a very good speculation for a boy." When Atkinson was fifteen, his father's firm fell upon hard times, and the boy was obliged to leave school and go to work. (Later in life he received an honorary Ph.D. from Dartmouth and was made an honorary member of Phi Beta Kappa.)

Atkinson found a job in the store of James Read, the distinguished Boston merchant and founder of the Boston Manufacturers, though that event was still eight years in the future. As was the custom, Atkinson worked from dawn to dusk, and his pay was $50 a year during the first two years, after which it was raised to $100. Read was more generous than the average employer of the time; on Atkinson's eighteenth birthday Read gave the young man a present of a year's salary and time off for a brief vacation, which Atkinson spent at Niagara Falls.

When Atkinson was nearing twenty-one, he left the Read store, where he had advanced to bookkeeper, to try to fulfill his ambition to be a salesman. "I passed from one occupation to another," he wrote when he was seventy-six, "seeking to be a salesman, but I wasn't cut out for that. I was made for an accountant, and later for a student of social and financial questions." Though a failure at selling goods, Atkinson was destined to become a master at selling ideas, notably the mutual idea.

Giving up his efforts to sell merchandise, Atkinson secured a job as a bookkeeper in the commission firm of J. C. Howe & Company. His natural talent for figures soon earned him a promotion, and before long he was receiving assignments as an accountant trouble shooter on the books of the various cotton mills the firm controlled. At twenty-four he was made treasurer of his first cotton mill. While maintaining his connection with the Howe firm, he went on to become a special financial assistant to a Boston entrepreneur, Benjamin E. Bates, who had developed the great textile mills at Lewiston, Maine. When Atkinson was thirty-one, he had straightened out the books and finances of nine cotton corporations and was serving as treasurer or assistant treasurer of six.

He had not, however, been so totally engrossed in his commercial affairs that he had missed participating in the liberal thought that centered in Boston in the years preceding the Civil War. He had strong thoughts on the slavery issue. In addition to raising money to equip John Brown and his forces in the struggle for "Bleeding Kansas," he worked with a friend, Edward Philbrick, in operating a hideaway for fleeing slaves in Brookline, Massachusetts. To allay the Southern argument that abolition of slavery would cause the ruination of the country's cotton textile industry, Atkinson wrote a fifty-two-page pamphlet which he titled *Cheap Cotton by Free Labor.* With a wide range of statistics and pertinent historical illustrations, Atkinson demonstrated the weakness of the Southern argument. The pamphlet was quoted in periodicals throughout the country, including Horace Greeley's New York *Tribune,* then the most influential newspaper in the country. Atkinson, who had prepared himself for a role as a pamphleteer by writing letters and articles for the newspapers of Boston, now emerged on the national scene. As an authority on the cotton trade as well as a man with distinct views on taxation and government finance, he was invited to meet with President Lincoln. "I had half an hour's close attention from the President himself," Atkinson wrote to his wife. "He is studying the cotton problem . . . and listened to my ideas with great interest."

Besides running the cotton mills with which he was associated throughout the Civil War, despite the difficulties of getting raw materials imposed by the embargo, Atkinson found time to continue spreading his ideas through writing for many important periodicals, including the *North American Review* and the *Atlantic Monthly.* His views were often unpopular with his associates because of their liberal tenor.

He cast his first presidential vote for the Free Soil party, vigorously opposed the candidacy of General Grant, and later joined the rank of the Mugwumps, the liberal Republicans who bolted the party ticket in the presidential campaign of 1884 to support Grover Cleveland. Furthermore, Atkinson was a strong believer in tariff for revenue only, not for protection, a stand which was far from popular with most New England textile men. In his later years, Atkinson became increasingly conservative. He never developed sympathy for organized labor, but he wished to assist the working classes. He felt that there was considerable waste in the way they cooked their food. To remedy this, he invented a cooking device called the Aladdin Oven, the use of which, he believed, would result in the saving of at least five cents a day to the workingman in the cost of food. The magic oven was not a spectacular success.

Though some of Atkinson's ideas may have been less compelling than others, no one can deny that they were wide, varied, and pungent. His daughter, in a written memoir, remarked, "It doesn't seem that there were many important events—whether local, state, national, or international—in which he was not actively interested and did not have a hand shaping in some way, although much of his work was done behind the scenes or through correspondence." Atkinson was a prolific letter writer. The Massachusetts Historical Society has fifty thousand pages of his letters. He also wrote two hundred and ninety pamphlets and magazine articles. He seldom said anything moderately, because he believed that an article was of little use if it did not, as he said, "stir things up."

Atkinson, like most men who hold pronounced views, was not universally admired, but even those who were not attracted to him willingly acknowledged that he was a remarkable personality. He was an accomplished speaker as well as a good conversationalist, and his manner was engaging. "He always liked both young and old people and made friends easily," his daughter has written. "If he liked the looks of any young female person's appearance, he was very apt to introduce himself by saying, 'My dear, I am sure I know your grandmother.' And," his daughter adds, "he always did!" Among other things, Atkinson carried on a strenuous campaign during most of his life against smoking and drinking. It was therefore a surprise when, on his seventieth birthday, newspaper reporters found him in his office smoking a big black cigar. Naturally, they reminded him of his frequently voiced opposition to nicotine. Atkinson replied tranquilly that they had misunderstood him. "What I have said all along," Atkinson remarked, flicking the ashes off his cigar, "is that no man should smoke until he's at least seventy years old."

Before his election to the presidency of the Boston Manufacturers, Atkinson, as we have seen, had been primarily a specialist in finance and administration, his particular field being the textile industry. His background did not include much practical experience in insurance, though he had served for the preceding thirteen years as a director of the Boston Manufacturers and had regularly attended the board meetings. Those meetings were, however, comparatively infrequent, being held only about once a year during Manton's all-embracing regime. Atkinson, well aware that he was not an underwriter by training, did not pretend to be one. Instead of trying to fulfill the function of a born underwriter, such as Manton, who was endowed with what amounts to a sixth sense for judging what will or will not burn, Atkinson selected as his basic approach the prevention of fires. That approach had, of course, always been implicit not only in the Factory Mutual System but in all mutual insurance; Atkinson, however, developed the principle to a new peak of thoroughness and efficiency. He turned an attitude into a science. Looking back years later, Atkinson wrote: "I think it never occurred to the founders of the Factory Mutual System, and I am sure that it had not occurred to myself, that we were engaged in developing an applied science." What Atkinson developed was the science of loss-prevention engineering. In so doing, he worked a gradual but profound revolution in Factory Mutual practice.

Atkinson's first step was characteristic. He wanted to find out how to prevent fires, so he sought statistics on what caused them. Within three weeks of taking office he had William B. Whiting's carefully kept records, covering 408 fires that had occurred during the preceding fifteen years, broken down into a statistical table, which showed, among other things, the place in the factory where each fire had originated as well as its specific cause. The three leading causes of fire, according to this analysis, were revealed to be faulty lanterns carried by watchmen, spontaneous combustion, and friction. Turning his attention to the first cause, Atkinson had his inspectors make an investigation of the lanterns then in use; they were found to be flimsily constructed and insufficiently guarded. Atkinson remedied this by working with the lantern manufacturers and encouraging them to develop safer designs. When he had four manufacturers turning out lanterns that met his specifications, Atkinson issued a circular to all policyholders, listing the four makes considered safe and advising that only those be purchased.

Friction and spontaneous combustion posed knottier problems. The first clue came in the discovery that well over 50 per cent of the fires owing to these causes pointed to inadequate oils used in lubricating mill machinery. It appeared that many of the lubricating oils used on the new and faster-moving machinery proved unequal to the load and frequently caught fire. This, however, was only informed speculation, and Atkinson wanted facts. He therefore took a step, which is now regarded as commonplace but was then plain pioneering; he decided to solve the problem through industrial research. He turned the matter over to the then comparatively new Massachusetts Institute of Technology. Professor John M. Ordway was placed in charge of the investigation. Since it was a new undertaking, for which no apparatus had been devised, Ordway was obliged to invent some. After three months he had achieved results that were so useful that Atkinson gave the findings to the New England Cotton Manufacturers Association for the benefit of the entire in dustry. Atkinson did not stop there. He arranged for Ordway to be financed in further research that lasted some five years and resulted in setting up standards for both lubricating and illuminating oils that revolutionized their manufacture, commercial handling, and industrial use.

As Ordway's research progressed, Atkinson kept mill-owners informed of the results—and their practical application—by issuing frequent reports and circulars. When the investigation revealed, for example, that the new kerosene burning oil that was then replacing whale oil for illumination was frequently dangerous, Atkinson put out a circular to mills, warning them to use no kerosene without testing and to beware of any having a flash point below 125 degrees. "Up to this date," Atkinson wrote, "there has been no loss to this office from the use of kerosene oil for burning, but the danger is evidently increasing and must be promptly guarded against if 'we would close the door *before* the horse is stolen.'"

Meanwhile, Atkinson had been issuing other reports that forcefully urged millowners to take additional fire-preventive measures. One of the earliest of these pointed out the need for a trained fire-fighting force composed of employees in each mill. During the next few years, as experiments were conducted and standards established, Atkinson prepared additional pamphlets, bearing such descriptive titles as *Fire Hose and Recommended Mill Design, Fire Ladders, Precautions against Freezing, Storage of Oil,* and *Report on Tests of Fire-Resisting Material.* After delving further into Whiting's loss record and making new breakdowns and discoveries, Atkinson printed his conclusions in a fifteen-thousand-word pamphlet, which was the most complete and valuable loss study that had yet been made. All of Atkinson's reports were distributed to policyholders and widely circulated among the mill managers of New England, who were soon made aware of the fact that something new and important had been added to the world of insurance, which had never before seen such a flood of printed instruction, practical advice, and timely warning. It became abundantly clear that the Factory Mutuals were dedicated to something of far greater consequence than simply providing indemnity in case of loss.

Carrying his crusade further, Atkinson turned his attention to fire doors. Whiting had been quietly educating industry to the advantages of the new tin-clad wooden door over the old iron door, which was supposedly fireproof but which actually often buckled and even melted in a fire. After a fire in a mill that was equipped partly with the old-fashioned doors, which failed, and partly with the tin-clad doors, which stood up,

Atkinson issued a report, using this experience as a dramatic example to drive home the point. Atkinson later made a direct contribution to the improvement of fire doors by inventing a device that caused them to close automatically in the presence of fire. This was a fusible link consisting of two pieces of metal held together by solder, which, when melted by the heat of the fire, broke the link and thereby permitted the door to slide closed. Atkinson, following the tradition established by Franklin, published the information on the fusible link and refused to patent it, as he later refused to patent other inventions of his own or of others connected with the System. "It is not consistent," Atkinson said, "with the position or duties of an executive officer in any mutual insurance company to have or to take any personal interest in or to hold any patents of any kind on apparatus used in controlling fires."

With unabated zeal to prevent fires, Atkinson next focused his attention on the inspection of risks. When he became president, the Boston Manufacturers employed three inspectors, who checked on the Boston's risks and those of certain of the Providence companies. Some of the other companies continued to leave the inspection work to their officers. The lack of uniformity in handling this aspect of the business seemed inefficient to Atkinson. He accordingly worked out an arrangement by which the Boston Manufacturers took over the inspection of all Factory Mutual risks and pro-rated the expense among the companies on the basis of the amount of insurance each had at risk. Whiting was placed in charge of the inspection force, which was gradually increased until by 1887 it consisted of twelve full-time inspectors and two clerks. At this point, in the interest of further efficiency, Atkinson secured the agreement of the companies to set up the inspection force as an independent unit which would make a general, thorough inspection of each Factory Mutual risk four times a year as well as a special, fifth inspection for the specific purpose of testing fire pumps. Thus was brought into existence the Inspection Department, which was to become one of the most remarkable fire-prevention and engineering organizations in the world. The department started conservatively, with an annual budget of $45,000. An indication of the steadily increasing scope of its activities is provided in the expansion of its budget, which within twenty-five years had reached $250,000.

In 1879, Thomas A. Edison produced the first commercially practical incandescent lamp. The discovery was enthusiastically greeted by the New York *Herald* with the headlines: "It Makes a Light without Gas or Flame—Cheaper Than Oil!" Within three years, eighty-two mills insured by Factory Mutual companies were partly or completely lighted by electricity. Long before this, Atkinson had realized that the use of electricity in mills might be hazardous and should be investigated. To this project he assigned his most able inspector, Charles J. H. Woodbury, who had been trained at the Massachusetts Institute of Technology and was the first graduate engineer to enter the Factory Mutual System. After spending weeks studying the installations in numerous mills, Woodbury traveled to Cleveland and Philadelphia, where he consulted with experts in the new field, and then went on to Menlo Park, where he received valuable assistance from Edison, who, at thirty-five, was already the grand old man of the new science. Woodbury's report, titled *Regulations for the Use of Electric Lighting Apparatus* and containing detailed rules for the installation and operation of electric lighting equipment, was gratefully received by the mills and by industry generally. The investigation was notable not only because it was the most thorough industrial research that had ever been sponsored by a fire insurance company but also because it treated a hazard from which the Boston Manufacturers had not yet incurred a penny's loss. This was loss prevention in its purest form.

Exercising his talent for selecting young men of great promise, Atkinson brought into the Factory Mutual System in 1886 its second graduate engineer, John R. Freeman, who was to become recognized as one of the world's foremost hydraulic engineers as well as one of the towering figures in the field of Factory Mutual insurance. Freeman started in the Inspection Department, which had become the System's training ground, but before long he was engaged exclusively in research. One of his first contributions was the development, after a series of elaborate and painstaking tests, of a set of statistical tables which made it possible for the first time to determine the quantity of water being applied to a given fire. Freeman's fire-stream tables, which are still used as the standard today, enabled firemen to apply the proper equipment to varying conditions and were therefore of inestimable value in the development of scientific fire-fighting techniques. For his investigation Freeman was awarded the Norman Gold Medal of the American Society of Civil Engineers.

Because there had been a rash of failures in the various types of fire hose then in use, Freeman conducted a thoroughgoing investigation of all the fourteen kinds then on the market. After testing the strength, conductivity, and general reliability of each, he found that many were of questionable value. He was not surprised by this discovery, especially since, as he noted in his diary, the people whom he had sent out to purchase hose for the investigation were often asked "whether they wanted hose for actual use in a fire department or hose only to put up in order to satisfy the insurance inspector." At the conclusion of his exhaustive tests, Freeman drew up specifications for rubber-lined cotton and linen hose and worked with the manufacturers to get high-quality hose produced. As soon as this was available, members of the Factory Mutual System were advised to buy only from manufacturers who had agreed to keep their product up to Freeman's specifications.

The third of Freeman's early, and major, contributions to the applied science of loss-prevention engineering was his development of specifications for the so-called "Underwriter" steam fire pump. The then novel idea that factories should be equipped with a pump reserved especially for use in case of fire had been advocated by William Whiting, and some such pumps had been installed. However, because they were used infrequently, the parts sometimes rusted or otherwise got out of commission, and the pumps proved inadequate at the time of a fire. The moving parts in the Underwriter pump that Freeman invented were made of non-corrosive metal, and with other improvements the new pump proved able to stand idle for years and yet deliver when suddenly needed. With modifications, the pump is in wide use today.

While giving direction and encouragement to Freeman, Woodbury, and the other members of the Inspection Department, Atkinson was also carrying on an unremitting campaign for improved standards of construction of mills and factories. This campaign began when, two years after assuming the presidency of the Boston Manufacturers, Atkinson delivered an address at the Massachusetts Institute of Technology on the subject, "The Relation of the Architect and the Underwriter." It was a vigorous attack on the faulty architecture,

JOHN R. FREEMAN, 1855–1932

'he second graduate engineer to join the Factory Mutual System, Freeman ·as elected president of the Manufacturers Mutual Fire Insurance Company in 896. He served in that post for the ensuing thirty-six years. Under Freeman's irection, the Factory Mutual companies increased their volume of business wenty-five fold. In addition to being an outstanding insurance executive, Freeman was recognized as one of the world's foremost hydraulic engineers.

Edward Atkinson, 1827–1905

Elected president of the Boston Manufacturers Mutual Fire Insurance Company in 1878, Edward Atkinson was the dominant figure in the Factory Mutual System until his death in 1905. A talented organizer, gifted speaker, and prolific writer he crusaded ceaselessly for a wide range of fire-preventive measures and devices particularly plank-on-timber construction and automatic sprinklers. During Atkinson's regime, loss-prevention engineering was developed into a science and became the keystone of Factory Mutual Insurance.

from the standpoint of fire prevention, of American business and public buildings.

His remarks caused a distinct cooling in the relations between himself and the architects and drew rebuttal in both newspapers and magazines. Atkinson was not displeased. He liked to stir things up, and he continued to press the attack against what he called "combustible architecture" not only before millowners and architects but before the general public as well. He contributed a ten-thousand-word article to the *Century Magazine*, a general periodical of wide circulation, wrote several articles for the *American Architect*, and spoke on the subject continuously. With characteristic lack of restraint, he would make dramatic statements, such as, "A good strong knotted rope is a good thing to have in one's trunk when passing a vacation among 'palatial' hotels and health resorts, many of which are most excellent examples of combustible architecture." And he went on to say that the country was burning an average of twelve hotels a week.

Atkinson's positive program consisted in trying to persuade architects and millowners to adopt a method of construction which he termed "slow-burning" or "mill construction," the two principal features of which were floors and roofs. The floors then generally in use in commercial buildings—and still commonly used in dwellings—were what architects and builders call board on joist. Atkinson was opposed to this type of floor because, as he insistently proclaimed, the thin joists, placed ten or twelve inches apart, not only burned like kindling but also resulted in many concealed spaces between the joists, which made convenient flues for the spread of fire. The floor construction for which Atkinson crusaded was the so-called "plank-on-timber" type. Instead of joists, this kind of floor is supported by large thick beams; dangerous, concealed spaces are thus avoided, and the flooring itself consists of thick planking. Against such a floor, with its great timbers and broad, flat surface, fire can beat with considerable ferocity but not readily catch hold.

The roofs then in use, as Atkinson never tired of pointing out, were also dangerous. They were mostly lantern, pitched, or mansard roofs, and all, from the standpoint of fire hazard, equally objectionable. Intended to be ornamental, they had the quality of tinderboxes. The kind of roof Atkinson advocated was what came to be known as the flat factory roof. As the term indicates, this is simply a flat, unornamented roof —merely a modification of the plank-on-timber floor. Like the floor, it presents a broad, thick, flat surface on which fire is slow to take hold.

The fact that these principles of slow-burning construction are today so universally accepted and such a commonplace in commercial and public buildings is all the evidence needed to demonstrate the success of Edward Atkinson's vigorous and enlightened crusade. He did not invent slow-burning construction, but he was, as a close student of his accomplishments has remarked, "the man who best made it known, who most strikingly and impressively defined it, and who thereby spread its influence over the architecture of American churches, schools, and public buildings—as well as over North American industry generally."

Of all Atkinson's accomplishments as a missionary of fire protection, none was more fruitful or of greater benefit to American industry than his crusade for automatic sprinklers. As in the case of slow-burning construction, Atkinson did not invent automatic sprinklers, but, as Marshall B. Dalton, president of the Boston Manufacturers, once said, "he took them in hand at an early stage, set up research to develop and perfect them, publicized them, fought for them, crusaded for them so vigorously that there is record of one exasperated mill owner, advising that Atkinson be sure to take a sprinkler with him when he died . . . and went to where a sprinkler would help protect him."

It is hard to realize that automatic sprinklers, now nearly as standard in industrial and public buildings as doors and windows, were first manufactured in this country only a few years before the first automobiles. Henry S. Parmalee, a piano manufacturer of New Haven, Connecticut, patented the automatic sprinkler in 1874. When four years later Atkinson became president of the Boston Manufacturers, several installations of Parmalee sprinklers had been made in textile mills, including those of Colonel Thomas J. Borden, an executive of several Factory Mutual companies. Atkinson expressed immediate interest in the new fire-preventive device and believed in its worth, but he hesitated to urge its wholesale adoption so long as it was a monopoly. Within the next five years, nineteen varieties of sprinkler heads had appeared on the market, and Atkinson decided the time had come for an exhaustive investigation. He assigned Charles Woodbury to the task. As he had in his earlier electrical investigation, Woodbury made extremely comprehensive tests and reported his results in a fifty-six-page pamphlet that not only set up standards for automatic sprinklers but also included Woodbury's careful study of the 128 known instances in which automatic sprinklers had actually performed in fires. Woodbury's report was a powerful endorsement of automatic sprinkler protection.

Now firmly convinced, Atkinson put his whole support behind the cause of automatic sprinklers. The going was tough. More than once, hidebound underwriters asked him, "Do you really expect to put out a mill fire with a watering pot?" Within a few years, however, Atkinson had provided himself with his favorite ammunition, a battery of statistics covering 965 fires. Of these, 759 had occurred in mills not equipped with automatic sprinklers, and resulted in an average insurance loss of $17,610. The remaining 206 fires had occurred in sprinklered mills and resulted in an average insurance loss of $1,080. The case for the "watering pots" was proved.

All the while that Atkinson was spearheading the dramatic public campaign to reduce the fire loss in American industry, he was also filling another, more private role as an administrator who was steadily enlarging the scope and efficiency of the Factory Mutual System. During his long association with the System, eighteen additional Factory Mutual companies were formed. One, the Spinners Mutual, was organized to handle only sprinklered risks. Others, such as the Paper Mill Mutual and the Rubber Manufacturers Mutual, were formed to specialize in insuring risks in those industries. Thus, under Atkinson's leadership, the Factory Mutual method began its expansion beyond the textile industry.

As new companies were formed and new fields entered, Atkinson saw the need for closer relations among the companies to establish uniformity in policies, classification and rating of risks, adjustments, and in myriad other matters. He accordingly brought about the establishment of the Associated Factory Mutual Conference. Made up of the chief executive officer of each of the companies, the conference became the governing body of the entire System and took on the functions of standardizing forms and rates and determining over-all policies. Establishment of the conference marked the more or less formal beginning of the close fellowship that has distinguished Factory Mutual operations ever since.

On December 11, 1905, Edward Atkinson died suddenly, in his seventy-eighth year. Of the many tributes paid to his long and remarkably fruitful career, perhaps none was more judicious than that of Thomas Wentworth Higginson, the well-known New England clergyman, soldier, author, and reformer, who said, "When the amount of useful labor performed by the men of this generation comes to be reviewed a century hence, it is doubtful if a more substantial and varied list will be found credited to the memory of anyone in America than that which attaches to the memory of Edward Atkinson." Even half a century later, an effort to review Atkinson's useful labor in the closely connected fields of loss prevention and mutual insurance imposes a singularly challenging task. However, a worth-while indication of the results of his monumental work can be gleaned from a few statistics, that tool which Atkinson himself always found so effective and illuminating.

When Atkinson became president of the Boston Manufacturers in 1878, the total annual volume of the Factory Mutual companies was about $200 million. When he died, the total annual volume was $1.4 billion. The increase was sevenfold. When Atkinson took over, the net cost of insurance to Factory Mutual policyholders was 26 cents per $100; when he departed, the net cost had been driven down to 6½ cents per $100. His skillful reduction of the cost of insurance to members of the Factory Mutual System had a beneficial effect far beyond that field. Confronted with such stiff competition, the stock insurance companies, which were still, at the time of Atkinson's advent, charging rates no lower than $1.25 per $100, were obliged to begin a steady reduction in their rates. The result was a reduction in costs for the benefit of all buyers of insurance.

It was no doubt this larger picture that was in the mind of Howard Stockton, the senior member of the Boston Manufacturers' board, when in 1905 he wrote of Atkinson, "His influence extended far beyond the limits of his own Company, not only to the Associated Mutual Companies, which looked to him largely for advice and guidance, but to the community at large, wherever the principles of fire protection were in question. He found the system of Factory Mutual insurance chaotic. He left it a perfectly organized machine."

CHAPTER IX

Three Men and an Idea—3

JOHN R. FREEMAN

TO THE contemporaries of Edward Atkinson, in 1905 the Factory Mutual System very reasonably gave the appearance of a "perfectly organized machine." No one of them without the gift of rare prescience could have foreseen either the gigantic expansion of American industry that lay ahead or the equally remarkable development of the Factory Mutual idea of insurance that not only kept pace with, but in important measure contributed to, that expansion. The foundations laid by Atkinson were solid, and the changes that have been made in the System during the close to a half century since his death have in the main been natural developments following logically upon the principles and practices in effect during his time. He was the first man in the System who turned to qualified, trained engineers to develop what he termed the new applied science of loss-prevention engineering. Since then, Atkinson's idea of fortifying and buttressing underwriting technique with engineering skill has been developed to the point at which the Factory Mutual System today is not only a conspicuously successful insurance mechanism but also one of the outstanding engineering organizations in the world.

It is fitting that the man who led the way in that unique development should have been brought into the System in the first place by Atkinson. He was John Ripley Freeman, a towering figure who was destined to take his place alongside Zachariah Allen and Edward Atkinson as the third member of the Factory Mutual System's "Big Three."

Born in a small farming community in Maine, John Freeman attended public schools and later entered the Massachusetts Institute of Technology, where he helped to pay his expenses by working during the summers for the Essex Company in Lawrence, Massachusetts. Freeman returned there after his graduation and spent the following ten years as the principal assistant to Hiram F. Mills, one of the greatest hydraulic engineers of his generation. Atkinson had heard of Freeman and hired him in 1886 as an inspector. He soon became assistant chief of the Inspection Department under William B. Whiting, and upon the latter's death in 1894 Freeman succeeded him. Besides engaging in an immense amount of original research himself, including development of the fire-stream tables and other fire-preventive discoveries already noted, Freeman brought into the department a corps of college-trained engineers who, working under his leadership, made enormous strides in putting the art of fire prevention on a genuinely scientific basis. The caliber of the men recruited by Freeman is indicated by the fact that some half dozen of them went on to become presidents of Factory Mutual companies. The permeation of engineering talent through the System, set in motion by Atkinson, was completed by Freeman. Today the head of every Factory Mutual company is by education and experience a trained engineer.

Freeman himself was the first graduate engineer to assume the presidency of a Factory Mutual company. In 1896, after ten years with the Inspection Department, he was elected president of the Manufacturers Mutual, the pioneer company founded by Zachariah Allen in Providence. Freeman was then forty-one. A man of prodigious talent and energy who thought nothing of working eighteen hours a day, Freeman not only provided dynamic leadership to the Factory Mutual System during a period of thirty-six years but also carried on a wide private engineering practice which won him world-wide fame. As a consequence of his imposing engineering accomplishments, Freeman was awarded seven honorary degrees (three of them from foreign universities) as well as an extensive list of other honors, including the Gold Medal of the American Society of Civil Engineers, which was awarded him three times. In 1929 another well-known engineer, who was then President of the United States, described John Ripley Freeman as "the foremost of American engineers."

As a jest, Freeman sometimes remarked that he led what he called a "Dr. Jekyll and Mr. Hyde existence," for among one set of his colleagues he was known as an expert insurance executive, while among another group of associates he was known as an expert consulting engineer. His insurance duties came first, and to them he devoted the greatest share of his time. It was Freeman's development of the engineering side of the insurance business that constituted his greatest contribution, a fact that was recognized in the resolution passed by the conference at the time of his death in 1932. "He brought into the Factory Mutual System," the resolution read, "and, in fact, into the whole field of fire protection, the spirit and practice of engineering, going to the bottom of things for all the facts on which to base final conclusions to give lasting quality to his work."

The unprecedented growth of the Factory Mutual System during Freeman's long tenure and in the years since is an impressive tribute to the lasting quality of his work. When Freeman succeeded Edward Atkinson in 1905 as the dominant force in the System, the companies together carried insurance totaling $1.4 billion. In 1949 the total amount of insurance in force had grown to $33.3 billion—an average increase of approximately three quarters of a billion every year.

Today the Factory Mutual System consists of nine companies. The present make-up of the System is the result of the orderly consolidation, started in the 1920s, of the thirty-five Factory Mutual companies that had been founded since Zachariah Allen established the first one in 1835. Of the nine companies that now comprise the System, four (the Manufacturers, Firemen's, Blackstone, and What Cheer) are located in Rhode Island; three (the Boston, Arkwright, and Cotton & Woolen Manufacturers) are Massachusetts companies; one (the Philadelphia Manufacturers) has headquarters in the city from which it takes its name; and one (the Protection Mutual) is located in Chicago. The four Rhode Island companies write more than half of the total insurance written by the System; in 1949 they carried 58 per cent. The three Massachusetts companies, in the same year, carried 33 per cent. Individually, the Manufacturers Mutual now writes the largest percentage of the total (29 per cent in 1949), followed by the Boston Manufacturers with 18 per cent, and the Firemen's with 14 per cent.

After one hundred and seventeen years of successful experience, the Factory Mutuals still require the highest standards of construction and fire-preventive equipment. Once an application for insurance is made, an engineer is assigned to make a thorough inspection of the plant. On the basis of his study, the company to which the application was originally made—the so-called placing company—decides whether or not to accept the risk. If it is accepted, the placing company issues the policy for the full amount agreed upon and becomes what is known as the guardian of the risk. Unless the risk is small, the placing company does not as a rule retain the entire amount of insurance, but instead distributes a portion of it among the other eight companies in the System. On the expiration of the policy, the participating companies pay the unabsorbed premium, or so-called dividend, to the placing company, which in turn transmits it to the policyholder or applies it to a new policy.

At first glance, the amount returned to Factory Mutual policyholders in dividends is altogether startling. At present, the average return is about 90 per cent on one-year policies and about 70 per cent on three-year policies. These arresting figures must, however, be viewed in the light of the Factory Mutual method of finance, which is unique in the insurance world. Though the Factory Mutuals have steadily reduced the net cost of insurance to their policyholders, they have kept the original premium deposit—that is, the amount of money the policyholder has to pay when he takes out a policy —at a comparatively high level. Today the average gross premium deposit is 50 cents per $100 of insurance. If, for example, a manufacturer insures his plant with the Factory Mutuals for $2 million, he is required to pay an original premium deposit of $10,000. On a one-year policy he gets back $9,000; on a three-year policy, $7,000.

The Factory Mutual practice of requiring a whopping original premium deposit—a practice whose origin goes back to the days of Zachariah Allen—has the advantage of giving the companies tremendous financial strength. Furthermore, the income from investment of the premium deposits contributes substantially to the payment of all of the System's operating expenses. The effect of the large premium deposit on the policyholders was described recently by the president of a large corporation whose plants are insured by the Factory Mutuals. "Making that first big payment is like taking a cold shower," the president said. "Afterward you feel fine."

That this philosophy is widely shared in American industry is shown by the spectacular growth of the Factory Mutual System. Seventy years ago the companies insured a total of 800 risks, all of which were located within 500 miles of the home offices. Today they insure close to 26,000 risks located throughout the length and breadth of the continent. "Our list of policyholders reads like a blue book of industry," a Factory Mutual executive has said with pride and accuracy. The list, to name a few in representative groups, includes General Motors, International Harvester, American Can, American Shipbuilding, Corning Glass, American Air Lines, Coca-Cola, National Cash Register, American Tobacco, International Shoe, Montgomery Ward, Campbell Soup, Aluminum Company of America, Eastman Kodak, American Woolen, General Foods, Crane Company, Otis Elevator, Proctor & Gamble, and the new United Nations Building in New York.

It is evident from this sampling that the Factory Mutuals no longer concentrate on insuring risks in the textile industry, as they did in the beginning. As late as 1880, cotton mills still represented 53 per cent of the total amount at risk. Though the next decade saw a gradual extension of Factory Mutual insurance to include rubber and paper manufacturing, it was John Freeman who provided the greatest impetus to carrying the System into the wide range of industrial fields in which it now operates. His success can be measured by the fact that the textile class now accounts for only 15 per cent of the System's total. The metal class, which includes automobile factories, machine shops, foundries, and a wide range of other manufacturing establishments, now heads the list, accounting for 42 per cent of the total. The paper class provides 8 per cent, the food class contributes 4 per cent, while another category known within the System as "other manufacturing" and including such risks as tobacco factories and warehouses, power plants and rubber mills, accounts for 22 per cent of the total. Thus, manufacturing of one kind or another now provides 91 per cent of the System's business. The balance is made up of non-manufacturing structures, such as hospitals, schools, office buildings, libraries, and a country club or two. Some of the risks in this group were originally taken on as gestures of good will, a practice started by Freeman to please policyholders who had other large risks insured in the System.

In the interests not only of good will but of good sound business, the Factory Mutuals have steadily led the way for more than a century in providing broader policy coverage—that is, to make the policy cover more and more hazards at no additional premium. In the beginning, the Factory Mutual policy covered only losses caused by fire. It has been gradually expanded until it now includes indemnity for loss or damage from lightning; sprinkler leakage; windstorm and hail; many types of explosion; riot; civil commotion; malicious mischief and vandalism; impact of airplanes, trucks, and other vehicles; and loss or damage from the faulty operation of furnaces. All these major extensions are provided at no additional premium. The Factory Mutual policy is further distinguished by its simplicity and lack of technicalities.

Every effort is made to avoid obscure clauses in fine print. The Factory Mutuals' unquestioned leadership in developing the policy form was initiated by Edward Atkinson. If he could have had his ideal policy, he often said, it would have read simply, "John Doe Company: You are now insured."

In spite of providing indemnity against an ever-increasing list of hazards, the Factory Mutuals' loss record has continued its uninterrupted downward spiral. In 1835, losses averaged 63 cents per $100 of insurance. By 1935, they had been cut to 3½ cents per $100. In 1950, the losses of the entire System averaged 3⅓ cents per $100 of insurance.

Not that there haven't been big losses. In the conflagration at Salem, Massachusetts, in 1914, the Factory Mutuals sustained a combined loss of $3,177,000. In 1917, the Union Switch and Signal Company at Swissvale, Pennsylvania, was destroyed with a total loss to the System of $2,185,000. Two years later, the destruction by fire of the Royal Mill in Riverpoint, Rhode Island, brought a loss of $1,220,000. And in 1948, the Factory Mutuals sustained their biggest loss when an explosion and fire destroyed the plant of the E. J. Brach Company, a Chicago candy-manufacturing concern, and resulted in a loss of $6 million.

Losses of this magnitude are, of course, unusual. As far back as 1918, losses had been reduced to the point at which 79 per cent of the total were for amounts of less than $1,000 each. This healthy trend has continued. Today 84 per cent of all Factory Mutual losses are under $1,000. And 99 per cent are under $25,000. But that remaining 1 per cent accounts for 51 per cent of the dollar volume in losses. The Factory Mutuals realize that until that ratio can be reduced their work is far from finished.

The reduction in losses over the years has naturally been reflected in the continual reduction of the net cost of insurance. The best that Zachariah Allen could do in 1835 was to bring the cost down to 84 cents per $100 of insurance, or less than half of the then existing stock company rates. When Edward Atkinson left the System, the net cost had been reduced to 6½ cents. Since then it has steadily been cut to the point at which the net cost of $100 of insurance in the Factory Mutuals stands today at less than 4 cents.

Behind the imposing record of the Factory Mutuals—a record highlighted by enormous expansion in volume of business combined with broader policy coverage and steady reduction in cost of insurance—lies a single concept: prevention of loss. This concept, implicit in the System from the start, takes practical form today in the Factory Mutuals' famous Engineering Division. An outgrowth of the Inspection Department created by Edward Atkinson and operating on the brilliant principles infused by John R. Freeman, the Engineering Division is today the lifeblood of the Factory Mutual System. The division's manifold services, provided without charge to Factory Mutual policyholders, can nowhere be excelled.

The Engineering Division has a total force of 835 people. With the exception of the clerical help, who number about 430, practically every member of the staff is a graduate engineer. The division's headquarters are in Boston; it also maintains district offices in the principal cities in the country; in addition, it has testing laboratories, covering seventy acres, outside of Boston. Operating on an annual budget of $4.5 million, the division is composed of seven main departments: Inspection, Appraisal, Plan, Standards, Laboratories, Publications, and Adjustment. Because of the combined work of these departments, the Factory Mutual System can rightfully claim to be the world's foremost loss-prevention engineers.

"The best insurance is that which protects the most," a member of the Engineering Division once remarked, and it is upon this principle that the division works. The protection begins when a prospective policyholder applies for insurance, and a member of the Inspection Department calls to make a preliminary or "candidate" inspection of the plant. If the risk is written, the policyholder will continue to be keenly aware of the Inspection Department as long as his policy is in force.

The Inspection Department, which is the first stepping-stone to advancement within the organization, consists of a staff of nearly four hundred, all of whom are graduate engineers. Upon going to work, they first receive an intensive ten weeks' training course at the Engineering Division's Boston headquarters and are then sent into the field accompanied by an experienced inspector. Large risks insured by the Factory Mutuals are thoroughly checked by a member of the Inspection Department about four times a year; medium-sized risks are inspected semi-annually. The inspections, which are not announced to policyholders in advance, may take anywhere from an hour on a very small risk to six weeks on a very large one.

Another protective service provided by the Engineering Division is performed by its Plan Department, which has a staff of 120. Their function is to prepare and keep up to date detailed plans of every risk insured. Three types of plans are drawn: sketches, data plans, and surveys. They range from the simple to the elaborate, the *pièce de résistance* being the survey plan. These are made on all large risks and are by far the most comprehensive. To prepare them, a so-called tape survey is made of the insured property, every jot and tittle of which are measured. This work is done by one or more of the twenty surveyors employed by the Plan Department; they may spend a month making the survey and three or four months doing the drawings.

The amount of insurance written on a risk is determined at the outset on the basis of the inspector's preliminary examination of the plant and on the combined judgment of the System and the assured. The figure thus arrived at represents everyone's best estimate of the amount needed. But since guesswork is anathema to the Factory Mutual System, the Appraisal Department works toward reducing the problem of determining the proper amount of insurance to a scientific basis. Members of this department, of whom there are forty, work with complete independence. They go into a plant without having consulted the inspector in the field, nor do they use the company's books in making their calculations, except that they do use the company's figures on the amount of stock on hand. The appraisers go over a plant with great thoroughness, placing a value not only on the building or buildings, but also on each piece of machinery. This requires that they be construction experts as well as specialists in a particular industry, such as metals, textiles, or food products. As a group, the appraisers must be able to recognize and place a value on more than one thousand different kinds of machines.

Up to this point in his experience with the Factory Mutual System, the policyholder has been able to observe, through the work of the Inspection, Plan, and Appraisal departments, the constant vigilance of the Engineering Division at first hand. Beyond these readily visible activities of the division are two other departments—Standards and Laboratories—

whose operations are seldom seen by policyholders, but whose work is of the first magnitude and importance to the System. Though they operate as separate departments, their work is closely interrelated.

Over the years, the Factory Mutuals have become famous for their unremitting efforts to improve standards of construction and fire-preventive equipment. Today the responsibility for continuing that work is in the hands of the Standards Department, which has a staff of forty-three, including thirty engineers. Their principal and unending assignment is to seek out the causes of fires and to devise methods and equipment for preventing them. One of the department's functions toward this end is to draw up specifications for approved fire equipment and then to work with manufacturers in getting it produced. Another function is to see that these specifications, once agreed upon, are maintained. The Standards Department is the final arbiter of the Factory Mutual System on whether approval of any particular equipment is granted or withheld. If granted, it can be installed in Factory Mutual risks; if withheld, it is not installed. The department also formulates the rules—or standards—of inspection.

In the great majority of cases, the standards thus established are the result of the tests and research conducted by the Factory Mutual Laboratories, which are no doubt the Engineering Division's most glamorous department. With a staff of thirty-four, including sixteen engineers and ten technicians, the Laboratories are located at Norwood, Massachusetts, fifteen miles outside of Boston. They are housed in a new, modern, two-story building set in the middle of a seventy-acre tract of land. One section of this, comprising four acres, is surrounded by a high wire fence. Inside the enclosure, in addition to the main building that houses the staff, are nineteen smaller structures of odd design and construction in which elaborate and frequently dangerous tests are made. The enclosed area is placed in the center of the seventy-acre tract in order to protect the surrounding countryside from ill effects that might result from the fires and explosions that are intentionally produced at the Laboratories in the course of research. No other organization, either government or private, is equipped to run the variety of tests that can be conducted by the Factory Mutual Laboratories, though some of them can be duplicated elsewhere. A unique organization, the Laboratories are a mecca for engineers, who trek there from all over the world.

The functions of the Laboratories are threefold: first, testing new equipment to determine whether it should receive Factory Mutual approval; second, testing products and equipment for the benefit of individual policyholders; third, conducting original research. The first function claims approximately half of the Laboratories' time; the balance is divided about equally between the other two.

The approval work done by the Laboratories consists of testing every new item of standard fire-preventive equipment that appears on the market. They are therefore constantly examining a tremendous variety of products, including fire extinguishers, valves, sprinklers, hose, various types of burners for ovens, flame arrestors, and containers for flammable liquids. This is but a tiny sampling. The book listing the equipment approved by the Factory Mutuals contains 146 pages. Every item listed has been rigorously tested by the Laboratories.

Along with these more or less routine duties, the Laboratories are frequently called upon by Factory Mutual policyholders to test equipment that they are in the process of developing. Also in the category known around the Laboratories as "risk service testing" is the work that is continuously being done on automatic sprinklers. While going through a plant, an inspector is very apt to detach a couple of sprinkler heads and send them into the Laboratories for a routine test to make sure that they are in proper working condition. The Laboratories test approximately eleven thousand individual sprinkler heads every year.

The Laboratories' third function, and one which has earned them world-wide fame, is their original research on the causes and means of preventing fire. These experiments are carried on in one of the nineteen specially constructed buildings that permit the engineers to simulate all the known conditions from which fires occur.

An example of an original research project performed by the Laboratories is the recent investigation they undertook as a result of changes in methods of industrial storage. These changes were, in turn, brought about partly by the invention and wide adoption of a machine called the fork lifter, which can pick up goods and pile them to heights that are impracticable when attempted by hand. The fork lifter has revolutionized industrial storage, particularly in the tire industry. Factory Mutual inspectors, visiting tire-storage plants and looking at stacks of tires piled by fork lifters to heights of thirty feet or more, were concerned over the new fire hazard thus created. A fire breaking out in between or on top of such stacks, they realized, would not only be extremely difficult to reach but also, since tires burn almost as viciously as gasoline and produce impenetrable clouds of smoke, almost impossible to extinguish.

Eventually the problem of finding means to deal with this new potential hazard was presented to the Laboratories.

They worked on it for two years, in the course of which they burned up some twenty-five thousand old tires. Not long ago they evolved what they believe to be the solution—an automatic sprinkler with a spray nozzle which creates a solid blanket of cold, wet vapor and thus tends to smother a fire as well as drown it.

Though spray nozzles are not new—they have been in use for many years to deal with certain stationary hazards—they had always been considerably more expensive than the conventional sprinkler head. In the course of research on the tire-storage problem, a staff member of the Laboratories invented a spray nozzle that can be mass-produced as cheaply as the orthodox sprinkler head. With these in use, the Laboratories believe that the fire hazard can be effectively reduced in tire-storage plants as well as in many other factories in which similar conditions exist. Like many of the Factory Mutuals' other research projects, the Laboratories' work on the problem presented by new methods of industrial storage comes under the heading of pure research. The investigation was undertaken before the System had incurred a single loss from this cause.

Every discovery made by the Factory Mutual Laboratories is promptly transmitted to all Factory Mutual policyholders through literature issued by the Publications Department of the Engineering Division. Edward Atkinson, who started the practice of spreading loss-prevention information to Factory Mutual members through circulars and bulletins, would be gratified to see how this program has been expanded. Today every policyholder receives a monthly eight-page magazine called the *Factory Mutual Record*, which has a circulation of twenty-one thousand and describes case histories of fires, new techniques in fire prevention, trends in industrial building, defense against industrial fires caused by atomic bombing, and a wide range of other topics. Policyholders are also provided with an abundance of other useful publications, including a comprehensive series of pamphlets called *Loss Prevention Bulletins*, manuals, booklets, posters, and literature for distribution among plant personnel. Altogether, the Publications Department publishes and distributes more than 600,000 pieces of literature every year.

It is likely that a Factory Mutual policyholder will have had contact directly or indirectly with all other sections of the Engineering Division before he suffers a loss and therefore has his first dealings with a Factory Mutual adjuster. The policyholder will no doubt be surprised, especially if he is acquainted with the practice of the general insurance companies, which usually employ outside adjusters or have one of their inspectors or other employees double in this capacity, to learn that the Factory Mutuals have their own separate Adjustment Department, staffed by twenty full-time adjusters who are all skilled engineers. Stationed in various parts of the country, the adjusters are empowered to handle all losses regardless of size—subject, of course, to home-office approval. Considering the character of the Factory Mutual System and the collective character of its members, it is not surprising that the System has never been involved in legal action by an assured in the course of settling a loss.

Working together, all departments of the Engineering Division have already made a tremendously impressive record in the field of loss prevention. However, it is not the past but the future with which the division is concerned. What new hazards it will be called upon to deal with cannot be foretold, but whatever they may be, the division has never been more fully prepared to cope with them than it is today.

It is strange but true that the division's primary future objective is also one of the oldest aims of the Factory Mutual System—"to improve the training of plant personnel in fire precautions and in the use of fire-fighting equipment"—or, in other words, to try to teach people to be smart about fire. "The only persons who can prevent loss by fire," Edward Atkinson said long ago, "are the owners or occupants of the insured premises. Upon them rests the responsibility for heavy loss, when any occurs, in nearly every fire."

The big fires in recent years have borne out this observation. In 1942, a fire at the Langley Mills, which involved a loss to the System of $3.2 million, got out of control because somebody had turned off a valve in the sprinkler system. In 1948 the System incurred a loss of $6 million in the E. J. Brach candy company's plant because a man forgot to turn off a kiln. The Engineering Division is therefore aware that its educational campaign must be never-ending. The millennium, when all the shortcomings and quirks of human nature can be controlled, does not appear to the Factory Mutual engineers to be just around the corner. As one of them not long ago remarked, "We can make things foolproof, but not damn-fool proof."

Back in 1895, an English engineer was sent to this country to investigate and prepare a report for the Royal Institute of British Architects on the construction and methods of American mills. He was so impressed by the Factory Mutuals that he devoted a section of his report to their work. "The prevention of loss by fire," he wrote, "is the chief function of the Factory Mutuals; the secondary purpose is to pay indemnity for actual losses." The fundamental principle, thus compactly stated, has never changed. As a consequence, just a half century later, another careful student of the Factory Mutual

System was able to report with accuracy: "The history of the Factory Mutuals is really the history of fire prevention in this country, for their pioneering work in the study and introduction of modern protective equipment not only reduced fire losses, inaugurated low-cost insurance, forced other insurance organizations to provide similar service and comparable rates on similar classes of property, but helped raise all standards of safety, and nearly eliminated danger to life from the manufacturing field."

Of the many efforts that have been made to summarize the philosophy of the Factory Mutual System, perhaps none is more instructive or more clearly reflects the thinking of the entire System today than a casual but succinct remark made recently in the course of conversation with a friend by Hovey T. Freeman, president of the Manufacturers Mutual, the pioneer Factory Mutual company. "We are ashamed of fires," Mr. Freeman said.

CHAPTER X

New Frontiers—1

FROM THE ATLANTIC TO THE PRAIRIES

BY 1852, one hundred years after its introduction into America, the mutual idea of insurance had sunk its roots deep into native soil and was thriving as lustily as the country itself. Branching out from Philadelphia, the mutual idea now offered protection to householders in a great many of the cities and larger towns and, by demonstrating its value to the millowners of New England, had set in motion the forces that would in time make mutual insurance the handmaiden of commerce. As it entered its second century, the mutual idea was in much the same stage of development as the nation it was serving: its principles had been proved, its growth had been sound, and it stood on the threshold of unprecedented expansion.

The half century following 1850 was a dynamic era whose predominant theme was the great westward movement that carried millions of Americans as well as millions of immigrants in an ever-swelling tide from the Alleghenies to the Pacific. In 1850, there were twenty-three million people in this country; fifty years later there were seventy-six million. And since the territory of the continental United States, except for the later addition of some twenty-three thousand square miles, was the same at the beginning of this era as it is today, there was plenty of rich land for all. Swarming over the great fertile Western plains and prairies, the hardy Yankees and hard-working immigrants brought more land under cultivation in the three decades between 1860 and 1890 than had been put under cultivation in the entire previous history of the country. With the ensuing sudden and tremendous growth in the rural wealth of the nation, which increased from four billion dollars in 1850 to sixteen billion in 1890, there developed a new and powerfully pressing need for the kind of fire insurance that would suit the special requirements of the country's farmers.

Though agriculture had always been the backbone of the nation's economy, the insurance needs of those who worked the land had never been adequately met. This rather paradoxical situation was partly due to the fact that in the earlier days the American farmer was a backwoodsman who had cleared a plot of land on the frontier and lived with his family in comparative isolation. Insurance was mainly an urban institution, and the companies then in existence were for the most part not interested in country business. When the stock companies did become interested and began a drive for the farmers' business, their rates were so high that most countrymen were obliged to forgo the protection. Gradually, however, as the backwoodsman gave way to the prairie farmer and the farming community became one of the largest and most progressive elements in the population, the mutual idea came to the fore and again proved its adaptability by furnishing the nation's farmers with sound insurance at cost.

The companies that provided this vital protection became known collectively as the farm mutuals. How well they fulfilled their function and the dominant position they now hold in the agricultural community can be seen from the fact that eighteen hundred farmers' mutual insurance companies are doing business today. Together they insure more than 60 per cent of all insurable farm property in the United States. Their policyholders consist of some four million farmers; and their combined total insurance in force is in excess of twenty-four billion dollars.

The farm mutuals are genuine grass-roots institutions. Their trials and successes, the social and economic conditions that brought them into existence and contributed to their growth, and the men who believed in them and fought for them combine to make a story as characteristically American as the covered wagon.

Though the opening of the West gave the greatest impetus to the development of the farm mutuals, they had previously taken root in a limited way in the settled East. Many of the pioneer Eastern companies, such as the 143-year-old Bucks County Contributionship in Pennsylvania, no doubt insured a large amount of farm property when they began, though their business is now primarily urban in character. When the Mutual Assurance Society of Virginia got under way in 1794, about half of its risks were on country property, but these were discontinued after a few years. Other companies later arose to provide protection on rural property in Virginia. Some of them had rather original bylaws. One company made the agent accepting the risk personally liable if a claim was made as a result of a fire originating in an adjacent property that was less than one hundred and fifty feet away from the structure insured. Another disclaimed liability if the insured at the time of a fire had more than five gallons of whiskey in his house. All things considered, it is not surprising that many of these companies did not survive. But the case is different with Virginia's oldest farm mutual. This company, the Mutual Fire Insurance Company of Loudon County, was founded in 1849, and today, after more than a century of successful operation, has in excess of sixty million dollars at risk throughout the state.

The experience of the Loudon County Mutual is, however, in the nature of an exception proving the rule that the early mutual companies whose business originally included a good deal of rural property were more than likely to change with the developing countryside into companies specializing in urban risks. More typical is the case of the New London County Mutual Insurance Company, of Norwich, Connecticut. Founded in 1840, this company was originally organized to insure rural risks, and as late as 1910 nearly 70 per cent of its business was still on farm property. However, by its one hundredth birthday, in 1940, its insurance in the farm class had declined to 22 per cent, and that trend has since continued.

The oldest existing genuine farm mutual in the United States—a farm mutual being defined as a company that has always written more than 50 per cent of its risks on farm property—is the New Jersey Association. In many respects it is typical of the pioneer farm companies. Founded in 1823 by eleven Quaker farmers in Crosswicks, New Jersey, which is situated in rolling farm country not far from the city of Trenton, the Association carries on today in much the same way as it did in the beginning. Its treasurer, John Hendrickson, who is in his eighties, is a great-great-great-grandson of one of the founders, Joseph Hendrickson, who insured his farmhouse, which is still the family home, with the Association more than a century and a quarter ago, and the insurance is still in force.

In its early years, the Association conducted its business on an assessment basis, each member giving a note making him responsible for his share of the losses. Later the company adopted the method of requiring a cash deposit of a certain sum for each hundred dollars of insurance, the rate depending on the kind and construction of the buildings insured. The rates, which are 1¾ per cent on frame or brick dwellings and 2 per cent on frame outbuildings, have not been changed in the past half century. Policies are issued for five years, and the initial deposit is collected when they are first written. At the same time, a charge of three dollars is made for the policy and four dollars for inspecting the risk. At the end of the five-year period and every five years thereafter, another inspection is made, and a fee of seven dollars is again collected, but the member pays no further deposit. When a sizable surplus accumulates, the company returns a portion of it to the policyholders in the form of what the Association calls a bonus. The last bonus amounted to 50 per cent of each member's original deposit. Members of the Hendrickson family have received so many bonuses during the hundred and twenty-nine years that their house has been insured that their insurance has long since ceased to cost them anything.

Being extremely conservative, the Association covers only fire and lightning and limits its risks to $2,000 on any one building and to $3,000 on any group of farm buildings. Though the Association is permitted by its charter to operate throughout New Jersey, most of its policies, which number 150, are on property in the three counties nearest the home office. Its risks aggregate $250,000, and its present comfortable surplus exceeds $100,000. Sound, conservative, and carefully managed, this tidy little company expects to go on rendering the same kind of service in the future that it has since the days of President Monroe. "The New Jersey Association," Treasurer John Hendrickson said not long ago, "is the only thing in this neighborhood that was started so long ago and is still in good shape, and we're proud of it. We've been very conservative in the risks we've accepted. We don't go out and look for members. If people come and ask us for insurance and we think they're a good risk, well, we're willing to give it to them."

Not all of the early farm mutuals were as well managed as the New Jersey Association, and many consequently had short lives. The number of farm mutuals that were born in the early days, only to disappear on the expiration of their charter or before, will probably never be known, since no official reports were at that time required of them. However, a report issued by the Massachusetts Insurance Department in 1880 provides a glimpse of the hectic nature of all insurance during that early period. In a section titled "The Wrecks of a Century," the report states: "Since the adoption of the State Constitution in 1770, four hundred and thirty-seven insurance companies (221 stock and 216 mutuals) have been chartered under general and special laws within the Commonwealth. Four hundred and eleven of these companies were Fire, Marine, and Fire-Marine, thirteen Life, twelve Health and one Steam Boiler. Of the whole number, one hundred and ninety-nine (115 stock and 84 mutuals) died in their cradles, and one hundred and fifty-four others (67 stock and 87 mutuals) closed their doors either by compulsion or voluntary decision, after longer or shorter periods of business life."

Of the farm mutuals that came into existence between 1830 and 1840, six are still doing business today—two in Pennsylvania, two in Connecticut, and one each in New

Hampshire and New Jersey. During this period, a number of farm mutuals were also organized in New York; their chief value to the movement was that they demonstrated quite clearly, by going out of business, how farm mutuals should not be organized. It was, however, the Empire State that, after serving for many years as a kind of laboratory for testing legislation governing the organization and operation of farm mutuals, at length produced a pattern statute that was successful and widely copied.

After the great New York City fire of 1835, which caused a combined loss of twenty million dollars and sent eighteen insurance companies to the wall, the surviving stock companies raised their rates radically, which in turn resulted in the organization of a number of new companies. In 1835 the New York legislature had chartered only two new insurance companies. In 1836, the year after the fire, more than fifty new companies were chartered, about half of which were mutuals; some of these were farm mutuals. "This demand for mutual companies," wrote James M. Cook, who, as state comptroller, then had supervision over insurance, "arose from the desire of the possessors of property in the interior of the State to place their risks in a company unconnected with that class of city companies, whose policies, as experience had taught them, were so concentrated in city risks as to make it possible to bankrupt them by a single fire." The trend toward mutual companies was further spurred, Cook observed, by revelations in the bankruptcy proceedings of the eighteen defunct stock companies, whose profits had been nothing less than handsome up until their collective demise.

The legislation under which the new mutual companies were chartered proved faulty, however, and the mortality rate of the companies organized during the decade after its passage was exceedingly high. Nor was any noticeable improvement made under a later statute which became effective in 1849. The act of 1849 permitted thirteen persons to organize a mutual company by giving notes to a total amount of $100,000, even though the property securing each note was valued at considerably less than the amount of the note. Thus, one mutual company that started with $102,000 in "assets" had actual insurance amounting to $24,675, and $121.25 in cash. "The summit level of folly, spurred on by avarice, had been reached," Comptroller James Cook observed a few years after this legislation had been in effect, "and as the ascent was with the speed and splendor of a rocket, the descent, as a matter of course, was like the stick that guided it upward." In less lovely language, failures were widespread.

Finally, in 1857, the New York legislature enacted a general law for the incorporation of so-called town co-operative fire insurance associations. Since "town," in this case, meant "township," the legislation applied particularly to farm mutuals and is, in fact, generally known as the first farmers' mutual insurance law. It provided that twenty-five or more persons, residing in any township, who collectively owned property of not less than fifty thousand dollars in value, could form a mutual fire insurance company to insure their buildings. The maximum risk on any single property was limited to two thousand dollars and the policy term to five years. Only detached dwellings and their contents and farm buildings and their contents could be insured, and all risks had to be situated within one township. The company was obliged to file with the town clerk an annual statement of its affairs on the day preceding its annual meeting, and the law even got down to the point of requiring that the corporate title of

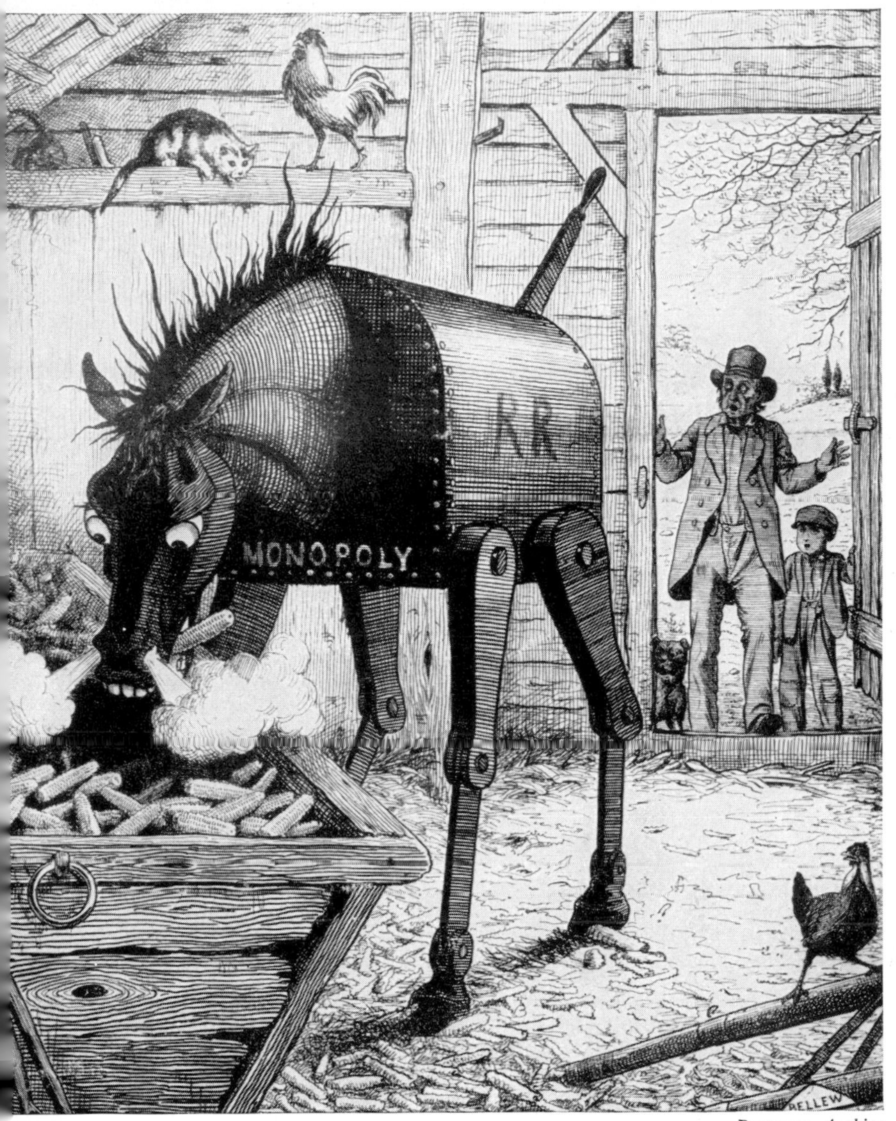

Bettmann Archive

"THE IRON HORSE WHICH EATS UP THE FARMERS' PRODUCE"

the above cartoon (from an 1873 issue of the New York *Daily Graphic*), the
mer is saying, "I can't afford this hired team; it takes every mite I can raise to
d him." Railroad freight rates in the latter half of the nineteenth century
re so high that farmers often burned their corn rather than ship it to market.
tes charged by existing fire insurance companies were also so high that few
rmers could afford the protection. To provide themselves with insurance at cost,
ey organized hundreds of mutual fire insurance companies.

Bettmann Archi

"THE FARMERS' MOVEMENT IN THE WEST"

Members of the Grange meet in the woods near Winchester, Illinois, in th picture from *Frank Leslie's Illustrated Newspaper*. The Grangers led the revo of the farmers against Eastern financial interests, elected their candidates t political offices, ended some of the more outrageous railway abuses, and taugl farmers the value of co-operative action. Of some 1800 present-day farm mutu insurance companies, several hundred were founded by members of the Grang the company include the name of the town in which the business office of the company was located. The fact that forty farm mutuals were formed in the five years after 1857 and that about half of them are in existence today is a singular indication of the improvement effected by the law of 1857.

Because the law aimed to eliminate the features of previous legislation that had resulted in widespread abuses and a wholesale perversion of the mutual principle, it was severely, perhaps unduly, restrictive, but it proved exceedingly important to the whole farm mutual movement. It served as the model for similar laws passed in Illinois, Iowa, Wisconsin, Michigan, Minnesota, Ohio, and Indiana before 1879, and eventually for those of ten other states in the South and West. Though patterned after the New York statute, the farm mutual laws of other states were generally more lenient in their provisions, or were made so by amendment. For example, the territory in which a mutual company was permitted to operate was usually extended to include a number of neighboring townships, a county, or several contiguous counties. And farm property of all kinds might be insured against lightning as well as fire.

With the way thus opened by legislation, the latter part of the nineteenth century saw a veritable tidal wave of farm mutuals sweep across the country, saturating the Middle West, and rolling on to the Pacific Coast. In the entire previous history of the country up to 1870, a total of 192 farm mutuals, still in existence today, were formed. In the thirty years after 1870, a total of 1,100 existing farm mutuals were formed. Approximately two thirds of all farm mutuals now doing business were organized in the flourishing years between 1870 and 1900. The insurance world had never seen anything like it.

The fact that enabling legislation existed is only a minor factor in the explanation of this sudden and phenomenal growth. Both the legislation and the mutuals were an expression—an effect rather than a cause—of powerful economic, social, and political currents that had begun cascading across the country after the Civil War. The most significant of these was the conquest of the West, a process that involved the greatest movement of population in our history.

In a literal sense, the westward movement had been under way for a hundred years, but it was the improvement in the means of transportation, particularly the building of turnpikes and canals in the early part of the nineteenth century, that gave the process its biggest initial momentum. It was quickened in the "fabulous forties," when settlers began moving out in increasing numbers over the long Oregon trail, when the Mormons made their spectacular hegira from Illinois to Utah, and when, at the close of the decade, the discovery of gold at Coloma, California, enticed a small army of farmers, clerks, lawyers, ministers, and assorted other adventurers to head West in quest of treasure. Within eighteen months after the first nuggets were found, some thirty thousand panting travelers had crossed the plains and reached the gold fields. However, not all those who moved West during this period were fired by the get-rich-quick fever. During the forties, Iowa and Wisconsin, having attracted several hundred thousand settlers, were admitted as states to the Union. And during the 1850s, the population of the eight states of the Upper Mississippi Valley increased by three and one third million, or more than 167 per cent.

Though the Civil War checked the Western movement, it

was still surprisingly large. During the war years, Illinois, Wisconsin, Minnesota, Iowa, Kansas, and Nebraska enlarged their combined population by 843,000 new settlers. A powerful stimulus to the opening of the prairie wheat fields of these states was provided in the Homestead Act of 1862, which gave to "any person who is the head of a family, or who has arrived at the age of twenty-one years, and is a citizen of the United States, or who shall have filed his declaration to become such," the privilege of obtaining a quarter section of land—160 acres—free of charge, except for a small filing fee. Some fifteen thousand homesteaders took advantage of the privilege during the war, but this was only a token of the rush that was to follow when hostilities ceased. Scores of thousands among the million disbanded soldiers, particularly those from the devastated South, headed West to stake out their 160-acre claims. The greatest period in Western expansion followed in the twenty years between 1870 and 1890. During this era, 200,000 square miles of farmland—an area equal to almost all of France—was added to the agricultural area of the United States.

One of the fundamental factors in the tremendous Western expansion was the growth of the railroads, which enabled the farmers to market their crops and secure equipment, tools, clothes, household furnishings, and other manufactured items from the industrial East. In 1865, there were thirty-five thousand miles of railroad in the United States, very little of which was in the Middle West. In 1900, there were close to two hundred thousand miles—more than in all of Europe—and there was scarcely a settlement in the Middle West that did not have access to a railroad.

In the beginning, Middle Western farmers regarded the arrival of the iron horse as a blessing sent straight from heaven, and though they were later obliged to revise this estimate sharply, they at first went all out to assist the spreading network. Individual farmers, municipalities, counties, and states bought bonds in order to attract the railroad to their section; as further encouragement, the states granted the roads liberal charters, gave them loans and subsidies, exempted them from taxation, and guaranteed to protect them from competition. Wisconsin contributed thirty million dollars in subsidies to the railroads, while Nebraska and Iowa each put up twice that sum. The states were niggardly compared with the federal government, which helped out the railroads by giving them 158,293,377 acres of public land—or an area almost as big as Texas. Holding some of this domain for speculative purposes, the railroads disposed of the balance, including the good farmland, at a price averaging around five dollars an acre. With subsidies from all sources, the railroads acquired enough money to cover their original costs of construction.

The need for cheap labor to build the railroads was one of the original factors stimulating the unprecedented immigration that took place in the latter half of the nineteenth century and contributed in a basic way to the settlement of the West. In the 1840s, more than a million and a half immigrants came to this country. Poverty and political unrest in Europe, together with the promising opportunities offered in America, combined to swell the tide of aliens flowing here in the following decades. In the 1850s, for example, more than a million people emigrated from Sweden alone—approximately a quarter of that country's total population. From 1860 to 1900, immigration reached a total of approximately fourteen million, bringing the population of the United States, at the end of that period, to seventy-six million.

The fifty years following 1860 saw the greatest agricultural expansion in our history. The number of farms increased from two million to six and one-third million, while the acreage more than doubled. The wheat crop increased from 173 to 635 million bushels, and the production of corn rose from 838 million to 2,886 million bushels. A great deal of this increase was the result of a spate of inventions of agricultural equipment and machinery. In 1834, Cyrus McCormick patented the reaper, and by the close of the Civil War more than a quarter of a million reapers were in use. Other important agricultural inventions of this period included the steel-toothed cultivator, the self-knotting binder, and the plow with a steel moldboard. The high cost of fencing, a problem that had plagued Western farmers, was solved in 1874, when barbed wire was put on the market. As a consequence of the improvements in agricultural methods and machinery, the time required to prepare the ground and sow a bushel of wheat was reduced from a half hour in 1830 to two minutes in 1900.

All the while that these tremendous strides were being made in agriculture, the plight of farmers as a group was steadily worsening. While their output was soaring, their income was declining. In 1860, farmers received 30 per cent of the national income; in 1890, they received 19 per cent. The trend of agricultural prices was generally downward. In 1855, a bushel of wheat sold for $2.50 on the New York market; in 1866, it sold for $1.45; by 1894, the price had fallen to 49 cents.

To get their crops to market, the farmers were totally dependent on the railroads, which charged them unconscionable rates. In the 1880s corn sold for around 70 cents a bushel in the east, but the Mid-western farmer received between 10 and 15 cents a bushel, the cost of transportation eating up most of the difference. When during the same period wheat was selling at Chicago for $1.00 a bushel, the railroads were charging 45 cents a bushel to move it from central Nebraska to the Chicago market. The farmers' animosity toward the railroads was enhanced when, as often happened, the countrymen's investment in railroad bonds turned out to be a total loss. To a homesteader who had bought railroad bonds that became worthless, the exorbitant freight rates charged by the railroads were an insult added to injury.

It was not only the railroads that were putting the squeeze on the farmers. Those being the days when the doctrine of *laissez faire* was rampant, practically all the producers of agricultural supplies and equipment had combined into trusts—the fertilizer trust, the farm-machinery trust, the barbed-wire trust—to maintain prices at artificially high levels. The farmers sold their products in a free world market, unprotected by tariffs, but nearly everything they bought—machinery, clothing, furniture, lumber, leather goods—was produced behind a high protective tariff wall, and as a result the prices were kept uniformly steep. The prices paid by the farmers for daily necessities were bad enough; what they were charged when they had to borrow money was worse. Interest rates were frequently above 20 per cent and seldom below 10 per cent.

As a consequence of all these factors, farmers were up against it simply to make ends meet, and their life was hard, mean, and harsh. Considering their circumstances, it is no wonder they felt that every man's hand was turned against them, and there seemed little they could do to improve their situation. The majority of both state and federal legislators were businessmen or lawyers, who were inclined to align themselves with the financial and industrial interests of the East. In 1870, though approximately half of the population was engaged in agriculture, only about 7 per cent of the members of Congress were farmers. The farmers' efforts to improve their lot through legislative action were hamstrung with discouraging frequency by the wily maneuvers of the Eastern legislators, who preferred that the Western farmers be maintained in their status, subservient and profitable. Reflecting this attitude was the supercilious remark of an Eastern editor, who said, "We do not want any more states until we can civilize Kansas."

Pressed on every side, the farmers at length took action to alleviate their burdensome condition and set in motion forces that were to assume the proportions of an agrarian revolt. They organized themselves into clubs and societies, the most important of which was the Patrons of Husbandry, usually called the Grange. This militant organization was founded by Oliver Hudson Kelley, a keen-eyed, black-bearded clerk in the Department of Agriculture, who, right after the Civil War, had been sent by President Johnson to survey agricultural conditions in the South. Appalled by the poverty, antiquated methods, and the widespread feeling of futility among farmers, Kelley established the Grange in 1867. According to its "Declaration of Purposes," the Grange was pledged, among other things, to "develop a higher manhood and womanhood among ourselves," to advance the cause of agriculture generally, to suppress "personal, local, sectional and national prejudices," and to "discountenance the credit system, the fashion system, and every other system tending to prodigality and bankruptcy."

However idealistic and nebulous its original program, the Grange appealed instantly to the farmers of the South and the Middle West, and though Kelley had said that the order had to be "advertised as vigorously as if it were a patent medicine," there was little need for high-pressure selling. Within three years after its organization, Granges had been established in nine states, and local chapters were being organized in seven others. Five years later, there were some 20,000 local Granges, and total membership was more than 800,000. Though the Grange had originally set out to improve the social, intellectual, and emotional life of farmers, it was natural, considering the times, that it should have become involved in politics.

So many farmers' political meetings, sponsored by the Grange and other agricultural societies, were held on Independence Day in 1873 that it became popularly known as the "Farmers' Fourth of July." Spearheaded by the Grange, farmers elected their candidates to office and were responsible for the enactment of a large amount of legislation, including the so-called Granger laws, which eliminated some of the more outrageous railway abuses. Though not all of the undertakings of the Grange and of similar societies were rewarded with lasting success, the one great beneficent effect of their combined activities was to teach the farmers that their salvation lay in co-operative effort.

It was against this background and in those times that the farmers' mutual fire insurance movement grew from infancy to adulthood. Fire was an ever-present menace to farmers living in the latter half of the nineteenth century, and their predicament was made more treacherous by the fact that they lived in comparative isolation; a fire on their property, once under way, was likely to rob them of all they owned. Very rarely did they have insurance. For in the matter of insurance, as in so many other respects, farmers were generally either neglected or exploited. In the Middle West before 1860, less than a dozen farm mutual fire insurance companies were in operation. If a farmer wanted insurance, he secured it from a stock fire insurance company, provided he could pay the exceedingly high premiums. He could, however, seldom afford this necessity because it was priced as if it were a luxury.

Furthermore, farmers were inclined to be distrustful of this kind of insurance. Their reasons have been made clear by A. F. Dean, a well-known stock company official, who, writing in 1900, explained: "The volume of farm business and its exceptional desirability led some managerial genius to conceive the idea that he could largely increase the premiums of his company from this source by sending out traveling solicitors through the country districts, after the manner of lightning rod, chain-pump, and patent-churn people. As these solicitors were selected for their glibness and push, rather than for their character or knowledge of the business, and as neither their judgment nor honesty could be trusted, the plan was adopted of taking payment in notes instead of cash. An elaborate application containing a cut-throat warranty was prepared, under which the assured surrendered every equitable right, and became responsible for any overvaluation of his property; and to make assurance doubly sure, every policy contained a printed stipulation that the company should be liable for only three-fourths of any loss that might occur. . . . In a few years the agricultural regions swarmed with traveling solicitors ready to sell a farmer a patent-churn, windmill, stump-puller, or fire policy with the same glib disregard of the truth. . . . In time, the adjustment of losses revealed the full iniquity of this plan, and in every farming community fire insurance came to be regarded as a swindle. Of the hundreds of fire institutions then doing business, not over four or five at most were implicated. . . . The industry of fire insurance became *non grata* in every state where the farmers had the controlling voice in legislation, and the entire insurance community has been made to suffer ever since for the sins of a few unprincipled adventurers."

To provide themselves with reliable insurance at cost, farmers turned to the mutual idea and vociferously demanded laws that would enable them to organize mutual companies. Securing passage of such legislation usually required some doing. In Minnesota, for example, farmers began agitating for a law permitting the formation of rural fire insurance companies in the early 1870s. "Strong opposition to such a law was encountered," V. N. Valgren, an outstanding authority on farm mutuals, has written, "which was no doubt fostered by commercial insurance interests, but was led apparently by the Insurance Commissioner of the State. The latter informs us in his annual report for 1874 that in the legislative session of the preceding year a bill was introduced providing for the 'indiscriminate organization of township mutual companies.' The bill passed both houses of the legislature, but the signature of the Governor, in the words of the Commissioner, 'was prudently withheld.' He further relates how in the legislative session of the year of the report two further attempts were made to pass such a law, the bill in both cases being defeated in the Senate after passage in the House." In spite of the commissioner's continuing efforts to block it, an act authorizing the formation of farm mutual fire insurance companies finally became law in 1875. Within ten years, Minnesota had 43 farm mutuals. By 1900, it had 122.

Farmers in other states had much the same experience. They fought for the legal right to insure their property by the method best suited to their needs, and they won. Starting from scratch in 1860, the farmers of Iowa had organized 142 farm mutuals by 1900. During the same period, farmers had established 55 such companies in Indiana, 167 in Illinois, and 174 in Wisconsin. In the country as a whole, 1,425 farmers' mutual fire insurance companies had been founded by the turn of the century.

The trouble with statistics is that they are as impersonal as the adding machine that computes them. For example, the fact that 55 farm mutuals were founded in Indiana in the forty years after 1860 is significant, but the cold figures fail to reveal anything of the people and events that produced them. Though the history of each of these companies is different, the story of one of them will perhaps bring to the fore some of the human factors that were responsible for the success of all farm mutuals. The Indiana Farmers Mutual Insurance Company, one of the 55 farm mutuals organized in the Hoosier state in the thriving period between 1860 and 1900, provides a useful illustrative example.

Like several hundred other farm mutuals in existence today, the Indiana Farmers Mutual was organized by members of the Grange. Founded in Crawfordsville, Indiana, in 1877, it was originally called the Patrons Mutual Fire Insurance Company. In the beginning, only Patrons in good standing, residing in the county where the company was located, could become members. As the company grew, the membership privilege was extended to farmers of good character in adjoining counties and eventually to those residing anywhere within the state, and the name of the company was successively changed to reflect its expanding operations.

Behind the formation of the company lay the farmers' desperate need to protect their property from the ravages of fire.

The founders had seen one or more of their neighbors wiped out by a fire that reduced their place to ashes and resulted in throwing them on the mercy of the community. When such a disaster occurred, neighboring farmers got together, felled the timber, and erected a new log cabin or other rude dwelling for the victims; to supply them with a few tools and other necessities, a wagon made the rounds of the community, and all the neighboring families contributed a few items from their own meager belongings. This was mutuality, but to provide a more certain and less arduous way of sharing each other's losses, the farmers around Crawfordsville decided to form a fire insurance company embodying the mutual principle. It took them seven months to accomplish their organizational work. By that time, fifty-two farmers had subscribed for insurance totaling $53,750, and the company was under way.

For two years and four months the company had no losses. Then trouble began. Fire destroyed the house belonging to the president of the company, the loss requiring an assessment of 50 cents on each $100 of insurance in force. Several farmers quit after that. Even more dropped out in 1884, after three fires had occurred within a period of little more than a month. Agents of Eastern insurance companies spread the word that the company was broke, wouldn't pay its losses, or would try to settle for much less than what was fair. Though this was all propaganda, members got the impression that incendiaries were responsible for the three fires, and many left the company for fear that their own buildings might be burned.

At the annual meeting of 1884, a great many of the members urged that the company be disbanded. The subject was debated most of the day, until finally an influential and well-to-do charter member named James Wilkinson rose and said to E. V. Brookshire, the secretary, "Vory, if your house burns, I will pay half of it. If mine burns, you pay half. Let's keep the company going." The statement had an electric effect on almost all the other members, who got to their feet and pledged that they, too, would carry on, and the company was saved.

But its troubles were not over. Competition from the stock companies was felt in many ways, one of which was a constant barrage of propaganda directed by their agents against the farmers' struggling organization. In 1885, the president of the company, James A. Mount, who was later elected governor of Indiana, decided to set the record straight and at his own expense addressed a circular letter to all members of the company. In spite of the losses that had required assessments, the letter pointed out, farmers were still getting their insurance at rates that were from 30 to 50 per cent less than those charged by stock companies. Referring to the six directors of the farmers' company, the president's letter asked, "Do you think six such men, having interests similar and consonant with yourself, would take any advantage of the trust and confidence? Or do you think that some kid-gloved, plug-hatted gentleman, perhaps getting off the train at your nearest railroad station and coming and looking over your heap of smoking ashes, would come nearer doing you right than your six farm friends?" Mr. Mount wound up with a few observations on "foreign insurance companies with millions of money, elegant and costly buildings and numerous salaried officers," and tartly added, under his signature, "P.S. It has been reported by insurance agents and others that I have become dissatisfied with the workings of this company and contemplate resigning as president. Such charges are false.

The company is in better condition than ever before, and I shall devote more time and energy in the future to make this Mutual Company a success than I have in the past."

Meanwhile, the treasurer of the company, Jacob M. Harshbarger, a wealthy and highly regarded farmer who was widely known as "Uncle Jake," was having some rather disquieting experiences. His enthusiasm for the company was boundless; he talked mutual insurance to everyone he met and recruited new members by the dozen. Finally, agents of one of the out-of-state stock companies made Mr. Harshbarger a rather interesting proposition. If he would drop out of the farmers' mutual, they said, their company would provide him and his children, free of charge, with all the fire insurance they needed for life. "I am not for sale," Mr. Harshbarger replied. "Every dollar I have is back of this company, just as every dollar of every other member is back of it. Nothing could be safer. Nothing is better. No, I am not for sale, and I am happy in any sacrifice I can make to help my friends and neighbors. I am not interested in your proposition."

In the three quarters of a century since its founding, the Indiana Farmers Mutual has developed into one of the country's largest and most progressive farm mutuals. During more than half of its career, the company was under the able leadership of Harry P. Cooper, who as secretary not only guided its destinies but also served continuously from 1913 until his death in 1947 as secretary of the National Association of Mutual Insurance Companies.

As a result of mergers with more than a dozen smaller Indiana farm mutuals, the company, from its headquarters in Indianapolis, now operates throughout the State. In addition to fire protection, it has for many years provided its members with both windstorm and hail insurance. Under some 90,000 policies, the company now protects approximately half of the insurable farms in Indiana. Its insurance in force exceeds $538 million, and its surplus, which was hit hard by catastrophic windstorm losses amounting to more than $2 million in 1948, is now more than $1.7 million. Though the Indiana Farmers has grown very large for a farm mutual, it has retained its original character. It still insures only farm property, and of its nineteen directors, fourteen are farmers or are directly interested in farming enterprises.

CHAPTER XI

New Frontiers—2

FROM THE PRAIRIES TO THE PACIFIC

IN THE first half of the twentieth century, the fortunes of American farmers have swung back and forth in a wide arc between prosperity and distress, reaching one extreme in war, the other in peace. During World War I, farmers were as well off as they had ever been. With the arrival of peace and deflation, their financial condition hit rock bottom. In 1920, farmers received 15 per cent of the national income; in 1933, they received 7 per cent. The disproportion is underlined by the fact that in 1930 farmers made up one fourth of the total population.

Though the farmers' plight began to be relieved with the payment of government subsidies beginning in 1933, real prosperity did not return to the farm until after the outbreak of World War II. As a consequence of the tremendous demand for foodstuffs, farm income, which had fallen to $5 billion in 1932 and had gradually increased to $9 billion in 1940, shot up during the next five years, reaching $22 billion in 1945. During the following years of uneasy peace and limited war, farm income continued to increase; in 1950 it stood at $28 billion. The value of farm property has also been subject to radical change. In 1920, farm property in the

United States was valued at $78 billion; by 1940, it had fallen to $41 billion. With war and inflation, the value of farm property soared, climbing to a peak of $88 billion in 1950.

Considering these widely fluctuating economic conditions, it might reasonably be expected that the collective history of farmers' mutual fire insurance companies in the first half of the twentieth century would reveal similar oscillations. The contrary is true. Though naturally affected by alternating economic currents, farmers' mutual fire insurance, with the exception of three years during the depression, has shown a steady and uninterrupted growth in every year of the twentieth century.

The past fifty years have seen the coverage of most of the remaining rural areas by farm mutual fire insurance companies. In 1900, there were only ten farm mutuals, existing today, in Kentucky, Tennessee, and Alabama. Since then, more than thirty have been added in those states, while more than forty have joined the ten or so that had been founded before 1900 in Texas, Oklahoma, and Arkansas. At the turn of the century, there were but two existing farm mutuals in all of Montana, Idaho, Wyoming, Colorado, and Utah; the total in those states now exceeds thirty. During the same period, about fifty new companies have joined those already located in the Southern states along the Atlantic Coast. In addition to entering new territory, the number of farm mutuals has increased in states where they had previously been well established. Since 1900, around fifty new farm mutuals have been formed in New York, Pennsylvania, and New Jersey combined; 115 in Ohio, Indiana, Illinois, Michigan, and Wisconsin; and 160 in Minnesota, Iowa, Missouri, North Dakota, and South Dakota. Altogether, more than five hundred farm mutuals have been formed in the first half of the present century.

In spite of this substantial addition to the ranks, there are fewer farm mutuals doing business today than there were fifty years ago. Several factors have contributed to this development. By 1900, the Western frontier was beginning to disappear, and though a tremendous amount of land was opened after that, much of it tended to be utilized as grazing land or in large farms. For example, in 1910 the average farm in the United States consisted of 138 acres; in 1945, it consisted of 195. In addition, the present century has been most noticeably marked by the growth of cities and the general urbanization of the entire country, resulting in a gradual decline of the farm population and a decrease in the number of farms. Between 1920 and 1945, farm population dropped from 31.6 million to 26.2 million, while the number of farms declined from 6.4 million to 5.8 million. With fewer farms spread over a larger area, farm mutuals were obliged to extend the limits of the territory they served. As a consequence, many of the farm mutuals founded in the past fifty years began by operating in an entire county or in several counties. Scores of other companies that were already in business consolidated to keep pace with changing circumstances. With the expansion of the larger companies, many of the smaller, inefficient companies either foundered or voluntarily retired from business.

The trend toward fewer and larger farmers' mutual insurance companies has been most marked since 1920. During the past thirty years, consolidations, voluntary retirements, and occasional failures have offset the numerical gains realized by the formation of new companies. But as the number of farm mutual companies has been steadily reduced, the amount of farmers' mutual fire insurance in force has grown by leaps and bounds. In 1921, there were 1,951 farm mutuals with $8 billion at risk. In 1949, there were 1,800 companies with $24 billion at risk. Thus, while the number of farm mutual companies has decreased during the last three decades by 8 per cent, the total amount of farmers' mutual fire insurance in force has increased by 200 per cent.

Another significant development in farmers' mutual insurance has been the growth of companies providing windstorm and tornado insurance. Tornadoes, sometimes called cyclones or "twisters," have always been among the most dreaded and costly natural phenomena with which prairie farmers have had to contend. Though one of the least extensive of storms, they are one of the most violent and terrifying. Occurring most often in midafternoon and heralded by a roaring, rushing noise like that made by several trains simultaneously speeding through a tunnel, they leave widespread devastation in their wake. In the thirty-five year period from 1916 through 1950, a total of 5,475 tornadoes—not including other kinds of severe windstorms—occurred in the United States; they caused 8,120 deaths and resulted in property damage in excess of $476 million. That is an average of 156 tornadoes a year and an average annual property loss of $13.6 million.

Being generally but by no means specifically predictable, tornadoes present an actuarial headache. Certain years have earned a dubious distinction for the high incidence of twisters. On February 19, 1864, sixty distinct tornadoes tore through the Middle West on a single afternoon. In 1925, on a single day in March, a series of eight tornadoes that cut through Illinois, Indiana, Missouri, Kentucky, and Tennessee caused losses approximating $16.5 million. In the month of May 1930, tornadoes occurred at the rate of three every day.

In 1948, a bad year, a total of 195 tornadoes occurred in thirty separate states, causing property damage of $54 million, or about four times the annual average. On three successive Fridays in 1948, beginning, ironically, on Good Friday, Indiana suffered the most disastrous windstorms in its history. Within those three weeks, one farm mutual company alone incurred more than 25,000 losses, the payment of which exceeded $2 million.

Though no part of the country is immune from the windstorm hazard (tornadoes have occurred in all states and in the District of Columbia), there is no place in the world more susceptible to tornadoes than the Great Central Plains east of the Rocky Mountains. With the exception of Missouri, more tornadoes have occurred in Iowa during the past thirty-five years than in any other state, the total number for the period reaching 498. Perhaps that is the reason why the first farmers' mutual company specializing in insuring against the windstorm hazard was founded in Des Moines, Iowa. That pioneer company, the Iowa Mutual Tornado Insurance Association, was incorporated in 1884; it now has more than a billion dollars of windstorm insurance in force.

Unlike the farmers' fire mutuals, which moved steadily westward, the windstorm companies spread out in an irregular pattern. Between 1885 and 1900, a total of 41 farmers' mutual windstorm companies were formed in ten states. As a rule, they were organized as separate companies by existing farm mutuals, often with the co-operation and active assistance of the state association of farm mutual companies, and were staffed by men experienced in farm mutual fire insurance. Today there are 66 farmers' mutual windstorm companies distributed throughout fifteen states, from Pennsylvania to Nebraska and from North Dakota to Georgia. In addition to the specialized farmers' mutual windstorm companies, there are approximately 300 large farm mutuals that write both fire and windstorm insurance. Altogether, the windstorm insurance on farm property provided by these two groups of companies now exceeds $8 billion.

After many years of loss-prevention research conducted by the Iowa Mutual Tornado Insurance Association and other farmers' mutual windstorm companies, it has been found that many traditional carpentry practices, handed down for generations from craftsmen to apprentice, are perpetuating unnecessary windstorm hazards. As a consequence, the windstorm companies are now embarked on a program to educate farmers and builders of farm property on the kinds of materials and methods of construction that most successfully withstand the onslaught of violent winds. It has been discovered that buildings of certain sizes and shapes, properly placed in relation to the prevailing winds, have a much greater chance of standing up against a fierce windstorm than have those that are designed and constructed simply to suit the fancy of the farmer's wife.

A detailed study of the proper bracing and anchoring of farm buildings has been made by the Farmers Mutual Insurance Company of Nebraska. The common, and apparently erroneous, belief used to be that, given enough weight, a building would stay put. "We've found that that just isn't true," Harold J. Requartte, president of the Farmers Mutual of Nebraska, said recently. "When one of these big cyclones passes over a heavy building, the suction is so tremendous that it can lift the house straight up off the ground. Perhaps the best solution is an anchor—that is, anchoring the house firmly to the foundation. There are several ways of doing this. One is to set bolts in the concrete when the foundation is poured. The bolts run up through the sill timber and thus anchor the top structure firmly to the foundation. Another method can be used for walls made of concrete block or cinder block. For those, you use long bolts bent at right angles. The lower part is set horizontally in the concrete foundation, while the vertical part extends up through the hollow openings in the blocks. Then the openings are poured full of cement. For small houses, you can simply drive long spikes through the sill timber into the concrete foundation while it's still soft."

Mr. Requartte recalls a time in 1935 when the power of a cyclone to lift a house straight up off the ground was extremely important to a policyholder. "It was out on Brushy Creek, in Frontier County," he said recently. "There had been a flood out there, but a tornado had preceded it. The problem was, which had done the damage—the flood or the twister—to the member's house. He didn't have any insurance against floods. Well, I went out to adjust the loss. The house had water lines up to its eaves and was 'way downstream from where it should have been. The refrigerator was more than a mile down that creek. Looking around, I noticed that the trees shading the spot where the house originally stood hadn't been disturbed at all. If the flood had done the damage the house would have had to go through those trees. We worked and worked on it, and finally the only explanation was that the twister that preceded the flood had lifted this nine-room house straight up, over the trees, and set it down upstream. Then it floated down past its old site. We paid the loss."

In addition to $24 billion of fire insurance and $8 billion of windstorm insurance, farmers' mutual insurance companies also provide their members with approximately $600 million of insurance against the damage or destruction of growing crops by hail. Specialized crop-hail mutuals have had an uneven history since the first one was founded in Connecticut in 1880. Many of those organized before 1920 adopted the post-loss assessment plan of the farmers' mutual fire companies and made no attempt to build up reserves. Because of a failure to realize that the hail hazard in its effects is actually more closely related to the windstorm than to the rural fire hazard, and hence that the accumulation of a surplus is of the first importance, the mortality rate among the early companies was very high. However, the companies that did accumulate reserves, such as the Farmers Mutual Hail Insurance Company of Iowa, founded in 1893, have had long and successful careers. This company also writes other lines of insurance, a practice that has become increasingly general among mutual companies writing crop-hail insurance.

Though mutual crop-hail insurance originated in New England, it was soon being offered in other sections of the country most susceptible to this kind of loss. There is great regional variation in the incidence of hail, which usually occurs during a severe thunderstorm. In a number of Northeastern states, the average appraised loss from hail is less than 1 per cent, while in parts of Colorado and in some sections of the Great Plains, the average appraised loss is more than 10 per cent. Approximately 80 per cent of all crop-hail insurance written by mutual companies covers growing crops in the Plains States and in the Middle West. In recent years, the largest increase in volume of crop-hail insurance has taken place in Illinois. Today one fifth of all crop-hail insurance in this country is written on growing crops in that state, a circumstance that can be attributed largely to the efficient operation of the Country Mutual Fire Company which is sponsored by the Illinois Agricultural Association, the Farm Bureau organization of Illinois. During the last few years the Country Mutual, which was founded in 1925 and now has more than $700 million of insurance in force, has written more crop-hail insurance than any other company in the United States.

The final important development among farmers' mutual insurance companies in the past fifty years has been the increasing use of reinsurance. Before 1900, reinsurance—the transferring of liability for part of a loss from one insurance company to another—was practically unknown among farm mutuals. The need for it was not great. Most of the companies then were small local organizations, and though their limit on a single risk may have been only a few thousand dollars, this was usually sufficient to accommodate the risks they were offered. As the companies increased in size and territory, larger values began to be offered, frequently requiring an amount of insurance above the top limit of the individual companies. In order to handle these risks and provide farmers having valuable properties with all their insurance in one company under a single policy, farm mutuals gradually started making use of reinsurance. Retaining in their own company an amount equal to their top limit on a single risk, they reinsured the remainder with another mutual company. This practice has steadily grown, until today something less than half of the country's farm mutual fire insurance companies make use of reinsurance.

To aid its further growth, facilities for handling reinsurance have been enlarged and perfected in recent years. At present, reinsurance is provided in several different ways in various parts of the country. In nearly all states, reinsurance is effected between ordinary farm mutuals on specific large risks. In Indiana and Ohio, there are reinsurance distributing agencies that act as intermediaries in arranging reinsurance on specific risks among member farm mutuals. Nine other states—Iowa, Missouri, South Dakota, California, Minnesota, Wisconsin, Nebraska, North Dakota, and New York—have specialized companies that insure specific risks. These specialized organizations are usually under the direct control of the state associations of mutual companies and operate throughout an entire state. Blanket reinsurance, which eliminates much of the record-keeping and bookkeeping required under the more common specific-risk insurance, is also available in Iowa and Wisconsin, as well as in Illinois. Much the same result is obtained in Michigan through the co-operative effort of a group of ordinary farm mutuals that reinsure one another by using a variation of the blanket method. In addition to the farm mutual fire insurance companies, more than a third of the farmers' mutual windstorm companies make use of reinsurance, as do almost all of the large mutuals that write crop-hail insurance.

In a fundamental sense, all of the eighteen hundred farmers' mutual fire insurance companies in the United States are alike, since they share a common purpose and fulfill a common function. But, in another sense, every company is unique, since each represents the hopes and labors of a separate and distinct group of people. Furthermore, there are farm mutuals in all stages of developments, providing varying degrees of service with varying proficiency. Some are more than a hundred years old, others are less than ten. Some operate in but a single county, others in an entire state. Some use the agency system for writing business, others write their business directly. Some provide extended coverage, others write only fire and lightning. And there are similar variations in their costs, methods of collecting premiums, loss-prevention activities, use of reinsurance, and in their financial and other practices. In short, there is no such thing as an "average" farm mutual.

There are, however, three characteristics that the majority of farm mutuals have in common. Approximately 85 per cent are fire insurance companies, writing fire and lightning; about a third of these write some form of extended coverage. Secondly, the majority of farm mutuals do business in from one to four counties. Finally, a substantial majority are assessment mutuals, operating on what is known as the post-loss assessment basis. Many of these companies collect little or nothing, except for a small policy fee, at the time the insurance is written. Income to pay losses is derived by levying an assessment on all policyholders after the losses are known. Originally, an assessment was made after each loss, but now most post-loss assessment companies borrow to pay their current losses and expenses, reckon the total at the end of the year, and make but one annual assessment. An increasing number of farm mutuals are adopting the practice of estimating their losses in advance, on past experience, and levying an annual assessment at the beginning of the loss year. The companies using this method are still in the minority, but there is a marked trend among farm mutuals toward adoption of the advance assessment plan.

Though an "average" farm mutual does not exist, there are scores of companies that in one way or another are typical or outstanding. The Svea Mutual Protective Insurance Company, which has its headquarters in Orion, Illinois, is both. It can be regarded as typical because it is situated in the Middle West, where the greatest number of farm mutuals are concentrated; because it was founded in 1872, more or less in the middle of the era when farm mutuals mushroomed; and because it is neither very small nor very large. It can be considered outstanding because of the low cost of the insurance it provides.

The Svea Mutual has a further subsidiary interest because it is representative of the large number of companies that were founded by farmers having common ties of nationality or religion. Many early farm mutuals were actually formed in churches, with the officers and directors being chosen from among the elders and policyholders being limited to members of the congregation. How many of the existing farm mutuals sprang from church groups cannot be determined, since many of the companies, with the passage of time, dropped the religious qualification for membership and removed a religious reference from the names of their companies. However, on the roster of farm mutuals it is still not unusual to find companies bearing names such as the Protestant Mutual Fire Insurance Association (Burlington, Iowa), the Roman Catholic Farmers Mutual Fire Insurance Company (Petersburg, Nebraska), the Lutheran Mutual Fire Insurance Association (Wellsville, New York), the Mennonite Mutual Aid Society (Bluffton, Ohio), and the Amish Mutual Fire Insurance Association (Parkersburg, Pennsylvania).

A great many other farm mutuals bear evidence in their names of having been founded by people who shared a common racial bond. There are, for example, at least nine farm mutuals that have the word "Scandinavian" in their names, twelve that have either "Swedish" or "Finnish," and four that have "Danish" or "Norwegian." About four dozen others identify themselves as "German," a dozen or so as "Bohemian," and at least one as "Czechoslovakian," "Italian," and "Hibernian."

The Svea Mutual was founded eighty years ago by a group of thrifty, hard-working Scandinavian immigrants who had settled in central Illinois. In the beginning, only those of Scandinavian descent were allowed to become members, but racial origin has long since ceased to be a factor in determining eligibility. The Svea Mutual, like many other more or less typical farm mutuals, has always done business in three contiguous counties; it operates, with minor variations, on the post-loss assessment basis traditional among farm mutuals, and its directors are farmers. At the close of 1950, the company had more than $70 million at risk on some 14,000 fire insurance policies and had extended its coverage to include smoke and hail without additional charge.

What distinguishes the Svea Mutual, however, is the fact that it has consistently provided fire insurance at a cost that is more than 50 per cent below the national average for farmers' mutual fire insurance companies. And the national average has been remarkably low. During the past thirty-five years, the cost to farmers of mutual fire insurance throughout the United States has averaged about 25 cents per $100 of insurance.

Throughout this period, certain areas of the country have had consistently better records than others. In 1947, for example, $100 of farm mutual fire insurance cost 57.9 cents in New England, where the cost was highest, and 19.2 cents in the West North Central States (Minnesota, Iowa, Missouri, North and South Dakota, Nebraska, and Kansas), where the cost was lowest. For the country as a whole, the cost has varied in the past thirty-five years from a high of 32 cents in

1932 to a low of 22.7 cents in 1942. Despite rising operating costs and an increase in farm fire losses, which jumped from $64 million in 1942 to $95 million in 1949, the average cost of farmers' mutual fire insurance has advanced only slightly from its all-time low. In 1949, the average cost per $100 of insurance stood at 23.2 cents.

Placed in relation to the national picture, the performance of the Svea Mutual is impressive. From 1872 until 1923, its members paid only 7.5 cents a year for each $100 of insurance. The cost rose gradually in the following years, reaching a high of 12.5 cents in 1932, compared to the national average for that year of 32 cents, but it has declined since. During the past five years, members of the Svea Mutual have paid only 10 cents a year for each $100 of fire insurance. Behind this outstanding record is the company's practice, begun eighty years ago and never changed, of inspecting every risk before issuing a policy on it, and continuing to keep a close check on all insured properties through frequent inspections. The company has divided the three counties in which it operates into thirty-six districts, each of which is under the supervision of a farmer who resides in the district and is also a director of the company. Together, these thirty-six district supervisors—or appraisers, as the company calls them—handle all inspections and appraisals, develop an exact and intimate knowledge of the risks under their care, and assume the aspect of local guardians. It is their work, together with the company's efficient management and the high character of its policyholders, that accounts for the notable record of the Svea Mutual Protective Insurance Company.

Among the farm mutuals, as among all mutual companies, the prevention of loss is a fundamental principle. The fact that farmers are able to buy mutual insurance at a cost that ranges from 25 to 50 per cent under that offered by competing companies stems largely from the successful efforts of the farm mutuals in reducing the causes and frequency of fires. The extent of the loss-prevention program varies, of course, from company to company. One that has done unusually effective work in this field is the Farmers Mutual Insurance Company of Nebraska, which has its home office in Lincoln. This company has additional interest because it is also more or less typical of a large farm mutual whose territory covers an entire state.

Founded in 1891, the Farmers Mutual of Nebraska grew to its present stature under the able direction of W. E. Straub, a farmer and breeder of registered livestock, who served as president and manager of the company from 1906 until his retirement in 1951. In addition, Mr. Straub served three terms as president of the National Association of Mutual Insurance Companies. When he was elected to the presidency of the Farmers Mutual of Nebraska in 1906, the company's premium volume amounted to about $115,000 and its surplus to about $15,000. At the close of 1950, his last full year in office, premium volume had risen to $1.5 million, surplus was $1.8 million, and assets were $2.7 million. In addition to fire and lightning with extended coverage, the company also writes windstorm and crop-hail insurance. It has more than $833 million of insurance in force, about 80 per cent of which is on farm property. Its policyholders number some 80,000, and the company insures more than half of all the insurable farm property in Nebraska.

Though it is now legally feasible for the Farmers Mutual of Nebraska to write on an advance premium basis, the vast majority of its farm policies are perpetual, and property valuations are adjusted every five years. After paying a premium of 70 cents per $100 for both fire and windstorm coverage when the policy is written, a member pays 30 cents per $100 a year thereafter for the combined protection; the fire insurance includes extended coverage. In practice this results in a saving of about 33⅓ per cent of stock company rates for the first five-year period, and of approximately 50 per cent for each year thereafter that the policy is maintained. Members who live in districts protected by rural fire-fighting organizations which meet the company's standards are given a reduction of 2 cents per $100 on their fire coverage.

Except for serious losses resulting from a severe tornado in 1913, the Farmers Mutual of Nebraska encountered no extremely serious problems until the Depression struck in the 1930s and fire losses shot up by nearly a third. Concluding that a large percentage of these losses was due to arson, the company engaged a former United States marshal named Tom Carroll as a special investigator. Using a combination of persuasion, religion, and threat, Carroll proved very effective. One day after working with a county attorney on a particularly difficult case, Carroll finally got a signed confession from a farmer who had set fire to his barn. "You know, Tom," the county attorney remarked, "over in India they believe in the transmigration of souls. They say that when a newborn infant comes into the world the soul of somebody who is dying passes into it. But I swear, when you were born, nobody was dying."

Sometimes help in solving arson cases came from unexpected sources. One morning Mr. Straub got a telephone call from a town in far western Nebraska. "Say, that Johnson fire was set," the caller said. "If you'll pay my expenses to Lincoln, I'll come in and tell you all about it." Mr. Straub agreed. Into his office a few days later walked a rangy, well-dressed rancher. "That fellow Johnson lives down the road from me," the rancher said. "I s'pose you think it's pretty queer for a neighbor to be comin' all this way to tell on another neighbor. But you know, I got so damned mad at him. Every time I go to town something disappears from my place. I kinda got even with him a little while back. I went to town and got a two-quart can of cylinder oil. Then I mixed in a handful of emery powder. I set it up on a shelf in my garage in a nice convenient place. The next time I went to town, sure enough, the can disappeared. About three or four days later, every bearing on Johnson's car burned out. Then he set this fire. You know, the fire department came out and put that fire out once. Later that night the place got afire again. When I got there the second time, the house was on fire in three different places."

Acting on this information, the company refused the claim, and the policyholder was brought to trial. He admitted that after the fire department had put out the first fire and left he and his wife had sat on their front porch and reviewed their situation. "Well," the farmer finally said to his wife, "we can't pay the mortgage, so we better go in and set it again." Besides being required to deed his property to the insurance company, he was sentenced to one year in prison.

The Farmers Mutual of Nebraska has always written its business through agents. Mr. Straub was an agent of the company for three years before becoming its president, and as soon as he took office he began building up an extensive agency force. "In those days, stock company competition was really tough," Harold J. Requartte, who is now president of the company, said recently. "Mr. Straub recruited his agents mainly among retired farmers. He just went out and *put* them into the insurance business. Our methods aren't hard to learn.

(For upper picture only) *Wide World*

TORNADOES RESPECT NO MAN'S PROPERTY OR LIFE

›re than 150 tornadoes occur in the United States every year, the majority ›eeping through rural areas. The upper picture, snapped on the scene by an ›ateur photographer using an inexpensive camera, shows the approach of a ›ster. The lower picture shows the destruction wreaked by a tornado that ›ped through Delaware County, Indiana, on March 19, 1948. Nearly 400 farm ›tual companies provide insurance against the windstorm hazard.

FARM FIRES

The barn fire in the upper picture was caused by spontaneous combustion. T
fire in the dwelling (lower picture) on a farm near New Lisbon, Indiana, w
caused by sparks on a wooden shingle roof. Both demonstrate how easily rural f
can get out of hand and why farm mutual fire insurance companies st
prevention.

To be an agent for us, a man needs to know more about farm buildings and people than he does about insurance." The company now has some eight hundred agents, who handle the inspections of risks and play an integral part in the company's aggressive loss-prevention program.

About ten years ago, Mr. Requartte, who was then secretary of the company, undertook the expansion of its loss-prevention activities. He had heard reports about the excellent work being done in this field by the Farmers Mutual Reinsurance Company, of Grinnell, Iowa, so he paid a visit to its headquarters. There he learned that this company, which was founded in 1909 to provide reinsurance coverage for farm mutuals in Iowa (in 1946, it extended its operations to include Illinois, Missouri, and Minnesota), had started its extensive loss-prevention program in the early 1930s with an exhaustive research project to determine the causes of farm fires. Results of these studies indicated that dwelling and barn losses made up more than 90 per cent of the total farm-building loss; in addition, they showed that the most important causes of dwelling and barn fires were construction deficiencies and lack of maintenance, both of which lend themselves to correction through inspection and education.

Putting the findings of its research projects into practice, the company began in 1934 to send teams of inspectors to check on the risks reinsured by the company. Since then, nearly 200,000 farms have been inspected. The results can be seen in the figures of Iowa farm-fire losses. Despite rising building and repair costs, the average annual farm-fire loss in Iowa has dropped from more than $3 million in the four years between 1930 and 1934 to approximately $1,350,000 in the past seven years. The inspection staff of the Farmers Mutual Reinsurance Company, Mr. Requartte learned, is made up of carefully chosen and well-trained men whose only responsibility is inspection and appraisal; they do not write insurance or engage in promotional work of any sort. The inspectors travel in the field in a house trailer.

After leaving the company's headquarters, Mr. Requartte joined one of the inspection teams and traveled with them for several days. Then, carrying with him a motion picture demonstrating the proper methods of inspection which the company had loaned him, he headed back to Nebraska. "We couldn't copy their system exactly," he said a while ago, "so we adapted it to make use of our agency foundation." To launch the program, the company's agents were brought together in district meetings, at which the newest methods of inspection and fire prevention were discussed and demonstrated and the entire program was outlined.

Now, when an agent of the Farmers Mutual of Nebraska calls to make an inspection, he comes equipped with a copy of a letter addressed to the company from the state fire marshal, a camera, and a fund of useful information. The letter from the fire marshal, written on official stationery, commends the company for its loss-prevention work, speaks of the terrible damage wreaked by fire on Nebraska farms, and suggests that the company's inspectors pay special attention to defective chimneys, electrical hazards, and the storage of gasoline and tractor fuel. If the inspector discovers an unusual or particularly glaring hazard, he snaps a flash-bulb picture of it. These photographs are used mainly in another part of the company's public education program, which consists of holding rural fire-prevention meetings. Enlargements of photographs taken by the agents which show cracked chimneys, damage from explosions, dangerously erected television aerials, or makeshift electrical wiring are passed among the audience to illustrate dramatically the points made in short talks and demonstrations. To stimulate attendance at these meetings, the company frequently gives away gadgets called Pellet Service Protectors, which ground lightning that has struck electric wires before it can reach the circuits inside a house and thus ruin electrical appliances. As door prizes, the company provides small fire extinguishers or wind-up fire alarms for use in the home, and the audience is told that both of these items can be secured from the company at less than cost.

Upon completing his inspection, the agent informs the policyholder of what defects, if any, have been discovered and how they should be corrected. He also makes a report to the company, and a form letter is sent to the policyholder, reminding him of the recommendations made by the agent. If the defects are not remedied within a reasonable time, the policy is canceled.

To keep its members alert to the fire danger and enlist their active co-operation in the loss-prevention program, the company frequently mails to all its policyholders leaflets, pamphlets, and other pieces of instructive fire-prevention literature. One of the most successful of these is a pamphlet, prepared by the company and called *Is Your Home Safe from Fire?* which explains the most common causes of fire and tells how they can be prevented. In drawings and illustrations the pamphlet shows thirty-one causes of fire around the home and eighteen around the barn. Other pages give advice on the construction and maintenance of chimneys and how coal- and wood-fired furnaces should be installed, while still others explain the dangers in overloading electrical circuits, why hand-fired furnaces with blowers are dangerous, how volatile liquefied petroleum, propane and butane gases should be handled, why lightning strikes where it does and what can be done about it, and how to avoid spontaneous combustion in such things as oily rags and stored hay. In conclusion, the pamphlet tells the reader what to do if he discovers a fire or if he's caught in a burning building. The language is simple, homey, and direct. For example, the section dealing with liquefied petroleum gas reads: "Speaking especially to wives, your husband may be right handy with tools. If he tries to fix that leaky pipe in the bathroom, about the worst that can happen is flooding the house. But don't let him monkey with the gas installation. The swedged and flared fittings used in gas piping should not be worked on by amateurs, no matter how strong and willing."

In 1945, there were only 53 fire trucks in the entire state of Nebraska available to respond to a rural fire. Today there are 170. A large share of the credit for this expansion in the facilities for rural fire protection also belongs to the Farmers Mutual of Nebraska, which not only helped to make the program possible but has also assiduously promoted it and provided it with substantial financial assistance. In 1945, a bill, which was written by Mr. Requartte, empowering farm mutuals to lend up to 20 per cent of their net surplus to volunteer fire districts at low interest rates for the purchase of modern fire trucks and equipment, was passed by the Nebraska legislature and became law. Since then, the Farmers Mutual of Nebraska has loaned, at 1 per cent interest, some $374,000, which made possible the purchase of 60 fire trucks. In addition, the company has made outright contributions totaling more than $25,000 to some 200 new fire districts. The low-interest loans are repaid in one of two ways: the more common is by organizing a volunteer fire district which has power to levy taxes; the other is by securing from farmers in the area served pledges that they will pay a small annual sum to their local fire department for protection.

To any group wishing to organize a rural fire-protection district, the Farmers Mutual of Nebraska furnishes without charge printed instructions and sample forms showing the step-by-step procedure. As soon as a fire-protection district has been set up, the company follows through by having its agent in the territory deliver to the new volunteer fire department three copies of a handsome fire-protection map of the county. Printed on heavy paper about a yard square, the map shows every road (and its type of surface) and every house, barn, church, school, and other structure in the county. The company also provides simple and practical but detailed instructions on how to number and letter the maps so that each structure can be quickly located when an alarm is received and the firemen can pick the best roads to reach the fire under prevailing weather conditions. The maps and instructions for their use are also supplied without charge.

All the loss-prevention activities of the Farmers Mutual of Nebraska might be described as a manifestation of highly enlightened self-interest—a description that would be quite accurate, in Mr. Requartte's view. "It's not charity," he says. "It's a hardheaded business proposition." The facts bear him out. Despite the soaring increase in the cost of labor and building materials since 1939, the pure loss cost of fire of the Farmers Mutual of Nebraska fell from an average of 9.5 cents per $100 of insurance in force during the years 1938–43 to 6.2 cents per $100 during the years 1944–50. That is a reduction of more than 30 per cent. Computed on the basis of insurance in force during 1950, it equaled a saving that year to the company's policyholders of exactly $94,222.99. As the

Farmers Mutual of Nebraska has shown, loss prevention—the basic principle of all mutual insurance—is good business.

"Not the Largest—But the Best"—that is the slogan of the McMillan Grange Mutual Fire Insurance Company, whose headquarters are located about four miles out of the town of Marshfield, Wisconsin, on the farm owned by Ben Lang, who helped to organize the company and has been its secretary for more than half a century. In many respects the McMillan Grange Mutual is typical of the great majority of farm mutuals, being moderate-sized, solid, and unpretentious, and in Ben Lang are combined many of the traditional and representative qualities of leadership that have carried farmers' mutual fire insurance through thick and thin to its present peak of success.

Like his company, Ben, as everybody calls him, puts on no airs. Now in his eighties, he has white curly hair, wears horn-rimmed spectacles, is bright as a dollar, and has a rugged constitution that matches his sturdy perseverance. He usually wears a hearing aid, but even without it he never seems to miss hearing anything he *wants* to hear. One recent summer morning, Ben, who was wearing a pair of faded overalls, sat down with a visitor in the dining room of his farmhouse and talked about a subject that is close to his heart—the McMillan Grange Mutual. The dining room also serves as the company's office and is furnished with two large desks, metal chairs, a couple of filing cabinets and other office equipment. Standing in a nearby hall is a medium-sized safe in which records are kept. Ben's memory goes away back, and so do the records of the company, which, unlike those of many larger companies, have been preserved intact.

"I was twenty-eight years old, just a kid, when we started this company," Ben said. "I'd lived around here most of my life. Came here with my mother and father when I was a child. It was nothing but woods then. My father went to work and cleared ten acres in nine weeks, using only an ax—no saw—just an ax. I was a pretty strapping kid, and when I got a little older I spent a year working in the woods. Saved a hundred and forty dollars and bought a forty-acre farm of my own. It cost me seven hundred and sixty dollars. I paid a hundred and ten down and paid the balance over a period of three years. I had it all paid off when I was twenty-two. The place was mine, free and clear."

Like thousands of other ambitious and progressive farmers, Ben became a member of the Patrons of Husbandry and was elected president of the local Grange. "We were interested in a lot of things, and one of them was insurance," Ben said. "We wanted cheaper insurance. All the line-company insurance was on a three-year basis, and you had to pay the premiums in advance, and the rates were steep as a wall. We couldn't afford that. They wrote all their business through agents, and they were paid a commission on their premiums. Write 'em high, that's the way those fellows worked. Write 'em high and cut 'em later if necessary. Some of those agents could lie faster than a horse can run. We talked it over at the Grange, and we decided to set up our own company. Three or four of the other locals around here had done the same thing, and they helped us get started."

The company was organized at a Grange meeting on May 28, 1898, but it did not begin in business until the middle of the following August. "We were all green," Ben says. "We had to find out how to run the thing. We had to get together the books—the minute book, the policy record book, and the other things. Also, we had to get the applications. The law was that we had to have at least twenty-five members and at least twenty-five thousand dollars of insurance value to set up the company. Well, we got applications from thirty-six members, and we incorporated on an assessment basis. When a member took out insurance, he paid a policy fee of a dollar and a half, plus one mill on the dollar—in other words, on a thousand of insurance, he paid one dollar. In those days, we didn't know anything about a surplus. We just figured to assess after we had losses. Of course we had a little left over from the policy fees. Mind you, out of each dollar and a half, the agent got fifty cents, and as secretary I got twenty-five cents. That wouldn't be enough to keep a chicken alive these days, but we weren't looking to get rich. We did it for the good of the farming community."

Three months after the company started business, it had its first loss. The modest dwelling owned by Fritz Kierhahn, a bachelor, burned to the ground at a total loss of $132. There was enough cash on hand from policy fees to pay this loss. Seven months later lightning struck Jacob Leick's barn, doing $5.00 worth of damage to the barn and killing one horse valued at $100. There being a paucity of cash on hand, Ben paid this loss by borrowing $105 at 6 per cent on a note from a friend who ran a tavern. "We didn't want to make an assessment right away," Ben says. "We didn't want to scare the fellows out." Ben paid two other losses, totaling $277, in the same way. "The big loss was on Fred Hopp's place," Ben said. "Not a stick left. We paid a hundred on the house and a hundred and seventy-five on the household goods. Those amounts seem small nowadays, but back then you could hire a carpenter for a dollar and a half a day."

After the company had been in business for little over a year, it levied its first assessment, which brought in $498.74. None of the fellows was scared out, and the company continued to grow steadily. At the close of its tenth year, in 1909, the company had 1,118 policyholders, insurance in force of $1,798,000, and cash on hand amounting to $1,638. "In those days, I did three quarters of the work, if not seven eighths, I might say," Ben recalls. "All day long I worked against a hired man on the farm and did the company business at night. Sometimes I was tireder when I got up than when I went to bed. That was all right. Work hard and keep close to God—that's what I believed then and that's what I believe now."

The darkest days for Ben and for the company occurred during the Depression. "The effects of the stock-market crash didn't reach out here until 1930 and 1931," Ben says. "Then things were hard. You could sell two cows and get sixteen dollars for the two. That happened in our family. Farm hands would work for fifty cents a day just to get something to eat." The company began to encounter trouble in the fall of 1930, and after that matters went from bad to worse. In 1931, the company paid a total of seventy-nine losses. It had had more losses in a single year before, but the losses of 1931 were singular in that nearly all of them were total. During the year, the company was obliged to levy two assessments totaling five mills, and although a letter sent to all policyholders explained that, even with these two assessments, members were still getting their insurance at more than 30 per cent under stock company rates, the double assessment was unprecedented in the company's history. In spite of collecting $69,825 in assessments during 1931, the company wound up the year with a deficit of $24,382.

Times being what they were, the assessments were not easy to collect, and to tide itself over the company had to borrow from banks at 6 and 7 per cent interest. "I was feeling worse by the day," Ben says. "The situation kept getting blacker and blacker, so I wrote Joe Kennedy—he's the secretary of the state association—and told him I was feeling pretty blue. Joe wrote back, and he said, 'Ben, I know you love that company like you love your child. Stick with it. Take new hope.' "

That was not easy to do. Losses continued to mount during the early months of 1932. The fires were nearly all of mysterious origin. One house caught on fire three times during a period of fourteen hours. It broke out first around noon, and neighbors rushed to the scene and helped put it out. At three in the afternoon people who were driving by saw smoke, stopped, and, finding the owner not around, extinguished the fire. At two o'clock the following morning the house finally went up in flames. During one nine-day period in the spring of 1932, the company suffered six losses, all total. "Any fool can tell that you can't have six fires in nine days," Ben says. "It was a bad time. My God, you were afraid to go to the phone. Every time it rang it was another fire."

In March 1932, the company's losses were $8,425; in April, $11,289; and in May, $12,921. At this point the directors held an emergency meeting, during the course of which they telephoned Joe Kennedy and arranged for him and an expert inspector to come immediately to Marshfield to inspect and revalue the company's insured properties. Kennedy and an inspector named Olson put in a hard stint inspecting the company's risks and reducing the insurance coverage in cases where they considered it out of line with prevailing property prices. In reducing the coverage, the company acted under the terms of its policy, which allowed it to write 75 per cent of the value of a property. "If anybody objected," Ben recalls, "we said, 'All right, hand over your policy and we'll cancel it.' Nobody did." After the inspection and revaluation, losses dropped abruptly. Whereas they had averaged $12,105 in April and May, they plummeted to $507 in June, and down to $184 in July. "By that time," Ben says, "we began to feel that we could see our way out of the woods."

Having weathered the crisis, the company decided in 1934 to go on the advance assessment basis. In March it levied an assessment of two and a half mills on all policies, out of which it paid all its losses and other liabilities, and wound up the year with $90.41 in surplus. Ten years later, in 1944, the surplus account had grown to $91,551, and by 1948 to $170,000. That year the company began paying an annual dividend of 10 per cent. The surplus account meanwhile continued to grow, and at the end of 1949 amounted to $181,000. (Total surplus and reserves of all farm mutuals in the United States amounted to $109 million at the close of 1949.) Now that his company has a comfortable surplus Ben feels much easier in his mind. "We don't have to worry any more about that '31 stuff," he says. "That pretty nearly drove me nuts."

The McMillan Grange Mutual now writes in four counties and at the close of 1949 had 2,511 policies in force and more than $19 million at risk. Approximately 90 per cent of its coverage is on farm property. It writes only fire and lightning, and its average rate in 1949 was 24½ cents per $100 of insurance. The company has twenty-two agents, who receive, on policies of $2,500 or more, a commission of $5.00 and a policy fee of $2.00. The directors, of whom there are ten, meet four times a year, or oftener if a need arises. Both the president and the treasurer are also directors of large insurance companies in Milwaukee and give the McMillan Grange Mutual the benefit of their experience, particularly on investment matters. The directors are paid $1.25 an hour, or $10 a day, while working for the company, in addition to a travel allowance of six cents a mile.

Ben's married daughter Margaret, who with her husband and children lives with Ben, has assisted her father in the insurance work for more than twenty years, and she is now assistant secretary of the company. Ben and his daughter together are paid an annual salary of $3,000. In addition to his administrative chores, Ben does a good deal of the company's appraisal work. When the phone rings and a policyholder says, for example, "Lightning killed our bull," Ben hops in the car and goes to have a look. He is rather proud of the fact that he can tell, among other things, whether an animal was killed by lightning stroke or lightning shock. "They can't fool this chicken," he says. "I've been in this game too long."

Besides his more than fifty years of service as secretary of the insurance company, Ben is also president of the Consumers Store Company, the largest office and commercial building in Marshfield, and of the Farmers Co-operative Produce Company, which he helped to start years ago with a cash outlay of $850 and which now does an annual business of more than $700,000. The produce company, like the insurance company, is operated for the mutual benefit of the farmers in the Marshfield area. The success of both is widely attributed to Ben's shrewd, down-to-earth ability as a businessman. His friends sometimes tell him that if he had spent his time on business for private gain he would be a rich man today. "I'm satisfied," Ben says. "The insurance company has been a wonderful thing for this community. It will continue to do good long after I'm gone. I'm glad I was able to do something about putting across this idea."

CHAPTER XII

The Risk That Nobody Wanted

AS A RESULT of the momentous era of agricultural expansion that followed the Civil War, the United States became one of the great granaries of the world. Side by side with this development marched the rise of the flour milling industry. By 1870, mills were springing up throughout the Middle West to convert the bumper wheat crops into flour for domestic use and for the ever-increasing export market. To store the golden grain until it was needed, wooden storage warehouses, or elevators, mushroomed on railroad sidings in towns and hamlets across the plains. The elevators, with their clean, simple architectural lines, topped by the familiar cupola, rose like a host of monuments to the rich fertility of the soil.

While their business was thriving, the millers and elevator owners were trying to cope with the same problem that a generation before had confronted the textile manufacturers of New England. In the West, as in the East, the cost of insurance was excessive, and for the same reason: there was no competition. The stock companies, with reason, considered mills and elevators as extra-hazardous risks; but the rates they applied to them, ranging from $4.00 to $10 for each $100 of insurance, were for the most part without reason.

Some mills and elevators, it is true, deserved exceedingly steep rates, but a great many others, whose owners maintained them in first-class condition and used the best methods of fire protection then known, did not. That made no difference. What was good enough for one was good enough for all, the insurance companies then in the field indicated, and they stood pat against requests for what to the millers and grain men seemed reasonable reductions. The situation was further aggravated as a result of the great Chicago fire of 1871. Soon after that conflagration, the stock companies belonging to the National Board of Fire Underwriters unanimously agreed to raise their rates on all classes of property. Rates on risks located in towns of less than thirty thousand population were increased 30 per cent; those in larger cities were stepped up 50 per cent. The increase was general, applying to the good risks as well as the bad.

Fortunately for the members of the milling industry, the mutual idea had traveled westward with the great migration and was ready to be adapted to solve their problem. Out of these circumstances developed a group of outstanding insurance firms—the Association of Mill and Elevator Mutual Insurance Companies. They are known collectively as the Mill Mutuals. Like other groups that were to follow in their footsteps, the Mill Mutuals are sometimes referred to as one of the "class mutuals," since they were originally founded to serve a special class of risks.

The first Mill Mutual was organized in Iowa. It grew out of the work of the Iowa Millers Association. At its first meeting, held in 1873, an energetic Scotsman named James G. Sharp, who owned a mill in Wilton, Iowa, addressed the members on what he described as the number-one problem facing the flour mill industry—the exorbitant cost of their fire insurance. The rates charged by stock insurance companies on mill property in Iowa at that time ranged from $3.00 to $7.00 per $100 of insurance. This was double what the rates should be, Mr. Sharp declared. Agreeing that something had to be done about the cost of their insurance, the members appointed a committee to study the subject. The committee's first step was to contact the National Board of Fire Underwriters and make a reasoned appeal for a reduction of rates on mill property in Iowa. The millers intimated that if some relief were not granted they might well feel forced to establish their own company. To judge from its response, the Board was not much concerned. Stock insurance companies, their reply stated, were not making a penny on flour mill risks, so instead of complaining about rates, the millers ought to be thankful that they could get insurance at all. However, if they thought they could do better by organizing a company of their own, the Board wished them luck, or so it said.

The millers believed they could. Statistics were gathered by the committee showing the actual loss on mill property by fire in the state during the previous five years. The figures indicated that the percentage of actual loss had not been more than one quarter of the premiums charged by the stock companies. At a three-day meeting of the Association held in April 1875, the insurance committee, which had previously sounded out a large number of millowners throughout the state, recommended the organization of a mutual fire insurance company to serve millers exclusively. The recommendation was adopted, and applications for $150,000 of insurance, the amount required by law, were soon secured. On May 11, 1875, the Mill Owners Mutual Fire Insurance Company issued its first policy to Dan Tyrrell in the amount of $3,000 on his mill in Des Moines. Mr. Tyrrell had been elected treasurer of the company, and Mr. James G. Sharp, who had worked unceasingly to bring it into existence, had been elected its first president.

To provide sound protection at low cost, the pioneer millers' mutual insurance company operated under very carefully considered bylaws. Insurance was limited exclusively to flour mills and the machinery in them. The maximum amount of insurance the company agreed to carry on one risk was set at $10,000. Liability was restricted to two thirds of the value of the property. When a policy was issued to a member, he signed a note "equal to the amount of one annual premium at the rate charged by a responsible stock company." In addition, he paid in cash a policy fee of $1.00, and $6.00 on each $1,000 of insurance he carried. These charges were made to create a fund to pay incidental expenses. As losses occurred, each policyholder was assessed in the proportion that his premium note bore to the premium notes of all other policyholders. Thus, in the beginning the liability of each policyholder for the payment of losses and expenses was unlimited. With the passage of time this liability was reduced successively to five premiums and then to one; in 1936, the assessment liability was removed entirely.

To both the management and policyholders of the new company, prevention of fire was a cardinal principle. The secretary of the company was required personally to inspect every property before issuing insurance on it and to repeat his inspection at least once every year thereafter. On his inspections he was accompanied by one of the nine directors, to each of whom was assigned a certain district of the state in which he was designated to act for the company. If the local director was personally interested in any way in the property to be insured, the secretary was obliged to call instead on some other member of the company to assist him. Policyholders were required to keep their mills supplied with ample water barrels and buckets, to provide access to the roof by ladders, and to take other simple but effective precautions. If a policyholder made any alterations on his property which either increased or decreased the hazards, he was required to notify the company at once, and the secretary was given authority to cancel or reclassify the risk. Failure of a member to comply with this rule voided his policy.

Adhering strictly to these rules of inspection and prevention, the Mill Owners Mutual made good progress from the start. Each year showed a steady growth under the capable management of the original officers and directors. When the first secretary was forced to resign because of failing health in 1879, he was succeeded in the chief executive position by Mr. James G. Sharp, who had been president of the company since its organization. Five years later his son, J. T. Sharp, who was then twenty-four and who had been operating the family mill since graduation from high school, joined the company as a general assistant to his father. Thus began a career of service with few parallels in the insurance business. By the time of his retirement in 1940, Mr. J. T. Sharp had served the company continuously for fifty-six years, more than half of that span as its senior executive officer.

In 1885, when the Mill Owners Mutual had been in business for ten years, it was insuring 290 of the approximately 650 flour mills that were then operating in Iowa. The company had $1.1 million of insurance in force. Its principles had been proved. During its first decade, the pioneer Mill Mutual had provided its policyholders with insurance at a cost that was only 42 per cent of that charged by stock companies.

Along with this notable accomplishment, the new mutual

company had established a reputation for full and prompt payment of claims. In fact, as early as 1876, when the company was but a year old, word of this important aspect of its business began circulating through the mill industry. One of the company's policyholders whose mill had been destroyed by fire was so pleased with the handling of his claim that he not only wrote an appreciative letter to the company but also addressed a similar communication to the *American Miller*, the industry's trade paper. It was given prominent space in that publication. "In less than half the time allowed the company," the letter said, "I have been paid every dollar that my policy called for," and added, "I feel doubly satisfied because if this mutual company had not been started, I would have had *no* insurance, as I would not pay the premium asked by other companies. I would recommend that all brother millers in Iowa join the Mill Owners Mutual. It is safe. Its claims are adjusted promptly. It is the cheapest and most reliable. Consequently, it is the best."

Under this letter the editor of the *American Miller* printed the following comment: "It is with no little pleasure that we give space to the above letter. Iowa millers are the pioneers in mill insurance, and we are glad to note the successful working of their company. The day is not far distant when every milling state will have its own millers' insurance company."

The editor proved to be a prophet with honor in his own industry, for by around the turn of the century millers' mutual insurance companies had been established in six milling states besides Iowa. In the order of their founding, these companies consisted of the Millers National Insurance Company (Chicago); Michigan Millers Mutual Fire Insurance Company (Lansing); Western Millers Mutual Insurance Company (Kansas City, Missouri); Pennsylvania Millers Mutual Fire Insurance Company (Wilkes-Barre); Millers Mutual Fire Insurance Company (Fort Worth, Texas); Millers Mutual Fire Insurance Company (Harrisburg, Pennsylvania); and the Grain Dealers Mutual Insurance Company (Indianapolis, Indiana). In 1933, the National Retailers Mutual Insurance Company, which had absorbed the mill business of the Ohio Millers Mutual Insurance Company, became a member of the Mill Mutual group.

With the exception of the National Retailers, a general writing company which will be considered later, all the Mill Mutuals were founded by members of the mill and elevator industry. Like the pioneer company in Iowa, they were usually organized under the auspices of millers' associations, and their respective founders were devoted and persevering. They contributed generously of their time and money to get the companies established, and their interest was enduring. Taking hold of the Millers Mutual, of Alton, Illinois, Mr. A. R. McKinney served as its secretary continuously for twenty-nine years, building it up from a promise to the place where it had more than $250,000 in surplus when he died. Another pioneer, Mr. A. D. Baker, was twenty years old and had just graduated from Michigan Agricultural College when he went to work in the office of the Michigan Millers Mutual, of Lansing, in 1889. He was the second employee hired by the company. The first was his uncle, A. T. Davis, who, as secretary, had for seven years constituted the company's entire office and field force. In order to impress millers whose insurance he wanted to write with the size and dignity of the company he represented, Secretary Davis virtually turned himself into two men. While working in the office, he was known as A. T. [for Thomas] Davis. While working in the field, he scrambled his name somewhat and was known as A. D. Thomas. When the company's first losses occurred, Secretary Davis, who was evidently a man of monumental optimism, lettered the claims A, B, C, and so forth, doubtless in the hope that the alphabet contained enough letters to designate all the losses the company would ever have.

When Secretary Davis augmented the office force with the addition of his nephew, A. D. Baker, Michigan Millers was getting well established, and there was plenty of work for both employees. Under his uncle's supervision, young Mr. Baker learned the insurance business and also absorbed other valuable experience gained from numerous chores, such as sweeping the office and, in the winter, keeping a fire going in the fireplace. On the death of his uncle in 1898, Mr. Baker, who had been carrying an increasingly large share of the work, was elected secretary. The company at that time had net cash assets of $166,000. At Mr. Baker's first meeting with the board of directors in the fall of 1898, he predicted that by the end of the year a net cash surplus of $200,000 would be reached, referring to that goal as "the mark toward which we have so long been striving." In succeeding years, Mr. Baker, who was senior executive officer of the company until 1935, when he became chairman of the board, has seen scores of successively more ambitious goals pass into history. Today, with a service record of more than sixty years, he has the perspective to appreciate the fact that his company's surplus now exceeds $4.2 million.

Though the spreading network of millers' mutual fire insurance companies throughout the milling states provided a solution to the insurance problem of millers, owners of grain elevators were for the most part still up against it for insurance adapted to their particular needs. Few, if any, of the Mill Mutuals were interested in writing insurance on elevators. Their reason was once explained by Mr. J. J. Fitzgerald, a mutual insurance executive whose knowledge of the subject was intimate and extensive. "There were elevators here and there that came up to flour mill standards," Mr. Fitzgerald wrote, "but on the whole it was a shabby risk. In the mind of the insurance fraternity, the country elevator of that day was merely a dismal warehouse on a lonely siding, difficult to reach and even more difficult to inspect. For that reason, no attempt was made to study the hazards of the business and suggest means for preventing fires—losses were recouped by increased rates. Grain dealers were all presumed to be speculators, ever ready to destroy their property when the market went against them. Under such a state of affairs it is not surprising that the burning rate of country elevators was high and the insurance costs excessive."

Elevator owners were thus forced to secure their insurance from stock companies, which regarded elevators as even more hazardous than mills and accordingly charged exceedingly high premiums. To grain dealers, there seemed to be no rhyme or reason in the way stock companies arrived at rates on elevators. As a correspondent writing in the *Grain Dealers Journal* of November 10, 1901, remarked: "The writer has in mind an old elevator written last year at 1¼ per cent. This burned and was replaced by a *new* structure now rated at 4½ per cent. Another elevator written last year at 1½ per cent is now charged 3 per cent. Still another, written in former years at 1¼ per cent, now pays 3.15 per cent. At this time, these rates are necessary to the stock companies. Relief will come only when the grain dealers co-operate and form an insurance company to make a specialty of elevator risks, offering competition and demonstrating a reasonable cost price for their class of hazards."

Less than a year later, on August 5, 1902, a group of thirteen men hailing from Indiana, Ohio, Illinois, Nebraska, and Michigan, who were prominently identified with association work in the grain trade, met in the Grand Pacific Hotel in Chicago to consider the advisability of organizing a mutual fire insurance company specializing in elevator risks. The man most responsible for bringing the group together was Mr. C. A. McCotter, who was then a special agent of the Millers National of Chicago. With twenty years of experience behind him, Mr. McCotter was a recognized authority on grain and elevator insurance. After considering the subject at length, the men who met in the Grand Pacific Hotel voted "that we incorporate the Grain Dealers National Mutual Fire Insurance Company [later shortened to Grain Dealers Mutual Insurance Company] with headquarters at Indianapolis, unless we find a more favorable location."

Funds to get the company started were contributed by nineteen grain dealers from Indiana, Illinois, and Ohio, who chipped in a total of $1,850. (This was repaid out of the first premiums collected by the company.) It was not a large sum, but not much was needed, since Mr. McCotter drew no salary during the period when the company was being organized; the only other original employee, J. J. Fitzgerald, was paid $75 a month.

Though he was then only twenty-four, Mr. Fitzgerald was already an experienced insurance man, having entered the business at fourteen. Born in Saginaw, Michigan, he finished grade school, spent a year and a half in a business college learning bookkeeping and shorthand, and went to work as a stenographer in the office of a local insurance company. Rising to the position of private secretary to the president of the firm, he emerged after six years with a good working knowledge of the insurance business. After that he worked for two other insurance companies in Michigan, meanwhile making the acquaintance of Mr. McCotter, who invited the young man to help him get the incipient Grain Dealers Mutual under way. Mr. Fitzgerald's first job was to send out notices of the formation of the new company to grain dealers and to solicit surveys of their properties. Mr. McCotter took to the road to drum up business. He met with such enthusiastic response from elevator owners that the amount of insurance needed to begin business was subscribed in exactly three months. This business covered 253 risks, given by 177 grain dealers, and made $691,000 at risk.

With this auspicious beginning, the Grain Dealers Mutual was launched. To make it a continued success, Mr. McCotter and Mr. Fitzgerald, who devoted all their remaining years to the company, gave their unstinting effort. "We imbibed the spirit of the secretary," Mr. Fitzgerald later wrote of Mr. McCotter, "and spread it throughout the length and breadth of the land. We lived and breathed country elevators; we ate with them; we slept with them. No one gave a thought to his personal fortunes; we were out to do one thing and one thing only. We were rich in confidence and the will to succeed." Mr. McCotter served as secretary and manager of the company from its founding until his death in 1927. He was succeeded as secretary by Mr. Fitzgerald, who was elected president in 1935, and continued in that position until his death in 1942. Today the Grain Dealers Mutual, which now also writes a great many other classes of business, is the largest writer of country elevator risks in the United States.

With the possible exception of the Millers National, of Chicago, the majority of the mutual companies founded by millers generally started out to provide insurance within a relatively limited area, usually confining their writing to one state. As they grew in size and experience, they branched out. The Mill Owners Mutual of Iowa, the pioneer company, decided in 1886, eleven years after its founding, to insure mills in surrounding states. Three years later, it was carrying $300,000 of insurance on mills in states other than Iowa. The Millers Mutual, of Alton, Illinois, confined its writings to its home state during the first eight years, spreading out after that into neighboring territory. The other companies followed a similar pattern. Today each of the companies in the Mill Mutual group operates in nearly all states, and three of them also write in Canada.

In addition to their territorial expansion, the Mill Mutuals have greatly enlarged the kinds of risks they insure. After they had become firmly established in the mill and elevator field, they found it expedient to begin writing a variety of other risks. This development resulted partly from changes in the flour milling industry. Toward the end of the nineteenth century, there began a large-scale movement of the mill and elevator business to the large cities, where mills of greater capacity were being built to derive shipping and transportation benefits. As this trend toward concentration of the industry near the terminal markets gained momentum, the number of available mill and elevator risks was sharply diminished. Adapting to the times, the Mill Mutuals began writing insurance on other kinds of property, such as dwellings and manufacturing and mercantile risks. Since then, all have evolved into general writing companies. Collectively, the Mill Mutuals now secure approximately 22 per cent of their total premium income from the mill and elevator class, and the balance from the field of general business.

As a consequence of their evolution into general writing

companies, the Mill Mutuals changed their method of acquiring business. Originally, they had been direct writing companies, securing all their business through salaried representatives. To write lines other than those in the mill and elevator class, each of the Mill Mutuals gradually built up an agency system. Today all their general business is written through agents. Their mill and elevator business, however, is still acquired and rigidly inspected by a staff of salaried employees, who receive specialized training in the recognition and elimination of the fire hazards peculiar to the industry.

Carrying the mutual principle into the operation of the companies themselves, the executives of the mill and elevator companies began during the early years of the century to meet informally for the purpose of discussing common problems, pooling experience, and working out fire prevention and other programs of general benefit. In 1910, this work was put on a businesslike basis by the organization of the Mill Mutual Fire Prevention Bureau, which was established by the various mill and elevator companies to carry on in an efficient and scientific manner a broad-scale program of prevention, inspection, and education.

In the more than four decades since its founding, the Bureau has done notable work in the field of loss-prevention engineering. It has developed standards and specifications covering the installation and operation of nearly every machine that is used in the flour mill and grain elevator industry. The Bureau has also developed its own electrical code, which is very stringent, and has performed important research and set up specifications and standards in the control of dust and in the safeguarding of mechanical hazards. All the Bureau's specifications are prepared with the collaboration of the engineering staffs of the several Mill Mutual companies. Each company maintains its own full staff of engineers and inspectors, who give direct service to the majority of its policyholders, while the Bureau's staff of expertly trained engineers act as technical advisers and inspectors of large risks or those requiring special service.

Originally founded to underwrite one of the most hazardous classes of fire risks, the Mill Mutuals today make up one of the largest and most progressive groups of insurance companies writing general business. Their combined assets, at the end of 1950, exceeded $81 million, while their policyholders' surplus amounted to $29.5 million. Their net premium writings in 1950 were more than $48 million, and in that year they returned to their policyholders $5.6 million in dividends.

The primary reason for the success of the Mill Mutuals stems from their original and never-ending campaign to prevent loss. "The very backbone of Mill Mutual Insurance has been its inspection system," Mr. H. C. Lee, assistant manager of the Mill Mutual Fire Prevention Bureau once observed. "From the very inception of these companies, inspection for fire hazards and practical corrections for such conditions have been fundamental reasons for success. Our competitors in the stock company field apparently knew little, and cared less, about the fire hazards of the grain handling and processing industry. They cannot today successfully point to one single, solitary constructive fire-prevention measure which they have ever originated for the benefit of the milling or grain trade. On the contrary, the Mill Mutuals, by their inspections and studies of the problems found, have increased the life expectancy of every mill or elevator in this country by at least twice."

In the field of loss prevention, Mr. Lee pointed out, the

Mill Mutuals "actively championed all-metal dust collectors and air-washing machines when such devices were absolutely untried in the mill field. They insisted on better machinery construction in innumerable cases. They forced the totally enclosed motor upon manufacturers. No group of insurance companies has done more for the industry it represents. As a consequence of its careful selection of risks and of its rigid inspection system, the Mill Mutuals reduced the cost of mill and elevator insurance by 50 per cent. They took a class which nobody else wanted, an outcast, an untouchable, and made of it a class which everyone else seems to want today."

CHAPTER XIII

Meeting the Need Again and Again

SINCE good news travels fast, the success of the mutual insurance companies organized by millers and grain dealers was soon being discussed by other groups of businessmen who were also concerned about the high cost of their fire insurance. Two of these groups that not only discussed but acted were composed of lumbermen and retail hardware dealers. Within a few years after the turn of the century, more than a dozen mutual fire insurance companies had been founded by leaders in the lumber and hardware fields to serve their respective industries. Like the Mill Mutuals, the Lumber Mutuals and the Hardware Mutuals were originally brought into existence to provide protection to specialized risks. Over the years they, too, have broadened the base of their underwriting operations and are now among the large writers in the field of general business. Their development, observed against the background of their origins, provides further evidence of the flexibility of the mutual idea.

Six companies now comprise the Lumber Mutual group. Four were originally organized by and for lumbermen, while two—the Central Mutual Insurance Company, of Van Wert, Ohio, and the Northwestern Mutual Insurance Association, of Seattle, Washington—were formed and have always operated as general writing companies, participating to a limited extent in the lumber field; they will be considered in a later chapter. Of the four companies founded by lumbermen, three were formed in 1895 and one in 1897. The states in which they began operations spread from Massachusetts and Pennsylvania to Ohio and Indiana.

Behind the organization of the Lumber Mutuals lay widespread discontent among wholesale and retail lumber dealers over the excessively high cost of their fire insurance. Whenever two lumber dealers got together in those days, the insurance problem seldom failed to enter their conversation, and it was invariably the subject of heated discussion at meetings of the lumber associations. Articles and editorials bearing on the topic also appeared with considerable frequency in the industry's trade publications, particularly in the *New York Lumber Trade Journal*. "While few merchants have any definite knowledge of the subject," the *Journal* said in its issue of September 1, 1894, "the majority believe they are over charged for insurance, and this is particularly true of lumbermen and woodworkers."

To demonstrate that members of these industries had cause for complaint, the article continued with an exhibit of figures covering lumber risks in Philadelphia during the preceding twenty years. They showed that the average annual loss of lumberyards, planing mills, woodworking shops, and similar risks in Philadelphia amounted to $52,209; the average annual premiums paid by these classes amounted to $219,750. By contrast, the exhibit showed that the average annual loss of cotton and woolen mills and of paper mills and warehouses in Philadelphia amounted to $410,068; however, the average annual premium of these classes amounted to $200,010. As the figures demonstrated, the textile and paper classes had annual losses of approximately twice the premiums paid, while the lumber classes had an average loss of about one fourth of the premiums paid. "The low rates obtained by the textile and paper industries," the *Journal* concluded, "are due to the fact that they have competed with the stock companies by independent insurance movements."

Three months after the appearance of this article, representatives of ten lumber associations in Pennsylvania, Massachusetts, New York, New Jersey, and Connecticut met in New York to delve into the insurance matter. Mr. Edward F. Henson, of the E. P. Burton Lumber Company of Philadelphia, presided, and in the course of his remarks supplied further statistical ammunition that he and other association members had collected. Based on the experience of 340 retail lumberyards, this study showed that over a five-year period these yards had paid a total of $108,633.80 in premiums; the losses incurred by all the yards together during the five years amounted to only $6,527.90. The lumber dealers apparently needed no further encouragement. Concluding the meeting, Mr. Henson said that he had been very pleased "to see the manner in which the subject of insurance has been taken hold of by the different associations, and if I am not much mistaken the outgrowth will be a matter of credit to us all, as well as dollars and cents in our pockets." Events soon proved him right. Within a year, three mutual insurance companies devoted to the interests of the lumber trade were in operation.

Mr. Henson was himself primarily responsible for the formation of the first, the Pennsylvania Lumbermens Mutual Insurance Company, which received its charter on February 26, 1895. "We started in business without a penny to our name," Mr. H. J. Pelstring, who has been associated with the company for more than forty years and is now its president, recently remarked. Though short on funds, the new organization had the enthusiastic support of the lumber industry as well as the energetic guidance of Mr. Henson, who served as president of the company from its inception until his death in 1931. "He worked untiringly day and night," Mr. Pelstring has said, "but he refused to accept a salary until the company was on its feet. Of course the stock companies at the time refused to consider our organization as a competitor and many jokes were made at our expense, but we didn't mind. We knew we were on the right track."

Following the same general pattern, lumber dealers in Massachusetts and Ohio also formed mutual insurance companies in 1895. The Lumber Mutual Fire Insurance Company of Boston was founded under the auspices of the Massachusetts Retail Lumber Association. The moving spirit behind the formation of the company was a well-known New England lumber dealer named William O. Curtis, who served as its treasurer as well as a director throughout the rest of his life, seeing the company's assets expand from a few thousand dollars to well over a million.

The first mutual company to relieve the insurance burden of lumbermen in the Middle West was founded in Mansfield, Ohio. Called the Lumbermens Mutual Insurance Company, it was brought into existence largely through the personal efforts of Edwin S. Nail, a prominent Mansfield lumber dealer. Between January and September of 1895, Mr. Nail devoted practically all his time and furnished all the funds needed to carry out the organizational work. Before the state of Ohio would grant a charter, it was necessary to secure applications for insurance on a minimum of 200 separate risks, with no application exceeding $5,000. Each application had to be accompanied by one annual premium in cash in addition to notes for three times that amount. Furthermore, each note had to be taken to a justice of the peace for certification to the effect that the signer was financially able to pay if payment were required. Of the necessary 200 applications, Mr. Nail personally secured 198.

The company received its charter on September 18, 1895, rented a small room for $100 a year in the Odd Fellows Building in Mansfield, and issued its first policy a week later. At the company's first meeting, Mr. Nail was elected president and held that office continuously for the next thirty-eight years, when he became chairman of the board. Retiring from that post in 1947, he continued as a director until his death the following year, having served the company for more than half a century. The company's first published statement, dated January 1, 1896, showed assets of $20,030, and a surplus of $6,831. Its growth since then is reflected in its annual statement dated December 31, 1950, which showed assets of $10.6 million and a surplus of $3.2 million.

The founders of the Indiana Lumbermens Mutual Insurance Company, which began business in 1897, were a very determined band of men. To secure a charter, they had to have an enabling law passed by the state legislature. That took sixteen months. Then the real trouble began. In its first six months, the company had three fires with combined losses of $2,753. After paying these, the cash on hand amounted to exactly $914.54. In its eighth month the fledgling company was staggered by another loss, this one amounting to $2,000. "Well, we were broke," Mr. G. E. Beall, the present secretary of the company, has remarked. "That, however, did not stop the board. They went to the Capitol National Bank and bor-

The description on this Currier & Ives print reads: "This terrible Conflagration commenced on Sunday evening, Oct. 8th, 1871, and continued until stopped by the rain on Tuesday Morning, Oct. 10th, consuming the whole of the Business portion of the City, all the Public Buildings, Hotels, Newspaper Offices and Rail Road Depots, and extending over an area of Five square Miles." A high wind fanned the fire, blowing flames and sparks across the Chicago River. Men, women, and children were forced to run to Lake Michigan and stand up to their chins in the water to escape. Even so, 300 people died and many more were injured. Eighteen thousand wooden buildings burned to the ground; half the city was wiped out; altogether $200 million worth of property went up in smoke. As a result, stock fire insurance companies raised their rates on all property from 30 to 50 per cent. This increase spurred the formation of mutual fire insurance companies organized by millers, the first of which began business in 1875.

THE HARDWARE TRADE

Volume IX. MINNEAPOLIS AND ST. PAUL, MINN., TUESDAY, MAY 2, 1899. Number 13.

The Hardware Trade

A Fortnightly Journal for Hardware Dealers and those in kindred lines.

Published each alternate Tuesday, by
COMMERCIAL BULLETIN COMPANY.
EDWIN HAYNES, President.
WILL S. JONES, Secretary and Treasurer.

WILL S. JONES, Manager.

Offices, 718-723 Boston Block.

ENTERED AT THE POST OFFICE AT MINNEAPOLIS, MINN., AS SECOND-CLASS MATTER.

The circulation of this journal is practically in Minnesota, Western Wisconsin, Northern Iowa, North and South Dakota, Montana, Washington and the Pacific Coast. It aims to reach the business men of every part of this territory. Advertising rates furnished upon application.

SUBSCRIPTION, $1.00 PER YEAR.

AUTHORIZED REPRESENTATIVE:
CHARLES S. LINDNER........Subscription Department.

EASTERN REPRESENTATIVES:
THE ROLAND B. REEVES CO.,
Room 1021 Park Row Building, New York.

Tuesday, May 2, 1899.

Plain Facts Told Plainly.

I attended this week a complimentary dinner to a friend who is about to change his residence. There were about sixty present to say their farewell to the guest of the evening, and among the number were high officials of the state, a judge of the state supreme court, judges of the district court, clergymen, lawyers and friends from various walks of business life. There was a significance about the gathering that will provide a very good text for a little talk here. The meeting of men high in position to honor a man who had not accumulated money was a hopeful indication in itself. Character, on this basis, counts for something after all. We grow pessimistic at times and feel the world is not improving in its estimate of worth, but little incidents of this kind from time to time give us new faith.

Socrates said: "Have no regard for what they may say of you, but for what the one man who has understanding of just and unjust will say, and what the truth will say." One of the reasons why these friends gathered was that in the man they honored were the strong lines of character, and it had been his policy for years to work out in his field of employment the principle outlined by Socrates centuries ago. Men like principles. We all admire the courage of conviction. It wins where trimming fails. It was not what this man said that won him friends, but it was his method, which stood for his character—the man. Men did him honor who had not agreed with all of his conclusions in semi-public capacity, but this did not interfere in the least with their enjoyment of the occasion, because they were there to enjoy the man and not his opinion.

The young man who has the confi- ... ...ity in which he ...

honored in so doing. There was true worth represented in his manhood, not triviality. This it was that appealed to those about him. The sunshine of character streamed out from his soul and left pleasant impression, helpful suggestion and uplifting influence wherever he went. The world has many men like him, and when the great history of man's evolution is completed it will be seen that their silent influence was great for the making of the world better.

Every man should in some way regularly brush against the opinion of other men. No mind is capable of knowing of itself all there is to be known of one subject, but by touching elbows with our fellows we learn the broadness of many subjects, we learn what our fellows know of these subjects and they in turn occasionally receive an idea from us. In this way new views and new facts are absorbed and we become broader minded men with more of self-reliance in opinion at our command. We sometimes hear it said of a man that he is conceited. Where this is true we usually have a man who fails to touch elbows with his fellow and so from a one-sided view of life he gradually takes on the belief that he has all the truth in his mind. This is an unfortunate position for any man to occupy. No man is independent of his fellow in the sense that his fellow has no rights. We all have the right of opinion and it is unfair for the superior mind to be unwilling to listen to the man who has made less progress with his thinking.

This idea of rubbing elbows can be carried to its logical length. There is a law underlying that works its result. This result may be up or down as affecting the personal character, for the law is one of companionship and judgment purely. Here is a man of exceptional business qualities but of defective personal character. We must learn to touch elbows with him, take all the good points from the association we can and not permit contamination of the principles we may have established for our working platform. By this rubbing together we learn how to meet people, not an unimportant thing by the way, and we thus broaden and grow in the ways of business, honest business if you please.

We occasionally meet the polished gentleman—not a policy gentleman. There is a difference and it is not usually difficult to distinguish between the two. The ring of sincerity cannot often be concealed in manners any more than in metals. This polished man had something in him to begin with instructive of gentlemanly quality, but his strength came with the growth and observation of years that followed the constant touching of elbows with men of strength. The rough edges have been smoothed down and the character is polished by the work of years. Make it a point to touch elbows with men. It will do you good. ELI.

METAL TRADING CHECKS O. K.

Judge Lochren Decides That Their Use is Not a Crime.

Judge Loc... of the ... this wee...

Hardware Men Launch Mutual Fire Insurance Plan.

The new mutual fire insurance plan of the Minnesota Retail Hardware Association has been fairly launched and before the end of the present year it will be in operation with a majority of the retail dealers of the state among its policy holders.

The initial steps to this end were taken at a joint conference of the board of directors and the fire insurance committee, held Tuesday, in the office of Secretary J. W. Clark. Secretary Clark was instructed to have the articles of incorporation drawn and to have the policies sent out to prospective members all through the state. This work will be undertaken at once, and practical results are expected to be obtained before June 1.

The meeting of the two committees was well attended and a great deal of interest was shown in the fire insurance proposition. There were present from the board of directors of the Minnesota Hardware Association the following:

James E. O'Brien, state president, Crookston.
W. C. Holmes, Austin.
Joseph Mason, St. Peter.
J. R. S. Cosgrove, Le Sueur.
G. W. Wells, Duluth.
A. A. Margoff, St. Paul.
H. B. Gardner, Minneapolis.
J. W. Berg, Little Falls.
J. W. Clark, Minneapolis.

The members of the fire insurance committee appointed at the last convention of the association were as follows:

A. C. Hatch, chairman, Battle Lake.
C. F. Stremel, Minneapolis.
E. H. Loyhead, Faribault.
H. Hause, Fairfax.
S. R. Nelson, Owatonna.
George W. Wells, Duluth.

At the joint meeting of the two committees, Secretary Clark explained what had been done in the way of securing the necessary legislation. He stated that it had been necessary to secure an amendment to the law permitting the organization of an insurance company among the hardware dealers, and that a great deal of work had been necessary in St. Paul to accomplish this, but that the amendment had been passed and nothing now stands in the way of organizing the fire insurance department.

There was considerable discussion of the best way to proceed in organizing, but most of the details were left for Secretary Clark to look after. He was instructed to have an attorney draw up the articles of incorporation at once. When these are drafted they will be printed and submitted to every hardware dealer in the state with blank applications for insurance to be sent back to the secretary. When $500,000 in insurance applications is obtained the charter will be filed with the secretary of state and the insurance company will be fully organized.

The joint committees named eleven men who will be voted on by the policy holders as directors when they return their applications. T...

...ment of this committee. Mr. Hatch is enthusiastic regarding the future of the mutual insurance plan. Following the meeting he said:

Will Be Operating by June 1.

"I have no doubt in my own mind that the mutual fire insurance plan of our association will be engaged in business before the end of the year, and I prophesy we will have applications for the required $500,000 insurance so that we can begin business by June 1.

"I have given the matter a great deal of attention and I believe we will secure applications from present members of the association amounting to $300,000, and applications from those outside the association who will become members at once, amounting to $200,000.

"In the Seventh congressional district, where I live, I have talked with many of the retail dealers, and I venture to predict that we will secure over $200,000 in that part of the state alone. They all recognize that the mutual insurance plan will save them a large amount of money annually, and a number of dealers who are not now members, have intimated to me that they would connect themselves with the association as soon as this thing went through and would at once apply for policies.

"It will be the biggest thing that ever happened for the Minnesota Association. It will build up the organization, and I would not be surprised to see our membership doubled in this state. Hardware risks are not at all hazardous. I believe the old line companies say they are next to stocks of boots and shoes in point of risk, and boots and shoes are the best risk among stocks of merchandise, so that we ought to be able to make our rate extremely low. All we need is honest management and we will meet with business success. We will manage the mutual insurance department honestly—that is guaranteed by the names of those whom we have selected to be voted upon as directors, and the men who are interested in our association.

"We do not intend to include stocks of implements now, although the majority of the hardware men carry implements. We are going to do business conservatively and carefully and take no risks that we are not absolutely certain about, so that losses will be reduced to the lowest possible point."

Secretary Clark has received an intimation of the interest taken in the fire insurance plan. During the past few days a number of letters from nonmembers of the association have been received inquiring about the matter, and asking for application blanks.

Advices are that the war in the Philippines is near an end. The energy of the Americans in suppressing the natives is unquestionably telling on their strength because they cannot endure a long campaign as against United States resources ...

ANNOUNCEMENT OF THE FIRST HARDWARE MUTUAL

On the right-hand side of this page of the May 2, 1899, issue of *The Hardware Trade* appears an account of the formation of the first mutual fire insurance company organized by retail hardware dealers—the Hardware Mutual Insurance Company of Minnesota. The basic principle of mutual insurance—prevention of loss—was uppermost in the minds of the company's founders. The chairman of the insurance committee is quoted in the article as saying, "We are going to do business conservatively and carefully and take no risks that we are not absolutely certain about, so that losses will be reduced to the lowest possible point."

rowed $1,000 on their personal security, collected a little additional in premiums, paid the losses, and closed the year with $527.75. But all that was too much for the man who had been hired as general manager at $125 a month. He figured he would have to eat in 1898, so he resigned at the board meeting in January."

Though faced with a rather bleak prospect, the tireless directors held a special meeting, devised measures for cutting expenses to the bone, dispensed with salaries to the president, treasurer, and members of the executive committee during 1898, and voted to hire a new general manager at the reduced salary of $50 per month. Soon things began looking up. By December of 1898, the company had cash on hand of $4,-281.98, and the board began to breathe easier.

However, the stock companies in the area began breathing somewhat less easily as they saw the mutual venture heading toward success. In fact, on December 5, 1898, the general manager of the Indiana Lumbermens received a letter from the state agent of one of the larger stock companies, stating that his company was prepared to reduce its rates from 5 to 15 per cent on planing mills and from 15 to 33⅓ per cent on lumberyards if the mutual company would retire from business. "As you may see," the letter said after listing the proposed reductions, "these are general effects. We will prepare a schedule which will meet with the above, and in some cases the reductions may exceed these per cents. We want to meet your officers and take hold of this matter in an intelligent manner, hoping for a happy and mutually profitable result." Needless to say, the officers of the Indiana Lumbermens believed that the most mutually profitable results lay in working harder than ever to make the mutual company succeed.

None worked harder than Mr. F. B. Fowler, who had devoted many months of his time to bringing the company into existence and had been unanimously elected its first secretary. During the first seven years, he did all the work single-handedly. In 1904, he finally hired a stenographer at $30 a month. Under his direction the company prospered. By 1909, its premium income exceeded $200,000; five years later, it had more than doubled. In those days Mr. Fowler personally passed on every risk. "He was always very dignified and very thorough," Mr. I. G. Saltmarsh, who is now president of the company, has said. "He had a very good head for analyzing the question—too good, we sometimes thought. He said he could always see the other side. We would bring in some fine risk, and he would proceed to explore the disadvantages so thoroughly we'd get discouraged and begin to think we must have made a mistake. But then the next morning he would come in and say, 'I didn't mean we shouldn't write that risk, you know.' "

In 1930, Mr. Fowler was elected president, giving up his duties as secretary but retaining his authority as general manager. Having headed the company for forty-six years, he asked in 1943 to be relieved of some of the executive responsibilities and was accordingly elected chairman of the board. "With fifty-three years of service to his credit," Mr. Saltmarsh remarked in an address in 1950, "he can rightfully take great satisfaction in the growth of that tiny acorn planted back in 1897, which now stands as a mighty oak, boasting assets of more than eleven million dollars."

Mr. Saltmarsh can himself look back on a career with the company spanning more than four decades. He joined the organization in 1910, going to work in the field at a salary of $125 a month. "Of course that seems very low now," Mr. Saltmarsh recently recalled, "but remember, ten dollars bought groceries for our family of four for a whole month in those days. I covered Missouri, Kansas, Oklahoma, and the northern part of Arkansas, writing the business, inspecting, and making all the adjustments. At that time, nearly every little town had its own lumberyard if it was on a river or a railroad. Some of the best yards were in small villages. Roads were terrible, of course, so we usually got around on freight trains, riding in the caboose. We would get into a small town and maybe I'd buy the crew their dinner so they would give me a whistle thirty minutes before they were ready to pull out. How long I stayed depended on how hard that town's lumberman was to sell. If he was hard-boiled and it took all day, you just didn't pay any attention to that whistle. Sometimes there would be two or three of us in the caboose—perhaps a tea-and-coffee salesman and a dry-goods salesman besides me—and in those cases we would get a team and buggy and work out an itinerary. We would try to hit as many little towns as we could, and then either come back to the same railroad or cut across the country to another line. At the end of the day we'd have a few hours' sleep in a dollar hotel room, and then get up and catch a freight at midnight. We had a wonderful time."

As the Lumber Mutuals grew in size and experience, they gradually branched out. As early as 1915, the Lumbermens Mutual, of Mansfield, began writing fire insurance on dwellings and household goods belonging to lumbermen whose business properties were already insured by the company. A few years later, it started furnishing automobile physical damage coverage to these same lumbermen, and around 1920 the company began the solicitation of fire and windstorm insurance on all classes of properties except farms. Less than 22 per cent of the company's annual premium income is now derived from lumber risks, and less than 17 per cent when reinsurance has been deducted.

The same pattern was followed by the other lumber companies, the Indiana Lumbermens entering the general business field in 1918, the Pennsylvania Lumbermens and the Lumber Mutual of Boston in 1930. With the exception of the Boston company, which still derives approximately 50 per cent of its premium income from risks in the lumber and woodworking classifications, the companies founded by lumbermen now secure less than one fifth of their total business from the lumber industry. All the Lumber Mutuals now write their general business through agents, but the lumber business of each is still, as in the beginning, written directly by salaried employees with many years of experience in the lumber field.

Loss prevention has always been a major interest of the Lumber Mutuals. Today all the companies formed by lumbermen, as well as the Northwestern Mutual, maintain staffs of engineers, inspectors, and other specialists to carry on this work. In addition to frequent and rigid inspections, the loss-prevention activities include constant study of the newest developments in fire-prevention methods and equipment, independent research, and a broad-scale educational program consisting of bulletins, posters, technical publications, and motion pictures to train plant employees in the recognition and elimination of fire hazards.

As a consequence of their loss-prevention program and of their efficient management, the Lumber Mutuals have accomplished their original purpose: to provide sound insurance at cost. When, for example, the Pennsylvania Lumbermens was founded, lumberyards in its area were charged a rate of $2.00 per $100 for their fire insurance. Today the better risks in this class are charged a rate that averages between 50 cents and $1.00. When the Lumbermens Mutual, of Mansfield, commenced business in 1895, the average premium rate on lumber and woodworking risks in its locality was $3.80. Today lumbermen in Ohio, Michigan, Kentucky, and West Virginia obtain insurance protection from the Lumbermens Mutual at a rate of not more than 75 cents. Thanks to the competition supplied by the Lumber Mutuals, the rates of all companies insuring lumber risks have been steadily forced down over the years.

Applying the same progressive methods in the general business field, the Lumber Mutuals have effected a tremendous saving to all their policyholders. Each of the companies in the group has paid dividends every year since its founding. Depending on the class of business, the dividend rate has ranged from 15 to 50 per cent. Since their establishment, the companies comprising the Associated Lumber Mutual group have returned to their policyholders dividends of more than $147 million. In 1950, their combined premium writings reached $52 million. Their combined assets amounted to $94.4 million, and their combined surplus exceeded $34 million.

Though the Lumber Mutuals have made notable progress, they do not consider their job finished. "Our biggest problem," Mr. Russell Davis, vice-president of the Lumbermens Mutual, of Mansfield, said recently, "is to bring home to the people the part their carelessness plays in the destruction of natural resources, economic resources, and human life. No nation on earth has a burning rate like ours. America is the world's biggest fire trap. If we could only bring home to the people the fact that they make their own rates, that we are not being selfish or trying to make money when we ask them to reduce fire hazards, half the battle would be won. To do the job right, a company must have something more to offer than payment for losses. What we are interested in is service to our customers, careful selection of risks, painstaking inspection, and making every effort to preserve the property we have insured."

In April 1897—the same month that the last of the Lumber Mutuals commenced business—the seed that was to grow into the first of the Hardware Mutuals was sown. On that bright April day a large group of retail hardware merchants from all parts of Minnesota, led by a dealer named Charles F. Ladner, met in the Chamber of the House of Representatives in St. Paul and organized the Minnesota Retail Hardware Association. One of its objects was to find a solution to the insurance problem confronting its members. Because they stored paint, linseed oil, and turpentine in their stores, hardware dealers were charged exceedingly high premiums by stock fire insurance companies. Time and again the dealers had pointed out to their insurance companies that their supplies of paint and other combustible items were either sealed or barreled and, furthermore, that these goods made up only a small part of their total stock, which consisted largely of implements, wire, metalware, nails, and other non-combustible products. The rates, however, were never lowered.

Since all efforts to secure relief from the existing companies seemed doomed to failure, Mr. Ladner turned to considering the formation of a mutual company that would insure hardware risks only. He discussed the idea with the secretary of the dealers' association, who was very enthusiastic and spread the word among the membership. However, when the proposition to form a mutual company under the auspices of the Association was presented to the dealers at their annual meeting, the suggestion failed to secure majority approval. A substantial number of dealers, including Mr. Ladner, decided to proceed nevertheless. On May 25, 1899, they met in Minneapolis, signed the Articles of Association of what was to be called the Retail Hardware Dealers Mutual Fire Insurance Company, and elected its first board of directors. To provide the company with funds to pay losses that might occur, the original board of directors, composed of twelve hardware dealers, signed a note for $20,000 at the Northwestern National Bank, thus giving a practical demonstration of their faith in the company.

Their faith was justified, the company prospered from the start, there were no early losses, and the note was soon paid. In the beginning, only stocks of hardware dealers were insured, but before long coverage was extended to include buildings and dwellings, and as time went on, the organization gradually developed into a general writing company. Under the leadership of Mr. Ladner, who was elected president in 1902 and served in that position and later as chairman of the board for thirty-five years, the company began expanding early in its career into states neighboring Minnesota. Now called the Hardware Mutual Insurance Company of Minnesota, the company operates in all states. At the end of its first year the company's assets amounted to $4,900.16 and its surplus to $704.71. The board of directors declared a 25 per cent dividend paid on all policies expiring in 1901; in the more than half century since then, the company has paid a dividend every year without interruption. At the close of its fifty-first year, in 1950, the Hardware Mutual Insurance Company of Minnesota, which identifies itself as the "Original Hardware Mutual," had assets of $16.7 million and a surplus exceeding $5 million. It now ranks among the three largest Hardware Mutuals in the country.

By the early part of 1903, some two dozen hardware dealers in Wisconsin, including the president and secretary of the Wisconsin Retail Hardware Association, had taken out policies in the recently founded mutual company in Minnesota. They were very pleased with the savings, amounting to about 40 per cent, which they had been able to effect on their insurance. However, as the president of the Association said in an address to its members, the Minnesota company had a top limit of $3,000 on any single risk, and many Wisconsin hardware merchants, including himself, would like to carry twice that amount. He accordingly suggested that the Association appoint a committee to consider forming a mutual insurance company for hardware men in Wisconsin. Following the favorable report made by the committee, a group of hardware dealers met on May 27, 1903, and drew up the Articles of Association for the Hardware Dealers Mutual Fire Insurance Company. The organizational work was completed by the following spring, and office space was engaged in Berlin, Wisconsin, at an annual rental of $50 a year, which included heat and light. The first policy was issued on April 4, 1904. Within a month, the new company had more than $500,000 of insurance in force.

Hardware dealers were kept informed of the company's progress through its punchy little advertisements in the *National Hardware Bulletin,* the industry's trade paper. An ad appearing in 1906 reported:

> $997,965 insurance written since we started. Have you any of it? We are young, but we are doing business. Why not with you? At this writing, expense and loss accounts are only 30% of premiums received this year. It is a good thing for you to write the undersigned about.

The undersigned was C. A. Peck, who was the first secretary of the company. In another advertisement, Secretary Peck discussed dividends and peaches:

> In 1905, we rebated 33½% and carried 28% to surplus. . . . What would you think of a man who owned a peach orchard full of luscious fine peaches, and went into the market and bought peaches at a big price, too? That is practically what you are doing if you fail to avail yourself of the benefits offered you by the above-named company. Don't let prejudice keep you from availing yourself of the benefits longer. The Company belongs to the policyholders and its profits are theirs.

In succeeding advertisements Mr. Peck pointed out, among other things, that the company was writing business at the rate of $4,000 a day, and, as he put it, "We have written considerable business in other states and are always looking for more." By 1909, the company was operating in thirty-eight states, was returning dividends of 50 per cent, and was apparently rendering good service to its policyholders, for as Mr. Peck reported with pride that year in an advertisement, "No party that has taken out insurance with this company has dropped the same."

After the death of Mr. Peck in 1911, Mr. P. J. Jacobs, who had been a director of the company and for twenty years a partner in a hardware business in Stevens Point, was elected to the position of secretary-treasurer of both the Wisconsin Retail Hardware Association and of the Hardware Dealers Mutual Fire Insurance Company. Within a few months after Mr. Jacobs took over management of the insurance company, its headquarters were moved to Stevens Point. The transfer was not exceedingly complicated, since the company had only four employees, and its office equipment consisted of two typewriters, one adding machine, one desk, its records, and, as an executive of the company once remarked, "plenty of American optimism." When Mr. Jacobs assumed direction of the company, it had $5.6 million of insurance in force and assets of $23,000. In 1935, when Mr. Jacobs retired as president, retaining his position as a director until his death the following year, the company was licensed in every state and had assets exceeding $5 million. Since then, the company has extended its operations into Canada and has grown to the point at which, at the close of 1950, it had assets of $21.6 million and a surplus of $7.7 million. A general writing company, less than 5 per cent of whose total premium income is now derived from hardware risks, the Hardware Dealers Mutual Fire Insurance Company is also one of the Big Three of the Hardware Mutual group.

The third number of this top triumvirate is the Federated Mutual Implement and Hardware Insurance Company, of Owatonna, Minnesota. It would probably not have come into existence if the implement dealers of Minnesota had been able to secure insurance from the Hardware Mutual of Minnesota during that company's early years. Since the original hardware company's bylaws did not permit extending coverage to implement dealers, they decided, through their dealers' association, to organize their own insurance company. As it turned out, they had undertaken an assignment that was to tax their ingenuity and perseverance. Their first step was to get introduced into the state legislature a bill granting permission to organize a mutual company to provide fire insurance to implement dealers only. After passage by both houses of the legislature, the enabling bill was vetoed by the governor, who gave as his rather novel reason his belief that the bill was "class legislation."

Dismayed but undiscouraged, members of the Association

continued their efforts. In the fall of 1906, they were able, with the approval of the Minnesota insurance commissioner, to acquire control of a small mutual fire insurance company in St. Paul, which had been organized two years before but had run into financial difficulties and had obligations amounting to $8,000. These had to be paid in full before the implement dealers could acquire the company's charter. They accordingly borrowed $8,000 from a bank, each of the directors, of whom there were nine, signing the note.

Having surmounted all the legal obstacles, the directors planned to hold their first meeting at the Ryan Hotel in St. Paul on January 22, 1907. Forgathering in the hotel lobby, they discovered that arrangements for a meeting room had not been made. Also in the lobby, however, was an implement dealer from Owatonna, Minnesota, named C. I. Buxton, who offered the directors the use of his room. This gesture was destined to change the course of Mr. Buxton's life. Though he had been a charter member of the dealers' association and had served on many of its committees, he had previously had no connection with its insurance activities. He was interested in the insurance project, however, and, being acquainted with its directors, sat in on their first meeting. At its conclusion, Mr. Buxton had not only been elected to the board but had also been appointed a member of its finance committee.

Progress of the new company was slow. Its aim was to insure only implement dealers, the number of whom was limited and many of whom in the early years proved hard to interest. Premium income in 1907 amounted to $15,159, and assets at the close of that year totaled $7,610. Two years later, premium income had shown no appreciable increase, and assets had shrunk to $5,466. Seeing little future in the enterprise, the young man who had been hired as secretary to manage the company turned in his resignation. There was still a little less than $5,000 owing on the $8,000 note, and it looked as if the company would have to wind up its affairs with the probability that the directors would be obliged to pay the balance of the note. At this critical juncture the position of secretary was offered to Mr. Buxton. He gallantly accepted, and the office of the company was moved from the Twin Cities to Owatonna. Mr. Buxton personally handled the transfer, going up to Minneapolis and carrying back all the company's files and records in one suitcase.

At the end of the first year under Mr. Buxton's management, the company showed a small deficit, but it wound up the following year with a surplus of $4,877. Five years later, at the close of 1916, the surplus account had grown to $94,574. Up to that time, Mr. Buxton, with the assistance of one girl in the office, had performed all the work, including passing on applications, writing policies, handling correspondence, adjusting losses, and, whenever possible, picking up his satchel and going out into the territory to solicit business. At the same time, he had been devoting part of his attention to the implement firm of which he was a partner. Early in 1917, when the company's premium income had reached $250,000, he sold his share of the implement business and after that devoted all his time to the insurance company. In 1917, the first year in which he gave his exclusive attention to insurance, the company's premium income shot up 71 per cent over the year before. Progress of the company since then has been uninterrupted.

During the forty-four years that Mr. Buxton, who died in 1951, was associated with the Federated Mutual Implement and Hardware Insurance Company—as director, secretary, president, and chairman of the board—he had the satisfaction of seeing the emaciated enterprise that he carried to Owatonna in a suitcase develop from a floundering company writing only one kind of risk in a small territory into a large general-writing mutual that operates throughout the country. In 1910, when he assumed leadership of the company, its premium income was less than $15,000; in 1950, its net premiums were more than $14.6 million. In 1910 the company had an indebtedness of $5,000; at the close of 1950, it had assets of $19.8 million and a surplus of $5.6 million.

In addition to the Big Three, the Hardware Mutuals include a number of other companies that were formed against a similar background and to achieve a similar purpose. Six of these companies were established between 1902 and 1916. In the order of founding, they consist of the Ohio Hardware Mutual Insurance Company, the Iowa Hardware Mutual Insurance Company, the Implement Dealers Mutual Insurance Company (Grand Forks, North Dakota), Nebraska Hardware Mutual Insurance Company, Hardware Mutual Fire Insurance Company of the Carolinas, and the Texas Hardware Mutual Insurance Company.

Originally organized to serve hardware merchants only, these companies have also extended the kinds of risks they insure. All now write fire, extended coverage, and automobile physical damage insurance, and a few also write additional lines. Their territory varies widely; one company (Texas Hardware) is licensed in but one state, while another (Implement Dealers, of Grand Forks) is licensed in thirty-one. On the average, they operate in twelve states. The average net premium writings of these six companies in 1950 amounted to $673,500. At the end of that year, their average assets were $1,155,265, while their average surplus was $495,389.

During the past half century, the Hardware Mutuals have become an important force in the fire insurance world. (In addition to writing fire and allied lines, the Big Three, directly or through companion companies, also write casualty insurance, a topic that will be discussed in later chapters.) In 1950, the combined premium writings of the Hardware Mutuals reached $40.5 million. Their combined assets at the end of that year amounted to $65.1 million, and they had a combined surplus of $21.3 million. From the smallest company to the largest, they adhere to the principle on which they were founded: to furnish sound insurance at cost. Their position today, as Mr. Arthur R. Craig, president of the Hardware Mutual of the Carolinas recently remarked, "is a tribute to the foresight and faith of those who in the early days contributed their money, time, and talent toward a goal which could be attained only in a country like free America."

CHAPTER XIV

Fire Insurance Comes of Age

IN CONTRAST to the Class Mutuals, which moved from the special to the general in the underwriting field, a substantial number of mutual fire insurance companies staked out the field of general business as their province from the start. Not infrequently, the companies that began as general underwriters reversed the characteristic pattern to a certain extent and later became specialists in certain lines. One such company is the Northwestern Mutual Fire Association, of Seattle, Washington. It is the largest general-writing mutual fire insurance company in the country.

The Northwestern Mutual was created by Frank J. Martin, an able and enterprising man who began his business career as the proprietor of a hardware store in the little town of McMinnville, Oregon. As a side line, he ran a stock fire insurance agency. During the depression of 1893, he was forced out of the hardware business and began to give his full time to insurance. Before long, however, he became involved in a disagreement with the special agent of the territory, who insisted that Martin increase the insurance on his clients' properties beyond a figure that Martin believed necessary and fair. The result was that he resigned his agency.

One of his clients, to whom he explained the reason for his

resignation, was a local merchant who had been considering setting up a mutual fire insurance company, and he suggested that Martin join with him and several of the other townspeople who were interested in the project. They selected Martin as the active organizer of the prospective company, which was to be called the Oregon Fire Relief Association. (Still in business, it is now called the Oregon Mutual Fire Insurance Company.) Securing the necessary number of insurance applications was Martin's first task. "He rode all over the county on his bicycle soliciting subscribers," one of the men originally interested in the organization has recalled. "On the front of his wheel was a basket in which, if he could not get cash, he carried home eggs, chickens, hens, or other farm produce that could be converted into cash." Within six months, Martin had not only developed a fine set of leg muscles, but had signed a total of 320 prospective policyholders. The company began business in January 1894, and Martin was elected its secretary and manager. He devoted his entire time to its development for the next six years. In 1900, owing to strife that had set in among the company's board of directors, Martin severed his connection and began thinking about organizing a mutual company whose scope would be greater than the one he had put on its feet.

Having set his sights high, he decided to move to Seattle, then a city of 80,000 and the center of the booming Pacific Northwest. His selection of Seattle was also prompted by the presence there of two former schoolmates, Martin Rhodes and Corwin S. Shank, a young attorney, both of whom gave advice and assistance in launching the new company. As a staff to go out and secure the necessary number of applications from prospective policyholders, Martin recruited three men experienced in exhorting and converting. Only one, a man named William Dent who had worked for the Oregon Fire Relief Association, had had insurance experience. The other two were ministers of the gospel. They were paid one dollar per application, and they put in three days away from their pastorates each week, soliciting subscribers.

The advent of the new company was not greeted with noticeable enthusiasm by the insurance companies already in the field. Anonymous circulars warning prospective policyholders against the new company were distributed wherever Dent and the other solicitors were working. Rougher tactics were also used. Upon leaving the Seattle railway station one night, Dent was waylaid, severely beaten, and then warned against continuing to work for the new company. Not being easily turned aside, Dent, having recovered, returned to his field work, and a second, more savage, attack was made on him. This time, however, his assailant was caught and convicted of assault and battery. When questioned by the police, the hireling admitted that he did not know Dent or anything about his business; he said he had committed both offenses because some insurance people had paid him twenty dollars "to beat up the old man."

In spite of all the unfavorable circumstances, more than enough applications to start the company had been secured within a month after the three agents had begun work. The Northwestern issued its first policy on April 24, 1901. Mr. Martin assumed the presidency of the company, and his friend, Martin Rhodes, became secretary. Within four months, the company had written insurance amounting to $605,413 on 1,221 separate risks and had collected premiums of $1,-620.10. Of this sum, 15 per cent, or $243, had been placed in the reserve fund. At this point, the company was examined by the deputy insurance commissioner. He concluded his report, which ran to a total of 111 words and included the foregoing figures, with this observation: "I find that the books of the Association are neatly kept in a businesslike manner. I also believe the Association is conservatively and economically managed and that it is furnishing good insurance at nominal costs."

That report, though somewhat laconic by current standards, could be used to describe with equal accuracy the Northwestern Mutual of today. The figures, of course, are considerably more impressive now than they were then. The gross insurance in force, for example, has grown from some $600,000 in 1901 to more than $6.3 billion in 1950. During the same period, premium income has increased from less than $2,000 to more than $17 million. The surplus account, which had not reached $250 at the time of the first examination, passed $10 million in 1950. That the company is continuing to furnish good insurance at nominal costs is indicated by the fact that the dividends it returned to policyholders in 1950 amounted to $1.8 million. With assets exceeding $30 million and some 800 employees, the Northwestern now writes throughout the United States and in Canada.

From the time it was five years old, the Northwestern has been a member of the Associated Lumber Mutuals. When the company was founded, the center of lumber manufacturing had shifted to the Pacific Northwest, and Mr. Martin looked with interest on the insurance possibilities in the booming industry at his front door. Rates on all classes of woodworking establishments on the Pacific Coast, as Mr. Martin was well aware, were high and were likely to remain so, mainly because the insurance companies then in the field faced little or no competition. He also knew that the Northwestern did not alone have a writing capacity large enough to handle the heavy insurable values offered by the lumber industry. Nor was any of the four Lumber Mutuals, with whose officers and operations Mr. Martin had become acquainted in the course of his inveterate attendance of mutual insurance conventions, sufficiently well established to begin expansion into the comparatively remote Northwest. Since the Lumber Mutuals were interested in the new business and Mr. Martin was interested in acquiring the reinsurance they could offer, he arranged in 1906 for the Northwestern to begin participating as an active member of the Lumber Mutual group. The energy with which his company went after business in the new field is reflected in the figures for 1907, which showed a 14 per cent increase in net premiums written in the lumber class.

Though the Northwestern still insures many of the largest and finest lumber risks in the West, its volume of lumber business has declined since the early boom days. Including reinsurance, approximately 9 per cent of the company's premium income is now derived from lumber risks. Today, as always in the past, the Northwestern Mutual concentrates on providing protection on the best risks in all classes of property. It has followed its original purpose for more than half a century, and it has been singularly successful.

The race for first place in the general-writing fire field wound up in 1950 practically in a dead heat. The Northwestern came in first with $17,024,000 in net premiums. In second place was the Liberty Mutual Fire Insurance Company, of Boston, with net premiums of $16,756,000. The distance between them was a matter of $268,000.

Seven years younger than the Northwestern, Liberty, like the bulk of mutual fire insurance companies, was originally founded to furnish protection to a group of specialized risks.

The genesis of the company goes back to the annual convention of druggists sponsored by the United Drug Company in 1907. One of the speakers at the convention, Archie W. Campbell, was the owner of a Rexall drugstore. He had chosen insurance as his subject. Druggists were being charged ridiculously high rates for fire insurance by the stock companies, Mr. Campbell said, and the remedy he prescribed was the organization of a mutual company by Rexall dealers to insure their own properties. Among members of the audience who were impressed by Campbell's idea was Louis K. Liggett, who was president of the United Drug Company. In a few months the idea had become a reality. The United Druggists Mutual Fire Insurance Company was incorporated in Massachusetts in October 1908, with Liggett as president and Campbell as secretary and manager. To provide the company with initial resources, Liggett had arranged for it to secure a bank loan of $100,000. Operating from a one-room office in Boston, the secretary transacted most of the business by mail. For about ten years the company concentrated on its specialized risks, paying dividends during that time of between 25 and 50 per cent, and gradually expanding to offer insurance on druggists' homes and on the property of certain doctors.

Meanwhile, the Liberty Mutual Insurance Company, a casualty company that will be considered in a later chapter, had been formed in Boston. Like many other casualty companies at that time, Liberty was not permitted by its charter to write fire, theft, and collision insurance on automobiles, and was interested in making an affiliation with a company that could. Mr. Liggett, who was a member of the casualty company's board, suggested that the United Druggists Mutual be used to provide this service. Accordingly, in 1918, the word "Druggists" was dropped from the title, and the United Mutual Fire Insurance Company began expanding into automobile and other lines. Known by its present title since 1949, Liberty Mutual Fire has close connections with its companion casualty company, S. Bruce Black serving as president of both companies. However, the vice-president and general manager of Liberty Mutual Fire, O. E. Ringquist, operates the company as an independent concern in many respects. It has an almost wholly separate board of directors as well as its own underwriting department.

Though the company's business expanded steadily from the beginning, the most notable growth has occurred since 1940. Net premiums that year totaled $5.2 million. They increased more than threefold in the next ten years. Approximately 55 per cent of the net premium income is derived from fire and extended coverage, around 30 per cent from the automobile class, and a majority of the balance from inland marine. Besides the standard fire coverages, Liberty has devised a special plan for superior farm property in New England, and it has also originated a new multiple location rating plan for chain-store risks. In addition, new coverages have been introduced in inland marine, a field in which Liberty does more business than any other mutual company. Accounting for only 12 per cent of the company's total business, inland marine premiums reached $1.9 million in 1950.

A leader in the field of loss prevention, Liberty now employs forty-three loss-prevention engineers in the United States and Canada. Their training begins with a three months' course of instruction in fire-prevention engineering, continues with a stint in the sales and underwriting departments, and winds up with work in the field under the direction of an experienced engineer. Quite literally, the inspectors' training never ends; they are provided, among other things, with loose-leaf notebooks which are kept up to date with the latest material on methods, processes, and developments in the industrial and fire engineering fields, and they are also required to do one technical problem by correspondence every month.

Members of the engineering department make a thorough inspection of each industrial risk before insurance is issued on it. In the course of the original inspection, a plan of the structure is drawn, and this is periodically updated. All inspectors are provided with cameras, and photographs are also made of the properties. Inspections are continued as long as the policy remains in force, the frequency depending on the nature of the hazards. Large high-hazard risks are inspected quarterly; small low-hazard risks are checked biennially. Each inspector has a dictaphone in his car. Upon completing an inspection, he immediately dictates a detailed report, covering prescribed topics. His reports are sent to both the home office and to the policyholder. The inspector then writes a follow-up letter to the policyholder, urging that the preventive measures that have been recommended be put into effect to bring the risk up to Liberty's standards.

Liberty also carries on an extensive educational program designed to alert the public to the value of loss prevention. One of its most effective items is a show called *Fire in Miniature,* which runs fifty-five minutes. It consists of a community of small-scale houses, schools, factories, and other structures that can be set ablaze and then extinguished. The show was put together in 1941, has toured the country constantly since, and is always booked solidly for weeks in advance. Very popular with children, it has been exhibited at scores of schools, as well as before numerous other groups and on television, and recently has been made into a sound movie.

With its loss-prevention program developed to its present high level of efficiency, Liberty thinks it unlikely that it will incur the kind of aggravating losses that occasionally cropped up in the old days. One of the more novel of these concerned a drugstore in Alaska that the company had insured at a very stiff rate, because, as the policyholder had reported, his town was without a municipal water supply system. A couple of years later he wrote that a system had been installed and asked that his premium be reduced. The company obliged, but hardly had the change been made when a wire was received saying the store had burned to the ground. The town, it developed, had put in water all right, but it hadn't got around to buying any fire hose.

One of the oldest and largest mutual companies founded to write general business is the Central Mutual Insurance Company, of Van Wert, Ohio, which was incorporated on April 7, 1876. It was originally called the Van Wert County Mutual Fire Insurance Company. "The company got started because the local merchants grew tired of paying exorbitant rates for fire insurance—when they could get it at all," F. W. Purmort, a vice-president of the company said recently. "Of course in those days there was no city fire protection and all construction was frame, but the rates were away out of line nevertheless. It was my grandfather who really got this company started."

From its inception to the present day, the Central has been continuously guided in its expansion by members of the Purmort family. In fact, the history of the company during its first half century divides itself naturally into three periods, corresponding with the tenures of office of its three successive secretaries—M. L. Purmort, Frank W. Purmort, and Clyde A. L. Purmort. During the first of these periods, the company was established, began building up its agency plant in Ohio, and sought admission to several other states. To reflect its larger scope, the company changed its name to the Central Manufacturers Mutual Insurance Company, later shortening the title to its present form. At the close of the second period, in 1908, the Central had become firmly established; it had a large agency plant in Ohio and was well on the way to building another in Indiana. After 1908, the company embarked on its third period, during which it not only developed into one of the country's largest general-writing mutual companies but also became a member of the Associated Lumber Mutuals. Over the years, the lumber business written by the Central has varied considerably, but it has never accounted for as much as 20 per cent of the company's total premium income. Through some 3,000 agents the company now operates throughout the country and in Canada.

In 1911, thirty-five years after the Central was founded, the Lumbermen's and Manufacturers' Insurance Agency was opened in Chicago for the purpose of inspecting and soliciting risks in the lumber and woodworking classes in the Chicago area. The general manager of the new agency was James S. Kemper, who had begun his insurance career with the Central and who later established, among many other insurance organizations, the National Retailers Mutual Insurance Company and the Lumbermens Mutual Casualty Company. The co-operation between the Central and the Kemper organizations has ever since remained very close; Mr. Kemper is a vice-president of the Central, and Mr. L. G. Purmort, president of the Central, is a vice-president of the Lumbermens Mutual Casualty Company. Today, still actively managed by members of the Purmort family, four of whom are among its officers, the Central has insurance in force of approximately $2 billion, assets of $25 million, and a surplus of $7.5 million.

Though it has always written general business, the National Retailers Mutual Insurance Company started out to specialize, as its name suggests, in serving retail mercantile establishments. The National Retailers operates under a New York charter as the result of a merger, effected in 1940, with the Glen Cove Mutual Insurance Company, which was founded by a group of Quaker farmers and businessmen in the village of Glen Cove, Long Island, in 1837. For a number of years before the merger, James S. Kemper had served as the company's president. Mr. Kemper also was, and is, president of the National Retailers, which was incorporated in Illinois in 1922. During the first year, premium income amounted to $144,000, much of which was derived from insurance written on stores belonging to members of the National Shoe Retailers Association. In the early days, the company successfully sought, and still retains, the endorsement of many other retail trade associations. Through the efforts of Mr. Kemper and other executives of the company, who frequently addressed association meetings, the National Retailers was endorsed by the Ohio Retail Clothing Dealers Association, the Minnesota Retail Furniture Association, the Chicago Meat Dealers Association, and many other similar groups. On risks in these classes the company paid dividends ranging from 20 to 33⅓ per cent, and business thrived. By 1931, nine years after its incorporation, the National Retailers had more than tripled its assets, and premium income had been pushed up to $1.4 million.

Mercantile and dwelling risks made up the majority of the company's business during the first decade. From the beginning, however, it had written whatever general business came into its agencies. As early as 1925, National Retailers issued its first physical damage automobile policy. With the passage of time and the development and aggressive selling of other coverages, the field of general business has come to account for an increasingly large share of the National Retailers' premium writings. In 1950, for example, the automobile class produced almost half of the company's gross premium income and more than a quarter of its net. An inland marine department, established in 1935, now accounts for approximately 10 per cent of net premium income. In 1939, National Retailers organized a yacht department; two years later it began offering aircraft hull insurance, thus rounding out a full line in the fire field.

Because of James S. Kemper's long and close connection with the lumber industry, National Retailers has also cooperated for many years with the Associated Lumber Mutuals, of which Mr. Kemper is Western manager. Though the company does not actively solicit business in the lumber field, it participates through reinsurance in a considerable volume of business in that class. With the absorption of the mill and elevator business of the Ohio Millers Mutual Insurance Company in 1933, National Retailers became a member of the Mill Mutuals; about 6 per cent of its net premiums, which had risen to $7.9 million in 1950, is now derived from mill and elevator insurance.

A company of marked diversification, National Retailers, which now has assets exceeding $11 million, is associated with three other groups of mutual companies that offer specialized insurance facilities. These are the Building Owners Federation of Mutual Fire Insurance Companies, the Food Industries Federation of Mutual Fire Insurance Companies, and the Improved Risk Mutuals. The first two were founded in 1917 and 1943, respectively, by James S. Kemper, who has continued to manage both organizations. The Building Owners Federation is composed of twelve large mutual fire insurance companies.[1] The organization specializes in carefully selected properties of non-hazardous occupancy and fire-resistive construction, such as office buildings, hotels, banks, churches, schools, and similar high-grade structures. Each member company assumes a specific proportion of each risk accepted either direct or by reinsurance. Coverage is provided in a single policy. The liability of the participating companies is several, not joint, and policies are written at tariff rates. Because of the high standard of the risks it accepts and the rigid inspection system maintained by its engineers, the Building Owners Federation returns dividends ranging from 25 to 40 per cent. It is able to write large lines, since the twelve member companies have combined assets of $123 million.

The same group of companies also comprises the membership of the Food Industries Federation, which was established to insure superior risks in the food-processing industry, such as fruit and vegetable canners and milk processors. Its technical operation, including the issuance of a single policy and the apportionment of liability among the entire member-

[1]The following companies are members of the Building Owners Federation: the Central Mutual Insurance Company; Grain Dealers Mutual Insurance Company; Indiana Lumbermens Mutual Insurance Company; Lumbermens Mutual Insurance Company; Michigan Millers Mutual Fire Insurance Company; Mill Owners Mutual Fire Insurance Company (of Iowa); Millers Mutual Insurance Association of Illinois; Millers Mutual Fire Insurance Company (of Pennsylvania); the Millers Mutual Fire Insurance Company of Texas; National Retailers Mutual Insurance Company; Pennsylvania Lumbermens Mutual Insurance Company; Pennsylvania Millers Mutual Fire Insurance Company.

ship, is the same as that of the Building Owners Federation. Dividends of 30 per cent are paid by the Food Industries Federation.

The Improved Risk Mutuals were formed in 1921. Among those most active in founding the organization were Frank J. Martin, A. D. Baker, then president of Michigan Millers, and E. S. Nail. The Improved Risk Mutuals are made up of eleven general-writing mutual companies.[2] Their combined assets exceed $144 million. The IRM insures large risks and issues either a combination policy written in the names of all the member companies or a policy written by one or more member companies with the liability reinsured 100 per cent in the IRM. In either case, the combined assets of all the companies are behind the policy. All loss settlements are made by the IRM in behalf of the member companies.

With headquarters in White Plains, New York, the Improved Risk Mutuals operate nationwide, insuring only properties in which construction, occupancy, maintenance, protection, exposure, and standards of management are above average. Unlike the Building Owners and the Food Industries Federations, the Improved Risk Mutuals do not confine their writings to special classes. The several thousand risks insured by IRM policies include a variety of industrial properties, department and specialty stores, warehouses, schools, hospitals, churches and other institutions, laundries, paper, textile and publishing plants, public utilities, municipal

[2]The companies comprising the Improved Risk Mutuals are the same as those that comprise the Building Owners Federation and the Food Industries Federation, with these exceptions: first, the Millers Mutual Insurance Association of Illinois and the Millers Mutual Fire Insurance Company of Texas are not members of the Improved Risk Mutuals; second, the Northwestern Mutual Fire Insurance Association is a member.

properties, and a wide range of other risks. All properties insured by the IRM are rigidly inspected from one to four times a year, the number depending on the hazards involved. The organization maintains an expert engineering department with a staff of forty men, seven of whom are attached to the home office; the balance make their headquarters in various key cities across the country. The general manager of the Improved Risk Mutuals, Howard F. Russell, is a graduate engineer from the Massachusetts Institute of Technology and has given the organization the benefit of his long and varied experience in fire underwriting and engineering. The Improved Risk Mutuals have paid dividends continuously since 1921, the current rate being 15 per cent.

In the past half century, as the experience of the general-writing companies demonstrates, the mutual fire insurance business has grown both vertically and horizontally. The volume of business has increased enormously. At the same time, the kinds of businesses written have been steadily enlarged. Fifty years ago, a man who took out a fire insurance policy was able to protect himself from loss if his house or business property was damaged or destroyed by fire. In some cases, he could also protect himself against loss from windstorm and from a minor number of other hazards. But for the most part fire insurance in those days was just what it said it was.

Nowadays a man can take out a policy with a general-writing mutual fire insurance company to protect himself from a great variety of hazards besides the basic one. For example, through extended coverage he can insure against loss from windstorm, hail, riot, civil commotion, as well as damage caused by smoke, vehicles, malicious mischief, and falling aircraft. He can insure himself against loss from earthquakes. If the property insured has a sprinkler system, he can take out insurance against sprinkler leakage. If his plant or store burns and his business is thereby interrupted, he can, through use and occupancy coverage, protect himself against loss of his net profits and also provide himself with money for necessary fixed expenses and salaries to keep his organization together during the emergency. If he leases a part of his plant to others, he can protect himself against the loss of rents as a result of damage to the property. If his company owns a private airplane, he can secure protection against its loss or damage. In addition to numerous other kinds of protection, he can, of course, also insure his automobile and the company's vehicles against fire, theft, and collision.

Along with all these are the varied and extensive coverages that come under the ineptly named category called inland marine. Insurance men have been trying for years to devise a term that would come closer to describing this branch of the business. About the best that has so far been offered is transportation insurance, but it has not replaced the old misnomer. By whatever name, inland marine is one of the most diversified kinds of insurance written by fire companies.

Generally speaking, fire insurance primarily covers stationary property or property at fixed locations, while inland marine covers property in transit or property that is at least portable. Individuals usually come into contact with inland marine through so-called personal-property or household floater policies, which cover clothing and other personal possessions either at home or away, and pay for damage or loss from just about every conceivable cause. Business firms use a great deal of inland marine to protect goods in transit, especially goods hauled by truck. Contractors use inland marine to protect tractors, steam shovels, and similar equipment.

Though bridges are not generally considered portable articles, they can also be insured under inland marine policies because they are connected with transportation.

Inland marine rates are frequently tailor-made to fit unique risks. For example, when Paul Revere's house was moved to a new site in Lexington, Liberty issued a policy covering the historic structure in transit. It also covered the moving of an entire sand-and-gravel plant from Pittsburgh to Chattanooga. The John B. Stetson Company once manufactured a line of hats to sell at $150 apiece, and as a sales-promotion feature presented each purchaser with an all-risk policy on his fancy headgear for one year. Liberty provided the insurance. One of its policyholders, a woman who owns several race horses, took out a personal-property floater policy that covered, among other things, the loss of railroad, theater, and other tickets up to the value of $500. She went to the track one day and, out of a sense of loyalty, bet $10 on one of her horses that was rated a long, long shot. After making her bet, she put the pari-mutuel ticket in her shoe for luck. It worked, her horse won, paying 40 to 1, and she ran out to congratulate the jockey. In the confusion her pari-mutuel ticket disappeared. Liberty paid her what the ticket had become worth—the full $400.

Since one of the standard witticisms in insurance circles is that it takes a crystal ball to arrive at inland marine rates, Liberty was momentarily nonplused when a Scandinavian baron who lives in this country and makes a living out of divining the future for the elite applied for a policy to cover the crystal ball he uses in plying his peculiar trade. Liberty issued a policy for $2,500. A while after that the baron was summoned by Princess Elizabeth to gaze into her future before her marriage; on his return voyage the crystal ball disappeared. Liberty paid the loss, and the baron is back in business.

According to the New York Insurance Department Report for 1900, all but 4 per cent of the premium income of fire insurance companies in that far-off day was derived from business described as "fire." The balance was classified as "marine and inland." In 1948, only 47 per cent of the total premium writings came from pure fire risks. In a sense, fire insurance is now fire in name only.

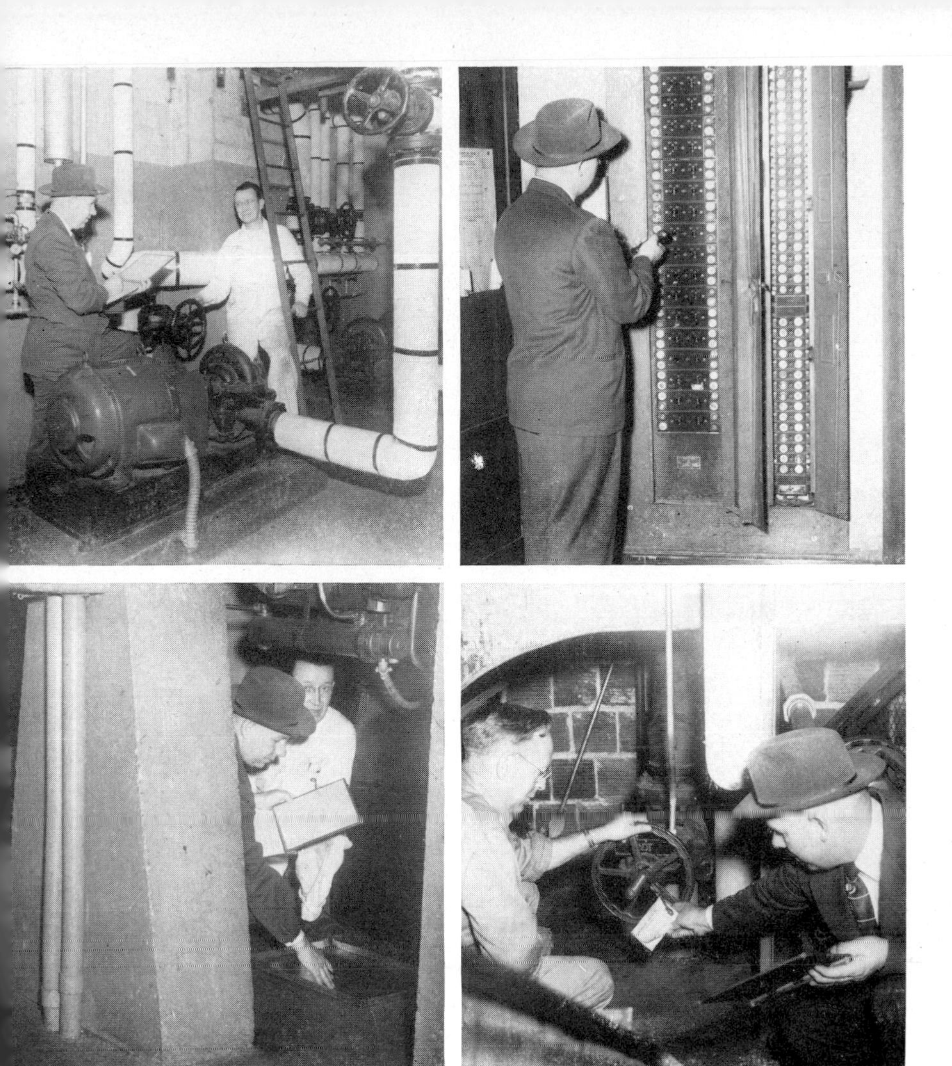

An Inspector in Action

'requent inspections of industrial properties—to discover and eliminate conditions hat might lead to losses—are an integral part of mutual insurance. The pictures bove show a mutual inspector in action. (Upper left) Accompanied by the plant ngineer, the inspector checks the heating plant, including the motors, pumps, and alves. (Upper right) The fuse box, the safety valve of the electrical system, is nspected. (Lower left) No spot where fire may begin is overlooked by the mutual nspector. (Lower right) Automatic sprinkler systems must be ready and able to perate 24 hours a day, 12 months a year. Here, the mutual inspector finds the prinkler valve in good order.

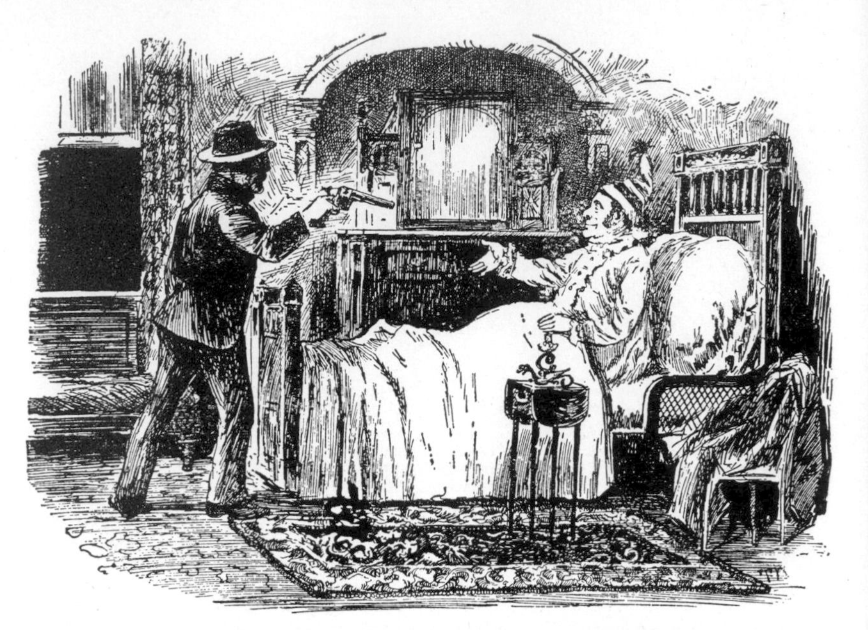

THE BURGLAR COULDN'T FRIGHTEN HIM.

"No, my burglarious friend, I shall throw up nothing at all! I am under the protection of the United States Mutual Accident Association, 320 Broadway, New York. If you wound me I get $50 a week. If disabled permanently I get $2500. If you hit me in the eye I get $1300; for both eyes I get $5000 for hand or foot $5000; for both $10,000. And if you should kill me my family get $10,000, and could live in opulence for the rest of their lives. Blaze away!"

Bettmann Archive

This cartoon, published in 1887, shows the effect that possession of an accident and health insurance policy, one of the early forms of casualty insurance, had on one happy householder.

CHAPTER XV

Background of Casualty Insurance

CASUALTY INSURANCE, a child of the industrial revolution, was reared in the twentieth century. In its earliest years, it was regarded by its elder brethren in the fire, marine, and life branches as a kind of gamin in the insurance family. But casualty proved to be an extremely lusty offspring, and its growth in the past fifty years has been phenomenal. In 1900, casualty premiums totaled $27.5 million. In 1950, they totaled $3.8 billion. That is an increase of 13,718 per cent. The rise of the casualty branch has been the most significant insurance development of recent times.

In large part, the advent of workmen's compensation legislation and the coming of age of the automobile made casualty insurance what it is today. Together, these two coverages now produce more than three quarters of all the business of mutual casualty companies. The other kinds of protection that come under the head of casualty number well over a hundred. Their extensive range and variety reflect the complexities and dangers of modern life and the efforts of the insurance industry to ease them.

Since the word "casualty" is broadly defined as an "accident," it might be assumed that casualty insurance provides protection against financial loss resulting from accidents. That assumption would be correct in the sense that claims made against casualty insurance companies arise out of events that are unexpected and generally afflictive or unfortunate. But that is also true of claims made against fire insurance companies. The basic difference between fire and casualty protection is that casualty provides protection against two kinds of losses: direct losses arising from an unfortunate event from which only the policyholder suffers, and indirect losses arising from an unfortunate event which causes injury or loss to some other person but for which the policyholder is legally liable. For example, a burglar enters your house and makes off with the flat silver; that is a direct loss, and the casualty company will reimburse you for the value of the goods removed by the unwelcome visitor. Say that you are driving your car and are involved in an accident for which you are responsible and which causes injury to some other person or damage to some other person's property; that is an indirect loss, and the casualty company will make the required payments to the person suffering the loss.

The bulk of casualty insurance provides protection against indirect loss, or what is technically known as third-party liability. In the automobile accident, for example, the policyholder is the first party; the insurance company is the second party, protecting the policyholder against damages to some other person, who is the third party. This illustrative example is plainly of the simplest kind. Besides automobile liability, burglary, robbery and theft, and workmen's compensation, other casualty coverages include accident, sickness and hospitalization, plate-glass breakage, fidelity, forgery and surety bonds, boiler and machinery and scores of others. Casualty insurance, tied as closely as it is to the protection of industry and the public and intimately bound up with the question of determining legal liability, is perhaps the most interestingly varied and, in its technical area, most complex branch of insurance.

There are now 204 mutual casualty insurance companies in the United States. Only a few of these were organized before 1900. Not actually casualty companies but in some respects their distant antecedents were the Schaghticoke Society for Apprehending Horse Thieves and Robbers, formed in Schaghticoke, New York, in 1832 and the Trambauersville Mutual Horse Insurance & Detection Company, formed in Trambauersville, Pennsylvania, in 1868. Their purpose was to furnish theft protection on the primary transportation instrument of their day. They remained in business for an average of seventy-three years and then retired, owing no doubt to the fact that the horse had meanwhile lost considerable caste in the social scheme.

The first genuine mutual casualty company was formed in Massachusetts in 1877. It was called the Mutual Boiler Insurance Company of Boston. Its field of operation was made plain by its forthright title. It was founded to insure a special kind of risk, and it has continued its specialization to this day. Now called the Mutual Boiler and Machinery Insurance Company, it confines its business to insuring all types of boilers and similar hazards, such as air tanks, refrigerating apparatus, steam tables, stills, and sterilizers, as well as mechanical and electrical machinery, such as generators, turbines, switchboards, and transformers. The company provides insurance to the policyholder for damage to his plant and equipment resulting from an accident like a boiler explosion (which, because of the company's skillfully developed inspection and loss-prevention engineering service, are happily rare) and for his liability to the person and property of others. This pioneer mutual casualty company is now the second largest writer of boiler and machinery insurance in the country. It is the only mutual company that limits its business exclusively to this field. Its premium writings in 1950 amounted to $6.3 million. Among the more interesting hazards it insures are the boilers in the Atomic Energy Commission's plants at Los Alamos and Oak Ridge.

The first mutual casualty company chartered to write multiple lines was founded in Shelby, Ohio, in 1880. For a great many years that company also insured only one specialized class of risk. Known during its early years as the Mutual Plate Glass Insurance Association, it confined its business to the writing of plate-glass insurance. This kind of insurance is unique in that the policyholder is usually indemnified in kind instead of in cash, the custom being simply to replace the glass. Having written only plate-glass insurance during its first half century, the second mutual casualty company to come into existence revised its charter in 1930 to permit the writing of all casualty lines. Now called the Shelby Mutual Casualty Company, it had a net premium income of $9.2 million in 1950. An indication of how extensively the company has branched out into other fields is the fact that of its total premium income in 1950 only a little more than $700,000 was derived from plate-glass insurance.

Another important new casualty coverage was pioneered in the nineteenth century with the establishment of companies founded to provide accident and health insurance. The first of these, the Franklin Health Assurance Company of Massachusetts, was organized in 1850 to write accident insurance on travelers. The insurance was issued in the form of a ticket that provided protection for a period of twenty-four hours and paid a lump sum of $200 for total disability lasting ten days or longer; if the disability lasted two months, the benefit was doubled. The premium was 15 cents. The coverage could hardly be considered extensive.

Considering the hazards that beset travelers in those days, the need for accident insurance was considerable. In the year 1864 alone there were 140 railroad accidents and 26 steamboat accidents, all of sizable proportions. Once accident insurance was introduced, a rash of companies sprang up to sell the new coverage. They issued policies labeled with very fancy names—Popular, Perfection, Excelsior, Excellent, and Extra-Special. For the most part, however, the benefits under these policies were something less than extra-special. Practically everything except total disability—and even that only when caused by special circumstances—was excepted. "Too often," an insurance historian has remarked, "the policy promised liberally on the initial page and on its reverse side reconsidered the generous impulse." Very few of the more than five dozen accident companies founded during this era survived for more than a few years. Gradually, policies were improved and broadened, health coverage was added, and the field of accident and health insurance began to make steady progress.

The largest mutual company originally established to furnish accident insurance to traveling salesmen is the Commercial Travelers Mutual Accident Association, of Utica, New York. Founded in March 1883, the company incurred its first claim two months later when one of its policyholders was injured in a panic that occurred during the ceremonies attending the opening of the Brooklyn Bridge. Having shown a steady, consistent growth for close to seventy years, the company is now under the direction of Edward Trevvett, secretary-treasurer and general manager, who represents the third generation of his family to guide the operation of the Association. With nearly 244,000 policyholders, the company had a premium income of $5.2 million in 1950, while its assets exceeded $8 million and its surplus was more than $5 million.

Following in the path of the Commercial Travelers of Utica, a number of similar organizations were established before 1900. Two of the largest of these were the Order of United Commercial Travelers of America, with headquarters in Columbus, Ohio, and the Illinois Commercial Mens Association, of Chicago. They were founded, respectively, in 1888 and 1892. Altogether, fourteen organizations now comprise the membership of the International Federation of Commercial Travelers Insurance Organizations. For the most part, these companies were organized as fraternal benefit societies and originally restricted their coverage to traveling men or to professional groups, such as ministers and physicians. Only two now operate strictly as fraternal societies, and virtually all have extended their coverage to other preferred-risk classes, including lawyers, executives, and men in a variety of other occupations. Some of the companies now also insure women, and many have added hospital and surgical benefits besides weekly indemnity for disability.

Collectively, the Commercial Travelers companies have come a long way since their founding members first adapted the mutual idea to accident and health risks. They now insure nearly a million persons. All the companies have an excellent reputation for fair handling of claims. Their combined premium income in 1950 amounted to more than $15 million, and they have accumulated assets of some $29 million. During 1950, their combined benefit payments totaled more than $10 million.

Today, as in the past, the Commercial Travelers companies

write so-called assessment policies. The directors of the various companies annually fix the premium rates for the ensuing year, based on the company's experience and earnings, and as a rule the premiums are paid quarterly. The companies are able to insure their members at very low cost largely because they have never, with few exceptions, sold through agents or direct representatives. Practically all of their business is obtained through mail solicitation or through the recommendation of existing policyholders. The operating expense of these companies is thus relatively small, and the proportion of each company's premium income repaid on its members' claims is unusually high. On the average, it ranges upward of 70 per cent.

In addition to boiler, plate-glass, and accident and health insurance, nearly two dozen other forms of casualty coverage had been put on the market before the close of the nineteenth century. Among the new coverages were bank burglary, messenger robbery, manufacturers' public liability, elevator, and teams. The teams' coverage was designed to protect owners of horse-drawn vehicles from damage done by kicking, biting, or runaway horses. The two major lines that were destined to give casualty insurance its great scope and strength—workmen's compensation and automobile—were still in the future. Even so, they were looming on the horizon. Automobile personal injury coverage was introduced in 1898. The market for it was somewhat limited; the year it was introduced, two hundred automobiles were manufactured in the United States.

Though the horseless carriage had barely entered the industrial arena, the United States had become the greatest manufacturing nation in the world by the turn of the century. The value of its manufactured products had risen from $1 billion in 1850 to $13 billion in 1900. In the same period, annual wages paid to American workers had increased from $237 million to $2.3 billion. A new phase in America's industrial revolution had set in at the close of the nineteenth century, when American manufactured goods began to invade the markets of the world. In 1850, the foreign trade of the United States had been $244 million; by 1900, it had reached $1.9 billion. The proportionate increase in the export of manufactured goods was far greater than that of raw materials and agricultural products. The national income had increased at an astonishing rate—from $7 billion in 1850 to $88 billion in 1900—and this in turn had brought about a substantial rise in the national standard of living.

The price of these giant strides in industry had been high. "We have been proud of our industrial achievements," Woodrow Wilson said in his first inaugural address, "but we have not hitherto stopped thoughtfully enough to count the cost, the cost of lives snuffed out, of energies overtaxed and broken, the fearful physical and spiritual cost to the men, women, and children upon whom the dead weight and burden of it all has fallen pitilessly the years through." The price of industrial leadership could be reckoned by the fact that the United States had more industrial accidents than any other nation on earth. Furthermore, it was next to impossible for a worker suffering an accident to receive anything resembling fair damages for his injury.

Under the common law an employee had the right to bring an action against his employer and recover damages for personal injuries sustained during the course of his employment. Legally, however, the cards were always stacked against the employee. The employer had three practically airtight defenses. First, under the so-called fellow-servant rule, the employer was not liable for injuries caused by the negligence or carelessness of fellow employees. Second, under the contributory negligence rule, the employer was not liable if the negligence of the injured employee, no matter how incidental, contributed to the cause of the accident. Third, under the assumption of risk rule, it was assumed that the employee had accepted all the customary risks of his occupation and that his compensation had taken these factors into account; thus the employer was not liable if he could prove that the accident resulted from inherent dangers in the occupation. In the face of these legal defenses, the injured employee was almost helpless. Even so, employers not infrequently required employees to sign contracts relieving them of all liability as a prerequisite to getting a job.

Employees were given a somewhat better break, theoretically, under employers' liability laws. Introduced in England in 1880, employers' liability laws were passed in Alabama in 1886, in Massachusetts in 1887, and later in most other states. These laws generally held employers liable for injuries resulting from defective machinery, and in some instances they modified certain of the employers' customary legal defenses. Concurrently with the passage of employers' liability laws came the introduction of employers' liability insurance. This was designed to indemnify the employer against loss resulting from legal liability for bodily injuries suffered by employees during the course of their employment. Some policies provided for the furnishing of medical aid irrespective of negligence.

The writing of employers' liability insurance did not solve the problem. It neither reduced the frequency or severity of industrial accidents, nor did it provide injured employees with adequate compensation. When a workman was hurt, the insurance companies sent investigators, who in nine cases out of ten decided the accident resulted from the workman's negligence or from some other cause for which the employer was not legally liable. In the usual course of affairs, the injured workman would then be approached by a hustling lawyer who would offer to take the case to court on a contingent-fee basis. "And all the time," President Taft, who favored changing the system, said in an address, "the ambulance chaser and the lawyers are thriving on the business—I used to be a lawyer and I dare say of the profession what I choose."

The members of the profession whom Taft had in mind usually charged the injured workman a fee in the neighborhood of 50 per cent of the hoped-for judgment or settlement; often it was more. If the workman won in the lower court, the insurance company appealed the case to higher courts. The litigation was exhausting and expensive. The settlement of one case took eighteen years. On the average it took between six and seven years to settle such cases in California. To avoid lengthy litigation, negotiated settlements became increasingly frequent; the cash settlements were usually low and unfair to the workman but were promptly offered and readily accepted because the injured employee lacked funds to support himself or his family. Occasionally a resourceful lawyer possessing a way with juries would win an award that was out of all proportion to the merit of the case. But approximately one third of the injured employees never received any settlement. The operation of employers' liability insurance congested the courts, engendered bad feeling between employers and employees, and brought but small relief to injured workers.

To provide a more just and less economically wasteful

method of handling the problem of occupational accidents, leaders of labor and industry advanced the idea of workmen's compensation around the beginning of the present century. Proponents of this concept held that the cost of industrial accidents should properly be considered one of the costs of production. An employer should be obligated to pay the cost of injuries to his employees just as he pays the costs incident to the repair and maintenance of his machinery, tools, and factories. Therefore, an employer should be responsible to his employees for every accident arising from employment, regardless of negligence. To avoid litigation, injuries sustained in the course of employment should be compensated in accordance with a definite schedule of payments, the amount determined by the severity of the injury. Under this plan the employee would surrender his right to sue for large damages; in return, he would have the assurance of receiving stipulated amounts promptly, with no expense or uncertainty. And since the expense involved in taking care of occupational accidents is a legitimate cost factor, it should be added into the employer's other costs of production and used to determine the price of his product.

Though workmen's compensation was a new concept in America, it had for years been an established practice in Europe. Germany passed compensation legislation in 1884, and by 1910 similar laws were in effect in every leading European country. In this country, compensation legislation was resisted on various grounds, such as the fear that it would prohibitively increase the costs of production, encourage habitual malingering, and even spell the end of free enterprise. An accident compensation law was nevertheless passed in Maryland in 1902 and a few years afterward in Montana and New York. All were declared unconstitutional by state courts, the opinion being that such legislation held the employer liable without fault, deprived him of property without due process of law, and denied to both employers and employees the right of trial by jury. The compensation movement continued to be pressed, however. It was given great impetus when a federal law, covering certain federal employees and actively sponsored by Theodore Roosevelt, was upheld in 1908. Nine years later, the United States Supreme Court declared that workmen's compensation legislation is a valid exercise of the police power. By that time, workmen's compensation laws were on the statute books of thirty-seven states and territories.

As soon as workmen's compensation became an accomplished fact, the industrial community was faced with the problem of providing itself with protection against liability for occupational accidents. To furnish this protection at cost, scores of mutual companies were formed by employers throughout the country. It was a logical and promising field for the successful operation of the mutual principle because, among other reasons, the opportunities for loss prevention were abundant. The mutual idea, having proved its value over a period of a century and a half in the field of fire insurance, was prepared to establish its worth in the field of casualty insurance.

CHAPTER XVI

Casualty Insurance on the March

ALMOST a quarter of a century before enactment of the first constitutional workmen's compensation law in this country, there was founded in Boston a company that was destined to become one of the leading writers of compensation insurance as well as one of the foremost mutual casualty companies. This was the American Mutual Liability Insurance Company, founded in 1887. A venerable and genteel organization, it can rightfully claim to be the oldest mutual liability company in the United States. It was founded to protect employers in Massachusetts against loss from damage suits arising from operation of the Massachusetts Employers Liability Law of 1887. When employers' liability legislation was superseded in the Bay State in 1912 by workmen's compensation legislation, American Mutual began writing in the new field. In 1950, it did $34 million of compensation business, thus ranking third in the writing of that line among all mutual companies. With its associated companies—the Allied American Mutual Fire Insurance Company and the American Policyholders' Insurance Company—American Mutual now furnishes practically all forms of insurance except life. It is the fifth largest mutual casualty company in the country.

During its early years, the company proceeded at a conservative pace. Its founders consisted of a group of Boston gentlemen, most of whom were executives in the textile and paper industries. One of them, William Croad Lovering, who was treasurer of the Whittenton Manufacturing Company, was elected the first president of American Mutual. He held the post for twenty-three years. Though he assisted in securing business, he never maintained desk space in the office, his position being largely titular. In 1897, he was elected to Congress and devoted his remaining years to politics. The company's original full-time employees consisted of a vice-president and general manager, a secretary, a safety engineer, and a bookkeeper. The last was Charles Edward Hodges, who was to become the outstanding figure in the organization. With the exception of the engineer, all the employees came to work in top hats and morning coats, a costume that was worn for directors' meetings as late as the 1920s.

Though Edward Atkinson, the Factory Mutual leader, was not a director of American Mutual, he was very much interested in it and frequently provided suggestions and advice. He is said to have rebuked the company for soliciting business. To Atkinson, the economic advantages of a mutual company were so self-evident that they should, he felt, appeal at once to the intelligence of any buyer of insurance. It was more dignified, he said, to wait for the buyer to recognize this obvious truth than to endeavor to persuade him. American Mutual, a company that has never lacked dignity, listened respectfully to this advice but did not necessarily subscribe to it, the officers being moderately anxious to avoid starvation.

In 1890, after the first two general managers had departed to seek their fortunes elsewhere, the directors of American Mutual appointed a lawyer named Russell Gray to that post.

Gray was not without eccentricities, one of which was his refusal to ride in an elevator with another passenger to reach the offices of American Mutual, which were on the upper floor of a large office building. Since he had made this emphatically clear to the building personnel, they worked out a plan of posting a man on watch each morning outside the building around the time Gray was due to arrive. When he loomed into sight, the lookout signaled the elevator starter, who sealed off an elevator for the exclusive use of the building's touchy tenant. A man who did not quickly embrace newfangled notions, Gray signed all letters and documents with a quill pen, and though he permitted installation of a telephone in the office, he conceived an aversion to the device and used it only in extreme emergencies. American Mutual was one of the last companies in Boston to employ female stenographers. "If they're pretty," Gray announced, "the boys won't do any work—if they're not pretty, I don't want 'em!"

The enterprising man in the company was Charles Edward Hodges. Born in Boston, he had set out to be a lawyer. Finding the law not to his taste, he went to the Orient and spent two years in Shanghai in the tea business. Back in America, he worked for a while in Chicago and Detroit and then returned to Boston, where he joined American Mutual at its inception. He was then twenty-eight. An ardent sailor in his spare time and one of the first men in the country to embrace the game of golf, Hodges made the building up of American Mutual his life's work.

During Gray's regime, Hodges assumed a steadily increasing amount of management responsibility. When Gray became president in 1910, Hodges was elected treasurer and thereafter took over to an even greater extent the active direction of the company, engineering its expansion into the national field. The first venture outside of Massachusetts was the opening of a branch office in Pennsylvania in 1911. Six years later, a period during which the company's assets increased from $858,000 to $3.7 million, Hodges succeeded Gray in the presidency. American Mutual continued to grow in territory and in volume. By 1920, the company was licensed in twenty-nine states. In 1923, premiums reached $10 million; in 1929, they climbed to $16.4 million. Expansion in territory, coverages, and volume continued under the close direction of President Hodges. He remained the dominant force in the company until his retirement at the age of seventy-six, in 1935. He was succeeded by his son, Charles E. Hodges, under whose direction American Mutual has grown to the point at which it now has some 3,000 employees and assets exceeding $100 million.

American Mutual has established a reputation for, among other things, the high quality of its claims and engineering service. In its claims work, the company is guided by a motto adopted many years ago by Russell Gray. A renowned Greek scholar, Gray chose as a slogan an ancient aphorism which, when translated, means "Deal with thine adversary promptly." (Carved on a panel of wood, the motto now hangs on a wall of President Hodges' office.) To see that this principle is carried into practice, American Mutual, unlike many companies which employ outside adjusters, maintains its own claims department staffed by salaried employees. Of all its claims, the company believes that approximately 99 per cent are not contested and that, of the remaining 1 per cent, more than half are settled to the company's satisfaction.

American Mutual, which employed a safety engineer the day it opened for business, has ever since demonstrated a marked and thorough interest in all aspects of loss prevention.

From 1920 to 1948, the company's activities in that field were under the direction of C. Eugene Pettibone, one of the leaders in the broad and enlightened approach of mutual casualty companies to loss-prevention engineering. American Mutual now employs 150 engineers, who survey all risks, carry on a constant inspection service, and work with policyholders to set up specific accident-prevention programs. Besides the work of its safety engineers, American Mutual provides its policyholders with numerous educational publications, such as a twenty-page magazine called *Loss Control,* which is issued quarterly and directed primarily toward management and supervisory personnel. Other material includes monthly safety bulletins and a wide range of technical material published in book form. One of these, written by a member of American Mutual's engineering staff and titled *Engineering Aspects of Property Damage in Open-Cut Construction,* has been used for many years as a textbook at the Massachusetts Institute of Technology. Another technical booklet, ninety-four pages in length and bearing the title *Foremanship and Accident Prevention in Industry,* was written by Arthur S. Johnson, the present head of the company's loss-prevention program. During World War II, when the training of foremen became an acute problem, Mr. Johnson's book was in great demand not only by industry but also by the armed services. It has been used all over the world and has so far been translated into ten languages, including the Hindustani.

"American Mutual does not treat injuries—it treats men," an executive of the company once said in describing American's approach to providing medical care for its policyholders' injured workers. Some six thousand leading physicians situated in all parts of the country are available to treat the company's patients. American Mutual also maintains three clinics—in Boston, Newark, and Baltimore—for the treatment of injured workers; the clinics are equipped to administer therapy and perform minor surgery. In severe cases, such as amputations, American Mutual provides rehabilitation treatment at the Institute for the Crippled and Disabled, in New York, or at a similar institution in other cities. The company is proud of the fact that it often invests time and money to provide treatment to an injured person when it is under no legal obligation to do so.

American Mutual has been a leader in sponsoring research in industrial medicine. One of its recent projects was a three-year study of low back pain, which is among the most common of industrial ailments. The results of that study, carried out with the co-operation of the Harvard Medical School and the Massachusetts General Hospital, have been published in a forty-two-page booklet under the title *Syllabus on Industrial Low Back Pain* and made available to the medical profession. Research sponsored by American Mutual on intervertebral disk injuries was set in motion ten years ago and is still going on.

Perhaps American Mutual's chief achievement in this field has been its sponsorship of a series of seminars on industrial medicine and surgery. The purpose of these meetings is to bring to physicians the best available and most up-to-date information on professional techniques and practices in the field of industrial medicine and surgery. The first seminar was held in 1939; sixteen others had been conducted up to the beginning of 1950. At these meetings, which have been held in a number of principal cities, leading physicians and surgeons present papers on a varied range of topics, such as "The Early Treatment of Severe Burns" and "Current Trends in the Management of Wounds," and in general discuss and pool their knowledge on industrial medical matters. At intervals, the papers presented at the seminars are collected and published in booklets, which are made available to doctors and others with an interest in the field. The company has also sponsored seminars for industrial nurses, twelve of which have been held since their inception in 1944. Through its seminars, American Mutual feels that it is making a long-range, practical contribution to the prevention of loss in industry.

In 1943, American adopted as a kind of trade-mark or talisman a fine-looking figure of a man to whom it gave the name "Mr. Friendly." The company has since built its publicity and advertising around him—he appears on all publications, on the air, and even on notices of overdue premium payments—because it believes that he epitomizes what one of the executives has described as "the spirit of prompt, friendly American service." Many other people are inclined to agree. Possessing a cheerful aspect and an air of gentility, Mr. Friendly is attired in a black suit, white vest, a derby reminiscent in style of the Gay Nineties, and a pair of spectacles attached to his lapel with a silk ribbon. Generally he carries a brief case and an umbrella. The total effect he produces is that of a conservative, honorable, unhurried Bostonian. Mr. Friendly observed, in a letter appearing over his signature in the company's 1950 report, that since its organization American Mutual had paid dividends to policyholders of more than $142.5 million—a piece of information that will do no harm to his popularity.

In contrast to the American Mutual, which, as noted, was originally organized to write employers' liability insurance and later entered the workmen's compensation field, a great many mutual casualty companies were founded for the specific purpose of writing compensation insurance exclusively. One of the earliest of these was brought into existence in Wisconsin, the state which has the distinction of being the first to pass a workmen's compensation law to be held constitutional by the courts. The law became effective September 1, 1911.

On that day one of the very first workmen's compensation insurance policies written in this country was issued by the Employers Mutual Liability Insurance Company, of Wausau, Wisconsin. The policy was issued to the Wausau Sulphate Fiber Company, now known as the Mosinee Paper Mills. The insurance is still in force. Up to the close of 1949, the Mosinee Paper Mills had paid premiums totaling $666,632 for their compensation insurance; they had received dividends totaling $131,779, or an average annual dividend of 19.8 per cent. Since the memorable day when its first policy was issued, the Employers Mutual has grown to the point at which it is now the second largest writer of workmen's compensation insurance in the United States.

Like many other mutual casualty companies, the Employers was founded by a group of industrial men who were primarily interested in forming a company to provide compensation coverage for their own firms. Most of the founders of Employers Mutual were members of the Wisconsin River Improvement Association, an organization composed mainly of lumber and paper companies. The founders gave their services to the new insurance company without charge. They were well acquainted with the mutual principle, since mutual fire insurance companies had already had a long and successful history in their state. Furthermore, the adaptation of the mutual idea to provide compensation insurance had been officially recommended by the legislative committee that framed the Wisconsin law. "Under section 26," the committee report stated, "we have given to employers an opportunity to organize, under the laws of this state, mutual insurance companies to carry the new risk. Strong mutual insurance companies clearly have been shown to be the cheapest, safest, and most reliable method by which the risk herein created can be taken care of."

Though aided by a climate favoring the mutual idea, the Employers Mutual was setting out to break ground in a new field of insurance, and it soon discovered that not all of the elements it had to deal with were so beneficent. The company embarked on the venture with a staff which, though small, was energetic and devoted. One of the first employees was a young man with a progressive social and political outlook named H. J. Hagge, who went to work for the company five weeks after its founding. He had had no experience in insurance. That was all right with the directors. "This is a new thing," they told Hagge. "We don't want to get old dogs and try to teach them new tricks." Within two years, the young man was elected secretary and general manager, and since 1931 he has served as president. Two other early employees were W. H. Burhop, who is now executive vice-president, and B. E. Kuechle, who is vice-president and claim manager. Before joining Employers Mutual, both had worked for the Industrial Commission of Wisconsin, which administers the state's compensation law.

The framers of that law, to make sure that it would not be declared unconstitutional, originally made its acceptance optional by individual employers and their employees. An employer who elected to come under the law was obligated to post a notice in his plant to that effect. Employees were then given thirty days to inform the employer whether or not they wanted to be bound by the law; in the absence of notice to the contrary, they were automatically covered. As a lever to encourage employers to subscribe to compensation legislation, the Wisconsin act deprived them of two of their important legal defenses if they did not. An employer who rejected the law was no longer able to escape liability in an action for damages for accidental injury by using the defense that the workman had assumed the hazards inherent in the occupation or that his injury resulted from the negligence of a fellow employee. Gradually, employers were deprived of their other archaic common-law defenses. Thus, it was made increasingly clear that it behooved them to fall in step with the parade.

They were, however, counseled to stay out of it by the stock casualty companies, which had been doing a very satisfactory business writing employers' liability insurance. They had exerted themselves in lobbying against passage of the compensation law and, having failed there, began an intensive campaign to urge employers not to sign acceptance agreements. According to the stock company propaganda, judgments in injury suits were bound to increase because of the removal of the employer's legal defenses. Therefore, stock company rates on employers' liability insurance would have to be doubled. But employers who chose to be bound by workmen's compensation—and thus make themselves financially responsible for every occupational accident—would have their rates quadrupled. This campaign was effective for a while, but eventually it petered out. Trying a new tack, the stock companies then blanketed employers with letters, circulars, and other published matter designed to discredit the Employers Mutual, its management, finances, philosophy, and practices. The most widely circulated of these was a twenty-page booklet that was not only mailed in great quantities to businessmen but was also distributed in stacks to offices, stores, banks, and even to barbershops.

"We were panic-stricken," Mr. Hagge has recalled. "We were just getting started. We didn't have the time or the money to spend trying to counteract that barrage. Our slogan was 'Insure for your men—not against them.' Actually, we didn't have a darned thing to sell except the idea. In those days, we sold insurance on the basis of the high standing and reputation of the men on our board. I remember going to see a prospect one day, but I hadn't gotten very far before he said, 'Why, I have never even seen one of your company's statements. What are your assets?' I told him they were $21,000. 'Uh-huh,' he said. 'And what is your surplus?' 'The present surplus is $3,000,' I told him. 'But never mind about those figures,' I said. 'Look at the men on our board,' and I went down the list. 'Now,' I said, 'you know these men wouldn't lend their names to a wildcat venture. They wouldn't be in this thing unless they considered it a sound idea.' Well, it worked, and we got the business, but all we had to sell was confidence in a good idea."

Despite a severe rate-cutting war launched by the stock companies in 1915 and terminated by intervention of the state insurance authorities in 1917, the Employers Mutual grew rapidly during its first fifteen years. In 1911, its first year, premiums had been $39,000 and surplus $9,000. In 1925, premium income had reached $2.8 million, and surplus had passed $1 million. During the first fifteen years, the company's operating expense had been held to 17.4 per cent of the earned premium, which was less than one half the expense ratio of stock companies. By that time, Employers Mutual was the leading writer of workmen's compensation insurance in Wisconsin, its business being greater than the combined compensation premiums of any twelve stock companies operating in the state. The Employers Mutual had begun to branch out and was also writing workmen's compensation business in Minnesota, Michigan, and Illinois. To provide its policyholders with other casualty coverages, the company organized the Employers Mutual Indemnity Corporation in 1923; its business was taken over by the parent company in 1937. Two years earlier, the Employers Mutual Fire Insurance Company had been founded and was managed by the same officers as its casualty companion. The two companies became known as the Employers Mutuals of Wausau.

Though some three dozen coverages were now being offered, workmen's compensation continued to be the predominant line. In 1934, Employers Mutual ranked tenth in compensation writings among all companies in the United States. By 1939, it ranked fifth. In 1950, it ranked second. The company now operates in all states as well as in Alaska and Hawaii; the bulk of its business has always been written by salaried representatives, and it offers complete casualty and surety coverages. In 1950, net premiums totaled $64 million. Of this amount, approximately two thirds was derived from workmen's compensation. Employers Mutual now has assets exceeding $100 million; surplus, in 1950, amounted to $16.4 million; and since its organization it has returned in dividends to its policyholders more than $60 million.

"To provide mutual protection and, by co-operation and the reduction of hazard, furnish the compensations required by the law at actual cost"—that was the way the Employers Mutual, in a booklet issued in 1911, originally defined its purpose. Four decades later, the purpose remains unchanged. Through the years, the brisk competition provided by Employers Mutual and by the other mutual casualty companies has had the salutary effect of forcing down the casualty rates of all companies, particularly in the field of workmen's compensation insurance. The results can be seen, among other places, in Wisconsin, the home state of Employers Mutual. Since 1911, when the workmen's compensation law was enacted, the benefit level has increased a little more than 150 per cent. Yet at the end of 1949 the compensation rate level was 3.5 per cent less than it was in 1911.

At the root of this notable accomplishment is the prevention of loss, a field in which mutual companies have consistently been the pioneers and leaders. "Reduction of hazard —to reduce the number of accidents—constitutes one of the chief purposes of this company," the Employers Mutual explained in a booklet issued at the time the company was launched. "WE DO NOT WANT YOUR MONEY," the statement continued emphatically, "nor do we want to carry your risk, unless you are ready to assist in an earnest effort to carry out the provisions of the Compensation Law, and will lend your aid in every reasonable manner to reduce the hazards and dangers tending to industrial accidents."

Besides requiring high preventive standards from its policyholders, the company early began its own efforts to discover and reduce the causes of occupational accidents. Soon after joining the company in 1914, Mr. B. E. Kuechle undertook the task of charting the causes of the first 8,000 accidents reported to the Industrial Commission of Wisconsin after passage of the compensation law. Since he had no tabulating machine, Mr. Kuechle performed his research with pencil and paper. In 1932, Employers Mutual established a laboratory in Milwaukee to conduct research into silicosis and other industrial diseases and to devise methods of controlling or eliminating the hazards that cause them.

The continued expansion of the loss-prevention activities of Employers Mutual has kept pace with, and in large measure been responsible for, the company's remarkable expansion of business. Through its corps of safety engineers, its industrial hygiene division, its industrial nursing service, its physiotherapy department, and its educational publications and films, Employers Mutual carries out a rounded loss-prevention program that ranks among the most progressive in the country. The company is especially proud of its prevention record during World War II, when it carried compensation insurance on dozens of government plants and installations, including powder plants and ammunition depots. One of its current policies covers some 7,500 workers on a mammoth government construction project on Guam. The premiums on this policy run to about a million dollars a year.

Probably no one is better qualified to suggest the reasons for the development of Employers Mutual in the past forty years from an idea into the fifth largest mutual casualty company in the country than Mr. H. J. Hagge, who has guided its destinies almost from the very beginning. "In a nutshell," he said not long ago, "it's absolute sincerity of purpose and square dealing—the application of a kind of hard-headed Golden Rule. It has never been our policy to short-change anybody, and we haven't made any exceptions. After forty years in business, we can still look every one of our policyholders, claimants, and employees in the eye. It's a comfortable feeling."

About thirty miles from Wausau, Wisconsin, where the home office of Employers Mutual is located, is the hustling town of Stevens Point. In 1913, this was the home of the Hardware Dealers Mutual Fire Insurance Company, which had been founded ten years earlier, and under the direction of its secretary and manager, P. J. Jacobs, had already become well established. With the advent of workmen's compensation, Mr. Jacobs saw the wisdom in organizing a mutual casualty company to provide compensation insurance to the hardware firms and other business establishments to which the company was already furnishing fire insurance. Under his leadership, the Hardware Mutual Casualty Company was accordingly founded in 1913, and began business the following year.

The casualty company's first employee was the founder's son, Carl N. Jacobs. A well-known insurance executive, Mr. Carl N. Jacobs is now president of both the Hardware Dealers Mutual Fire Insurance Company and the Hardware Mutual Casualty Company, which are among the leading mutual companies in their respective fields. In its compensation writing, the casualty company started out to specialize in the smaller business firms, or what Mr. Jacobs describes as "Main Street risks," in Wisconsin. The company has since expanded its scope and territory until it now writes the full casualty line, except for fidelity and surety and boiler and machinery, and operates in all states through more than six hundred full-time salaried salesmen. Net premium writings in 1950 totaled $38.8 million, of which $23 million was derived from automobile coverages. The Hardware Mutuals, as the fire and casualty companies are jointly known, offer a striking example of the development of casualty insurance. Though ten years younger than its companion fire company, the Hardware Mutual Casualty Company does more than three times as much business.

As workmen's compensation laws were enacted in state after state, mutual casualty companies sprang up to provide protection against the new risk. In Michigan, workmen's compensation legislation became effective September 12, 1912. The same day the Michigan Mutual Liability Company began business. It now writes more compensation business in Michigan than any other company. The Michigan Mutual operates throughout the country, offering most casualty coverages, and in 1950 had net premium writings exceeding $24 million. In 1913, the Texas Legislature passed a compensation law, and as part of that legislation created a mutual company—the Texas Employers Insurance Association—to provide business and industry in the Lone Star State with workmen's compensation insurance at cost. In 1950, the Texas Employers Insurance Association wrote $15.3 million of workmen's compensation insurance, and, in keeping with the principle on which it was founded, returned to its policyholders $1.8 million in dividends.

Between 1910 and 1920, forty-two states and three territories passed workmen's compensation laws. During that eventful decade, premiums of mutual casualty insurance companies increased from $1.1 million to $53.1 million.

CHAPTER XVII

A Midwestern Saga

IN 1911, forty years after the much-maligned Mrs. O'Leary had testified under oath that she was safe abed the night the great Chicago fire broke out and knew nothing about it until roused by a friend of the family, Chicago had become the commercial and industrial metropolis of the West. High on its list of booming industries was the lumber business. At that time, Chicago was the lumber capital of the country. Into its harbors came the schooners of Lake Michigan, laden with timber from the virgin forests of Wisconsin, Minnesota, and northern Michigan. Sailing up the Chicago River, they discharged their cargoes at the mammoth lumberyards that honeycombed its banks. Business was humming. Lumbermen were prosperous and influential.

They were also preoccupied with a common problem. Illinois was preparing to enact a workmen's compensation law, and lumbermen were concerned for two main reasons. First, more than ordinary hazards attended their industry, and accidents were frequent. Second, lumbermen had been informed that stock company rates for coverage under the projected law would be four times higher than the rates then being charged for employers' liability insurance. It was therefore natural that insurance matters should have been the inescapable topic of conversation at meetings of the Lumbermens Association of Chicago and of the Illinois Retail Lumber Dealers Association. The members of both groups concluded that the stock company rates for coverage under the impending legislation, scheduled to become effective on May 1, 1912, were excessive. Early in 1912, each association accordingly appointed a committee to explore the feasibility of organizing a mutual company to provide its members with workmen's compensation insurance.

Working closely with the investigating groups was an up-and-coming young insurance man named James S. Kemper. Though then only twenty-six, he had already begun to cut quite a figure in Midwest insurance circles. Destined to become one of the most successful men in the industry, he had chosen insurance as his life's work at an early age. He was born in Van Wert, Ohio, and attended the public schools there. His father was a lawyer and many of his ancestors had been either lawyers or clergymen. At the age of eleven, James made up his mind that he would not pursue the ministry. One stormy Sunday morning, being the only boy in his class to appear at church, he was placed in the Bible class which was composed of adults. There he heard a report from a missionary recently returned from China. At the close of the missionary's address, James questioned him closely. He was disturbed to learn that, having once been exposed to Christianity, heathens who then rejected it automatically went to hell. Those who had not been exposed to the gospel fared better, since they were eligible for heaven if they lived up to the tenets of the only religion they knew. As Kemper has since jokingly remarked, he decided then and there that he would steer clear of an operation that might damn as many souls as it saved. Though not choosing to follow one of the ancestral professions, he has been very active in the work of religious institutions. He has served as president of the Presbyterian Union of Chicago, and he is also a trustee of McCormick Theological Seminary.

Having decided to enter business, Kemper went to work upon graduation from high school in 1905 for the Central Mutual Insurance Company, of Van Wert. As an apprentice at a wage of one dollar a day, he worked in the company's home office, learning the business. One of his first jobs was to make copies of all letters in an old-fashioned letter press. To the astonishment of his superiors, Kemper requested and was given permission to read all the day's mail each evening. He had decided that by studying the day's correspondence he could most quickly become familiar with all phases of the company's business. Before long he had acquired the reputation of being able to pinch-hit anywhere in the office.

Possessing a native talent for selling, Kemper was promoted after two years in the office to a job in the field. He traveled through western Ohio and Indiana, contacting agents and policyholders, inspecting risks and writing business. By the time he was old enough to cast his first vote, he was an experienced fire insurance field man, ready for further promotion. Two positions were offered him. One was a partnership in an insurance agency in Dayton, Ohio, and the other a partnership in a brokerage office in New York City. Kemper elected to by-pass both opportunities, although each offered a considerably larger income than he was receiving. His ambition, based on a number of conversations with Frank W. Purmort, secretary and general manager of the Central, was to open a mutual insurance agency in Chicago. The opportunity to realize this ambition came when the Associated Lumber Mutuals decided to select a committee of one man from each company to explore the reasons for the adverse loss of ratio the Lumber Mutuals had experienced in Wisconsin, Minnesota, and the Dakotas. Kemper was selected to represent the Central.

The upshot of the investigation was the organization of the Lumbermens and Manufacturers Insurance Agency of Chicago, with Kemper as manager, to represent the Lumber Mutuals in Cook County, Illinois, northern Michigan, Wisconsin, North and South Dakota, Iowa, Nebraska, and Canada from the Sault to the Rocky Mountains. Renting a small office, he sold insurance by day and wrote up policies by longhand at night. The first major insurance order he received in Chicago came from a large agricultural implement manufacturer. "I'll never forget the satisfaction that order gave me," Kemper has since recalled, "nor, for that matter, my embarrassment when at the conclusion of our interview the insurance manager said, 'Now that we have disposed of that, there is one question I should like to ask—how old are you, anyway?' " Soon afterward Kemper grew a mustache.

Meanwhile, he had also been working with the committees of the two lumber associations that were considering the organization of one or more mutual companies to provide themselves with workmen's compensation insurance. There was considerable sentiment favoring the establishment of a separate company by each association. Kemper became convinced, and was able in turn to convince the two associations, that their needs would best be served by the founding of one company to serve all members of the industry.

During the year and a half that he had managed the mutual agency in Chicago, Kemper had won the support and confidence of several of the city's leading businessmen, including influential members of the lumber associations. When it came

WISCONSIN WORKMEN'S COMPENSATION FORM
GUARANTEE FUND PLAN

POLICY NO. 1

Employer's Mutual Liability Insurance Company

OF WISCONSIN

In consideration of the premium required for this Policy and of the statements set forth in the application herefor, the EMPLOYERS MUTUAL LIABILITY INSURANCE COMPANY of WISCONSIN, hereinafter called the "Company"

HEREBY INSURES AND AGREES TO INDEMNIFY

Wausau Sulphate Fibre Company

as a member of said Company, and hereinafter referred to as the "Insured,"

of Mosinee, County of Marathon, State of Wisconsin

beginning on the first day of September, 19 11, at 12 o'clock noon,

AGAINST LOSS OR EXPENSE BY REASON OF THE LIABILITY ON ACCOUNT OF THE CLAIMS ARISING, AND IMPOSED UPON THE INSURED BY CHAPTER 50, LAWS OF WISCONSIN, 1911, AND KNOWN AND REFERRED TO AS THE WORKMEN'S COMPENSATION ACT

and such insurance and agreement of indemnity shall continue while this policy remains in force by compliance with its conditions and requirements during the period covered by the stipulated premium and renewals thereof:

1. (a). The Company's liability under this Policy, for compensation on account of accident resulting in injuries to or in the death of one employe,—in addition to the medical and surgical treatment required under the law,— is limited to Three Thousand Dollars ($3000.); and subject to the same limit for each employe, the Company's liability for any one accident, resulting in injuries to or in the death of more than one such employe is limited to Twelve Thousand Dollars ($12,000.),—in addition to the medical and surgical treatment required under the law.

(b). PROVIDED, HOWEVER, that for indemnity under this Policy on account of accident resulting in bodily injuries or in the death of one employe, who, prior to such accident by notice to the insured, had elected not to be subject to the compensations of Chapter 50, Laws of Wisconsin, 1911, the Company's liability,—in addition to the necessary first aid for medical or surgical attention,—is limited to FIVE THOUSAND Dollars ($5000.); and subject to the same limit for each such employe, the Company's total liability for any one accident resulting in bodily injuries to or in the death of more than one such employe is limited to TEN THOUSAND Dollars ($10,000.), and in addition to such limits, the Company will assume and have charge of all settlements and pay all costs and expense in the trial and defense of suits and legal proceedings against the insured; provided also, that if the said Chapter 50, Laws of Wisconsin, 1911, be repealed or decided unconstitutional while this Policy is in force, then and in either such event the Company's liability shall be as provided in this sub-division and be governed by all the conditions and provisions applicable thereto.

(c). The Company shall not be liable on account of any accident resulting in injury to or in the death of any person employed contrary to any law of the State, nor for those employes whose compensation or wages are not included on the pay-roll upon which the premium contributions to the Company for the year are based, provided that this policy while in force shall extend to those employes whose compensation is included in the pay-roll for the adjustment of the premium for the year.

2. Upon the occurrence of an accident the insured shall give immediate written notice thereof, with the fullest information obtainable, by mailing such notice and information to the Home Office of the Company. The insured shall also mail to the Company the original or a copy of the notice to him of claim for injury by the employe, and a copy of all reports to the Industrial Commission of Wisconsin relating to such accident, and the original or copy of all communications received by him in relation thereto from said Commission.

3. The insured at the time of the accident shall provide such immediate surgical relief as is imperative and required, employing for such purposes, if obtainable, the Company's regularly appointed surgeon, and if not obtainable, the nearest qualified physician, and all bills for the necessary medical and surgical treatment incurred during the disability caused by such injury, not exceeding ninety days, shall be verified by the insured and promptly forwarded to the Company for payment or reimbursement.

PIONEER WORKMEN'S COMPENSATION POLICY

ne first constitutional workmen's compensation law was enacted by the state of isconsin and became effective September 1, 1911. On the same date, the above licy was issued. It is one of the first—if not the first—workmen's compensation surance policies written in the United States. The insurance is still in force.

Movies in the Making

As part of its crusade to save the lives of young drivers, the Lumbermens Mutu Casualty Company has produced two dramatic sound motion pictures, *Last Da* (above) and *Sergeant Bruce Reporting* (below). The latter was made with th technical assistance of the Los Angeles Police Department. Both movies have wo several awards, and each has been seen by millions.

to selecting a manager for the new company to write compensation insurance, Kemper had many sponsors promoting his candidacy, and he was chosen for the position.

The solicitation of applications for insurance began in October 1912, and the organizational work was completed in record-breaking time. The company received its charter on November 18, which coincided with Kemper's twenty-sixth birthday. One week later, the Lumbermens Mutual Casualty Company (known within the organization as LMC) began active business with the issuance of workmen's compensation policies to twenty-nine lumber and woodworking firms.

To secure a license, it was necessary that the company have $20,000 cash in the bank. Kemper and Edwin E. Hooper, secretary of the Lumbermens Association of Chicago, borrowed this sum from a Chicago bank and repaid it a few weeks later when the new policies had been issued and the premiums collected. At the year's end, Lumbermens had written premiums of $29,000; it had assets of $28,000, and a surplus of $8,000.

Even before the company had received its license to do business, Kemper had engaged a safety engineer and a chief surgeon. Shortly thereafter he also hired a combination publicity man and safety committee secretary, H. L. Kennicott, who is now secretary and public relations director of the company. From the beginning, Kemper followed a special principle in selecting men for the organization. "Whenever a likely applicant came along," he has recalled, "we hired him—and decided afterward what job he best could handle."

Operating exclusively in Illinois at the outset, LMC wrote only workmen's compensation and manufacturers' public liability insurance on lumber and woodworking risks. No agents were employed. The company solicited business through salaried field men, who, under Kemper's constant encouragement, went to work with a will. Before long, the new company numbered among its policyholders most of the leading lumber and woodworking concerns in Illinois. "This result was rather a remarkable demonstration of sales genius on the one hand and confidence on the other," an official of the company later observed, "for it must be borne in mind that the principal asset of the new company in its first few years was adherence to a program and that at the outset the policyholders became subject to an assessment liability of five times their deposit premiums." In time, this liability was reduced to one premium, and in 1935 dropped altogether. Since then the company has issued only non-assessable policies. The company's early success was made more dramatic by the fact that Chicago at that time was a stock insurance stronghold.

In the beginning, LMC set its rates at half those charged by the stock companies. Since it was virtually impossible to ascertain costs in advance, the new mutual decided to collect only half a year's premiums and adjust the rate for the second half of the year on the basis of the first six months' experience. At the end of the first six months, losses were so small that the collection of the second premium was waived. At the end of a year, it was found that the losses incurred and the operating expense together amounted to only 40 per cent of the premiums collected for the first six months' coverage. Accordingly, the board of directors voted to declare the company's first dividend, which amounted to 25 per cent of the six months' premium. This made a total saving to the policyholders of 62 per cent of the stock company rate for the full year.

The dramatic disparity between LMC and stock company rates during the first year brought about developments that were not altogether unexpected. Soon the company was faced with intense and often cutthroat competition from scores of companies, many of which had been hurriedly organized by promoters to try to cash in on the new business provided by the compensation legislation. Very few of these, incidentally, lasted long. One of the large New England stock companies set up a branch in Chicago to tap the newly created market and to drive out, if possible, the competition that had sprung from the native soil. This company advertised that it would undercut any rate quoted by LMC by 50 per cent.

Despite such reckless competition, LMC continued to grow and to pay dividends of 25 per cent during its first four years, or until 1916. That was a year of minor crisis for the young company. It was faced with a sudden upsurge in claims arising in part from a rapid expansion of production for war and export. Increased claims were received in advance of any increase in premiums based on pay-roll re-evaluations. The directors of the company were concerned, and dividend payments were temporarily suspended, awaiting a final tally: At the end of the year, it was apparent that increased premiums would cancel out most of the increase in claims and that a moderate dividend might safely be declared. However, apprehensive of what the next year's experience might bring, Kemper suggested that all policyholders be notified that they would be paid a "basic" dividend of 10 per cent with an "additional" 5 per cent dividend for the year.

The response from policyholders to the notice of dividend rates was rather surprising. Kemper received scores of letters of commendation. This mystery was solved when he discovered that dividends received by many of the policyholders had been automatically entered into their companies' accounts by bookkeepers and that the companies' executives had been unaware until then of the amount of the dividend they had been receiving.

The directors of LMC were aware that a specialized company operating in a limited area was particularly vulnerable to cutthroat rate competition and to catastrophic losses. Consequently, they decided to extend the business into new territories and to diversify it with the addition of new casualty lines. Coverages like general public liability insurance, property damage, and teams' liability were added soon after the company was established. So was automobile insurance, which was to prove of tremendous importance. The company ventured into automobile liability insurance—and with dire predictions on the part of some contemporaries—as an accommodation to policyholders who were car owners.

The first order for an automobile policy was secured by James S. Kemper before the issuance of the company's charter, at the time that he was calling on lumbermen to solicit applications for workmen's compensation insurance. He was asked by one of the prospects upon whom he called, Frank J. Heitmann, if the new company would also insure his car. Kemper said it certainly would. The two men then began bargaining over setting a fair rate, based on the hazards involved in the use of the newfangled machine. Heitmann insisted that an automobile was at least twice as safe as a team of horses hauling a wagonload of lumber. Kemper contended that the thing might prove four or five times more dangerous. They compromised on a rate that was exactly twice the rate then charged for teams' liability insurance, and LMC's first automobile policy was subsequently issued to Heitmann and patterned in form after a teams' liability policy. Apparently, LMC's first automobile policyholder was satisfied. Now, forty years later, he serves on the company's Advisory Board.

In 1912, premium income from automobile insurance amounted to $123. In the following year, the figure shot up more than fivefold, to $694.35. Though not all of his associates agreed with him, Kemper was very much in favor of promoting the automobile line. By 1917, after incurring unusually heavy claims and being faced with intense competition in the workmen's compensation field, the company began going after automobile business with vigor. By 1921, automobile premiums went over a million dollars, outstripping compensation and becoming LMC's leading line. Today automobile insurance accounts for 57 per cent of the company's total premium income.

To round out its service, LMC steadily added other coverages, including plate glass, burglary, fidelity bonds, boiler and machinery, group health and accident and family hospitalization insurance. The company now writes the complete casualty line. Of its total premium income, 25 per cent is now derived from workmen's compensation. With the 57 per cent from automobile, these two lines now produce 82 per cent of the company's total premium income. An indication of LMC's growth in recent years is the fact that total premiums produced by the so-called minor lines (that is, excluding automobile and workmen's compensation) were greater in 1950 than total premiums produced by all lines in 1933.

From a local trade mutual, LMC gradually evolved into a company operating throughout the continent. Within six months of its founding the company was doing business in

Illinois, Indiana, and Wisconsin; by the end of its second year, branch offices had been established in several key cities. Today LMC operates in all forty-eight states, the District of Columbia, all of Canada (except Prince Edward Island and Newfoundland), Alaska, Hawaii.

With the expansion of its territory, LMC altered its method of acquiring business. At the start, as related earlier, all business was written by salaried employees. In order to write casualty insurance for their regular clients, some of the lumber fire mutuals represented by the Kemper agency also began in 1915 to sell LMC policies. As time passed, more and more business was written through agents in the home territory. Kemper soon decided that it would be feasible to operate under an agency plan in other regions as well. By 1919, it became necessary to set up an Eastern department with headquarters in Philadelphia, and by the close of 1923, several hundred well-established agencies were representing LMC in New England. The company now writes insurance only through agents. Kemper himself is interested in several Midwest agencies. The Lumbermens and Manufacturers Mutuals, Incorporated, which he established in 1911, has continued to operate as the Kemper agent for the lumber trade in the Chicago region and now collaborates with James S. Kemper and Company, LMC agents in the Chicago region.

From the time of its organization, Lumbermens followed two practices that were unique in casualty insurance. One was to provide policyholders each year with a complete list of all securities owned; the other was to issue all financial statements on an actual market-value basis. As a result of a conservative investment policy, which stemmed, in part, from these two procedures, Lumbermens was in a position during the difficult 1930s to take over, through merger, the business of several mutual casualty companies, whose business added substantially to LMC's volume.

In 1930, it absorbed the business of the Federal Mutual Liability Insurance Company, of Boston, which had been organized as a contractors' mutual in 1905 and had later expanded its writings to include compensation and liability for manufacturers. In 1931, LMC reinsured the outstanding policies of the Twin Mutual Liability Company of Boston, and in 1933, it reinsured the Illinois Manufacturers Mutual Casualty Association, founded in 1912 by a group of Illinois industrialists to write compensation insurance.

Today, forty years after its founding, the Lumbermens Mutual Casualty Company is one of the three largest mutual casualty companies in the country. Except for the two-year war period—1943–45—when, because of substantial rate reductions granted on automobile insurance in recognition of reduced hazards resulting from gas rationing and speed controls, premium income declined slightly, LMC's premium writings have expanded every year since the company was organized. In 1950, its total premium income exceeded $90 million. The company's surplus has increased every year, without exception; at the close of 1950, net surplus stood at $14 million. Dividends have been paid annually without interruption. By the end of 1950, the company had returned in savings to its policyholders dividends totaling more than $118 million.

From the day of its inception, the Lumbermens Mutual Casualty Company has been under the able management of James S. Kemper, who is now chairman of the corporation. The president of the company is Hathaway G. Kemper, a younger brother of the chairman. In 1912, when he was seventeen, Hathaway Kemper left his home in Ohio to go to work in the Chicago agency managed by his brother. After six months, during which he performed a variety of duties, he left to enter the University of Wisconsin to study mathematics, then as now one of his chief delights. With his brother's help and by working in his spare time, he remained in school for a year. Returning to Chicago, he resumed work in the agency as assistant manager of the claims department. Later he enlisted for service in World War I, after which he put in a spell selling insurance in Indiana. In the early twenties, he became manager of the Chicago agency. In 1928, he was elected executive vice-president of LMC, and has served as its president since 1946.

Considering that the Lumbermens Mutual Casualty Company was founded on the mutual principle, it is not surprising that one of the first departments created in the new company was a Division of Inspection and Accident Prevention. In the first year, an experienced safety engineer was employed to supervise inspections and to "reduce the cost by eliminating the cause." Despite aggressive selling, risks were selected carefully and efforts made to reduce accident hazards. As the company grew and as automobile insurance bulked larger in its business, LMC expanded its campaign for accident prevention beyond the confines of its own policyholders.

To formulate and direct a nationwide campaign for safe driving, LMC, in 1917, organized the Automobile Safety Committee. The oldest organization in the field, the Automobile Safety Committee has held more than 409 meetings since it was founded. Under its direction, a public safety advertising campaign was begun during the twenties. A number of effective safety handbooks, including *Accidents Are Preventable*, *Drivers Handbook*, and *Children's Safety Lessons*, were published and widely distributed.

Meanwhile, the Committee had made many discoveries contributing to highway accident prevention. It pioneered in "safe-braking" distance charts; it emphasized the hazards to children in running from behind parked cars; and it discovered and widely publicized the fact that the driver who weaves in traffic multiplies his chances of accident by seven. In 1940, the Committee summarized its studies in a report, *Why Ask for Accidents*, a booklet that has been kept in print to meet a steady, continuing demand. Through its Automobile Safety Committee, LMC has employed almost every medium of communication, including radio, magazine advertising, and motion pictures, to focus the nation's attention on the need for less speed and more conscience in driving.

In recent years, the Committee has concentrated its campaign on the teen-age, "accident-prone" group. Coining the word "teenicide," which has already found its way into one standard dictionary, the Committee has brought the problem of the younger driver before the public in a dramatic twenty-page booklet titled *Teen-Age Drivers*. "If a single catastrophe took the lives of 7,100 of our teen-agers and injured 320,000 more, the entire nation would be stunned," the booklet states. "Yet that was one year's tragic toll of young people killed and injured in traffic accidents." Originally published in December 1949, the booklet met immediately with great demand, 150,000 copies being distributed in the first six months. It has since been constantly reprinted.

The campaign to reduce teenicide has been further pressed by the initiation of annual college newspaper contests (289 entries in 1950) and by enlisting the aid of radio disk jockeys who have the ear of teen-agers. In 1950, LMC produced and distributed a sound movie titled *Last Date*, which tells a dramatic story of four teen-agers whose lives are tragically affected by the carelessness of one. It was received with such enthusiastic response, winning two noted awards and being seen by more than twelve million people, that the following year LMC put out a group of movies bearing the title *Sergeant Bruce Reporting*. Produced with the technical assistance of the Los Angeles Police Department, each of this series of thirteen separate, six-minute talking pictures deals graphically with a different, important aspect of safe driving. Tackling the safe-driving problem from the law-enforcement side, the Kemper Foundation for Traffic Safety annually awards eight competitive scholarships and eight fellowships to the Northwestern University Traffic Institute. There specialists in traffic problems train police officers in the latest and best methods of traffic control.

Separately administered but allied in general purpose is the James S. Kemper Foundation, which was incorporated in 1942 "to assist worthy persons in securing an education designed to be particularly useful in the insurance business." The Foundation is supported by contributions from the Lumbermens Mutual Casualty Company, James S. Kemper, and other individuals and firms in the Kemper organization. The Foundation has granted scholarships for postgraduate work in industrial medicine and surgery at Northwestern University Medical School and the University of Pittsburgh. Other grants have been for courses in actuarial science at the University of Manitoba, fire-protection engineering at Illinois Institute of Technology, industrial hygiene at Harvard University, and for the regular course in Ripon College with postgraduate training in one of several universities.

Though the oldest and largest, the Lumbermens Mutual Casualty Company is but one of a group of closely affiliated companies founded by, or under the direct management of, James S. Kemper. This group comprises an extensive fleet known collectively as Kemper Insurance. The flagship is, of course, the Lumbermens Mutual Casualty Company. Sailing with it is the National Retailers Mutual Insurance Company, considered in an earlier chapter. Another component is the Federal Mutual Fire Insurance Company, of Boston, which became part of the organization in 1928; later, the Twin Mutual Fire Insurance Company was merged with the Federal. The company writes general fire business through local agents, and in 1950 the premium writings totaled $1.6 million. Joining the fleet in 1946, the American Farmers Mutual Insurance Company was founded to specialize in automobile and other casualty lines in rural areas. Its premium writings in 1950 amounted to $4.8 million.

Supplementing the facilities of the mutual companies, the Kemper group includes three stock companies, two of which operate on a participating basis; the third is a reinsurance carrier.

Altogether, the companies comprising Kemper Insurance had combined total premium writings in 1950 of more than $123 million. Their combined assets exceed $181 million, and they have accumulated a surplus of more than $25 million. Since starting business, the companies have returned more than $144 million in dividend savings to their policyholders. Together, the companies employ some five thousand people. In 1948, the Lumbermens Mutual Casualty Company purchased the forty-two-story skyscraper which when completed in 1930 was called the Chicago Civic Opera Building. Now known as the Kemper Insurance Building, it will eventually harbor the entire fleet.

Today, as in the past, James S. Kemper is at the helm of all the companies. He is chairman and a director of each, and also serves as president of two. His other insurance posts, as indicated earlier, are manifold. Aside from his insurance role, Kemper has figured on the national scene as president of the United States Chamber of Commerce and as the holder of numerous offices in the Republican party, most recently as treasurer of its National Committee. Having a particular interest in hemispheric relations, he served as president of the United States delegation to the American Conference of Associations of Commerce and Production in Montevideo. Later he served for three years as president of the Inter-American Council of Commerce and Production, and continues as a member of its executive committee. For his services in promoting inter-American friendship and solidarity, Kemper was decorated by the President of Brazil as a Commander of the Order of the Southern Cross and by the President of Ecuador as a Commander of the National Order of Merit. An indication of his other interests is the fact that he has held office or is a member of some three dozen other commercial, political, social, educational, and philanthropic organizations.

One of the outstanding and most successful men in the insurance industry, James S. Kemper in the past forty years has erected a towering and diversified insurance structure, writing practically every kind of insurance except life. Underlying the growth of Kemper Insurance are many factors, one of which has been voiced by the founder. "We started with certain ideals," James S. Kemper has said. "We never grew careless of them."

CHAPTER XVIII

Mutual Insurance on Trial

IN MANY RESPECTS, New York has provided an uncommonly useful laboratory for testing mutual casualty insurance, particularly in the field of workmen's compensation. The Empire State was among the first to enact compulsory compensation legislation. Being the largest manufacturing state in the nation, it has the greatest number of workers covered by a compensation law. And from the beginning, the State of New York has actively competed with private insurance companies by offering workmen's compensation insurance to New York employers through a state-controlled and state-operated fund. In New York, therefore, mutual casualty companies have had to prove themselves in competition not only with stock companies but also with an enterprise enjoying the blessings of the state.

Because of New York's large and progressive labor force, agitation for improving the legal position of employees in their unequal struggle under the employers' liability doctrine began late in the nineteenth century. This effort culminated in the passage of an accident compensation law in 1910. The state courts declared the law unconstitutional the following year. However, a state constitutional amendment paved the way for remedial action, and New York enacted a compulsory workmen's compensation law in 1914. The benefits it provided to injured workmen were then the highest in the country, or in the world. They still are.

The New York law allowed four plans of insuring compensation. First was the State Fund, to be set up and administered by the Workmen's Compensation Commission. The State Fund was authorized to collect premiums from employers and to apply the premiums in the payment of compensation to claimants. The administrative expenses of the State Fund were to be paid for the first two and one half years by the State of New York. Second, employers were permitted to self-insure their compensation, provided proof of their financial stability was established to the satisfaction of the Commission. Third, stock companies authorized to write employers' liability in New York were permitted to transact compensation business. Fourth, the law not only permitted but encouraged the formation of mutual companies by groups of New York employers to provide compensation insurance.

Before enactment of the law, the only mutual company writing casualty insurance in New York was the American Mutual Liability Insurance Company, of Boston. To stimulate the organization of domestic mutuals and to give them an opportunity to become established under favorable circumstances, the New York statute prohibited mutual companies from other states from writing workmen's compensation insurance in New York for a period of three years after the law became effective.

Under the law, a domestic mutual could be formed by an association of thirteen employers who, after taking the necessary legal steps, secured applications for insurance from a minimum of forty employers who together employed no less than twenty-five hundred workers. "The theory upon which mutual companies are to establish and gain public favor is that they will enable the employer to secure insurance at actual cost," a publication issued by the New York Insurance Department in 1914 observed. The publication, designed to acquaint employers with mutual principles and practices, further remarked: "Mutual associations of employers are perhaps in a better position to enforce rules for prevention of accidents than any other corporate body of insurers. The personal interest in reducing the number of accidents and the cost of compensation should manifest itself to a greater extent in such associations banded together for mutual protection than in any other form of corporate insurance."

Between March 16, 1914, when the Workmen's Compensation Law was enacted, and July 1, 1914, when it became effective, fifteen mutual companies were founded by New York businessmen to provide themselves with compensation insurance.[1] With very few exceptions, the original companies were formed by employers in a particular business or industry, and their names—Bakers Mutual, Lumber Mutual, Printers and Bookbinders Mutual, Brewers Mutual—were frequently indicative of the fields they served. Of the companies founded to operate in more than one industry, the most successful was organized by a group of prominent manufacturers in upstate New York and called the Utica Mutual Insurance Company. Managed since its founding by John L. Train, a well-known executive who has been a lead-

[1]In addition, the American Mutual Compensation Insurance Company, which was organized by interests identified with the American Mutual Liability Company, of Boston, was licensed to write compensation insurance in New York on March 9, 1914. At the expiration of the three-year period during which foreign mutuals were banned from operating in New York, the American Mutual Compensation Insurance Company was absorbed by its parent organization.

ing advocate of mutual insurance, the Utica Mutual is now the largest domestic mutual casualty company in New York.

The mutual companies, the State Fund, and the stock companies were all ready to go by July 1, 1914. Shortly before that, the competitive situation had been outlined by Mr. Leon S. Senior, who was then an official of the New York State Insurance Department and who later became manager of the Compensation Insurance Rating Board, in an address before representatives of the insurance industry. "The State is about to enter upon a new experiment," Mr. Senior said. "It will establish an insurance fund in competition with private companies. It will have certain advantages over private insurance. The employer will be released from individual liability to his workmen, and the fund will have a subsidy from the State in the way of administrative expenses for the first two and one half years. It remains for you gentlemen to demonstrate whether, in spite of these advantages, private insurance is superior to state insurance. The race will soon begin. We in the Insurance Department, as impartial spectators, will watch with keen interest, and with best wishes to all participants, the result of this contest."

Starting from scratch, the mutual casualty companies got off to a good start and soon secured a strong foothold in the compensation field. In 1915, their combined premium writings in that class totaled $1.3 million. In 1920, they reached $9.6 million. Meanwhile, three of the original sixteen companies had dropped out of the race. They were small companies, none of which had written premiums exceeding $50,000 in any year. Each of the three liquidated companies paid all its claims in full.

By 1924, six other New York mutual companies had been formed to write workmen's compensation insurance; half of these were so-called trade mutuals, having been organized to specialize in particular industries. That the mutual companies were making a good record is indicated by the praise given them by the superintendent of insurance in his annual report covering the year 1924. "Mutual insurance in relation to the older lines of insurance has been an unquestionable success," the report stated. "Since the latter companies have been permitted to organize, viz., since July 1, 1914, no companies of this kind have failed to pay their policy obligations in full, and many of them are showing remarkable growth with dividend distribution, resulting in lower cost to policyholders."

The tribute was earned. Behind it lay a decade of constant struggle. From the beginning, the mutual companies were up against the tough competition of the well-entrenched stock casualty companies. Foxy underwriters and indefatigable propagandists, they harried the mutuals on a wide front. One of their most popular, and entertaining, charges was that the mutual insurance business was in the hands of Bolsheviks. "The average citizen does not detect the Red danger that lurks in mutual insurance," the president of one of the largest stock casualty companies said in winding up an address before a convention of insurance agents in 1920. "You field men, however, not only know it but you also have the greatest possible opportunity to kill it. And I want to attend the funeral."

The facts were sufficient to deal with the stock companies' propaganda. A much more ominous threat came from the pressure groups that were determined to give the State Fund a monopoly in the writing of workmen's compensation insurance. This design was fostered partly by certain labor elements and partly by extreme left-wing political groups. The campaign to make the writing of workmen's compensation insurance a state monopoly antedated passage of the compensation law. Meeting with no success then, its sponsors had continued to press their cause vigorously and without interruption. In 1923, they succeeded in having introduced into the New York legislature a bill entitled "An Act to amend the Workmen's Compensation Law in relation to insurance carriers." Translated, that meant the creation of a monopolistic state fund. It also meant that private insurance in New York was about to go on trial.

The thirteen domestic mutuals and the six mutuals of other states that were then writing compensation insurance in New York selected John L. Train, general manager of the Utica Mutual, to present their case. Mr. Train had the right qualifications for the job. A lawyer, he had been admitted to the Bar in 1904, the year he graduated from Syracuse University, and had worked from 1905 until 1914 in the New York Insurance Department, starting as a clerk and winding up as assistant chief examiner. Having then spent nine years managing the Utica Mutual, he knew his subject.

In a comprehensive six-thousand-word memorandum replete with facts and figures, Mr. Train laid the case for private insurance, particularly mutual insurance, before the members of the legislature. His approach was down-to-earth. In considering the adoption of a system of state monopolistic insurance, he said, the legislators should determine on the basis of actual results whether such a system would be "better for the employees, better for the employers, and better for the public."

Looking at the subject first from the employees' viewpoint, Mr. Train pointed out that one sound way to measure the service rendered them by the three principal forms of insurance was to examine the loss ratios of the three respective carriers. The lower the loss ratio, he explained, the larger is the share of the premium available for expenditure on accident prevention. Thus, employees benefit most from the insurance system that operates with the lowest loss ratio. On the basis of the first seven years' experience in New York, the records showed that the ratio of losses incurred to premiums earned was 61 per cent in the State Fund; 58 per cent in the stock companies; and 51 per cent in the mutual companies. Continuing, Mr. Train observed that the prompt payment of claims is also of the highest importance to employees. The records of the mutual companies showed that in 80 per cent of all compensable cases the first payment was made within thirty days after the accident. "We invite comparison of that record with the records of the state insurance fund in the State of New York or any monopolistic state fund anywhere," Mr. Train said.

Turning to consider the interest of employers, he observed that they were apparently being well served by mutual insurance, since 95 per cent of those who insured in mutual companies in the beginning were still insured in them. This would indicate that employers had not found the State Fund to be more economical, as its advocates maintained. Nor did the figures offer proof of real economy. They showed, the memorandum acknowledged, that the combined loss and expense ratio of the mutual companies was 2.7 per cent more than that of the State Fund. But nearly 2 per cent of the mutual companies' expense was represented by taxes, and as the memorandum added, with emphasis, "THE STATE FUND PAYS NO TAXES." Furthermore, the expense figures of the mutual companies included the money they spent on accident prevention, on maintaining a high standard of efficiency in handling claims, and on providing other services, all of which were evidently regarded as superior by employers.

Perhaps the best way to test the employers' preference, Mr. Train went on, was to see which carriers were increasing their business. Since workmen's compensation legislation became effective, the mutual companies had increased their business every year, and they were the only insurance carriers that had. In the period between 1914 and 1921, the New York workmen's compensation business of the stock companies had decreased 10 per cent; the business of the State Fund had fallen 3 per cent; but the business of the mutual companies had increased 12 per cent.

The public has a real stake in the cost of compensation insurance, Mr. Train reminded the legislators, since the employer adds the charge for his compensation insurance to the cost of his product. In this connection, it was pointed out that all the expenses of the State Fund, amounting to more than $360,000, were paid by the taxpayers during the Fund's first two years. The memorandum also reported that the mutual companies, in their first seven years, had returned to their policyholders in New York savings in the form of dividends amounting to $7.2 million. Furthermore, the public has an enormous interest in the prevention of accidents to industrial workers. Preventing accidents reduces suffering and economic waste, some portion of which must be borne by the general taxpayer. "It follows, therefore," Mr. Train stated, "that the general public is interested in seeing that there should be competition as to service by various insurance carriers, especially in accident prevention, since each carrier is thus endeavoring to excel not only in reducing suffering, but also in preventing the consequent loss. The results shown by past experience prove conclusively that the state insurance fund has not equaled the other carriers in accident prevention and reduction of losses."

Woven throughout Mr. Train's report was the underlying theme that no single form of insurance—state, mutual, or stock—should be forced upon employers. All forms should be offered in the market place. Employers should not be compelled to buy one kind or the other. In buying insurance, as in all other phases of conducting their business, they should have a choice. "If the employers of this state," the memorandum observed near its conclusion, "as a result of the actual facts and experience of the past eight and one half years, are not convinced of the advantage of mutual insurance, we do not believe in compelling them by legislation to insure under the mutual system or any other system. We believe that employers are entitled to their own opinions, and that in the long run such system or systems will prevail by automatic selection as will best suit the needs of the employers and employees of this state."

As a result of Mr. Train's advocacy, combined with that of other segments of the insurance industry, the proposal for a monopolistic state fund was defeated in the 1923 legislative session. However, the specter of monopoly did not vanish. In every session of the legislature during the next twelve years, one or more bills proposing a monopolistic state fund were introduced and defeated.

Meanwhile, the mutual companies writing compensation insurance were growing at a quick pace. In each succeeding year, they increased their premium volume, their assets, and their surplus. In 1930, their premium writings reached $13.8 million. That year also marked the beginning of the great depression, a period in which the strength and stability of mutual companies were put to their severest test. During this period, two mutual companies that had been founded in 1914 and one that had commenced business in 1920 were absorbed by the Utica Mutual. Neither the companies that were taken over nor any other mutual company defaulted on their policy obligations during the dark depression years.

That record takes on added significance when compared with the record of other insurance companies. In the years between 1927 and 1934, eighteen stock insurance companies writing workmen's compensation in New York became insolvent and were taken over by the Liquidation Bureau of the State Insurance Department. This debacle brought a renewed and widespread demand for a monopolistic state fund. A bill to give the State of New York a monopoly in the writing of workmen's compensation insurance was, as expected, introduced in the 1935 session of the legislature. The proposal now had many influential supporters, including Governor Herbert H. Lehman, whose party controlled both houses of the legislature, and Industrial Commissioner Elmer F. Andrews, who was an outspoken champion of the bill. Mr. Andrews said he favored the bill "primarily as a measure of justice to the wage-earners of this state. The most compelling reason for considering the establishment of the State Fund as an exclusive underwriter for workmen's compensation insurance is the appalling suffering that has been visited upon thousands of injured wage-earners, their families and survivors by the failure of eighteen stock companies which have been placed in liquidation by court order since June 1, 1927. Of these, three failed in 1934. These eighteen companies have a total workmen's compensation liability estimated at about $2,600,000. Approximately 6,500 claims for workmen's compensation are on file against these insolvent companies."

To meet this crisis, all segments of the insurance industry, numerous associations of businessmen, and many other groups that disapproved of the measure on principle banded together to oppose it. John L. Train was again selected to represent the mutual companies and subsequently appeared before the Senate Insurance Committee that held hearings on the proposed legislation. "When the Workmen's Compensation Law was adopted in this state," Mr. Train began, according to the minutes of the hearing, "the legislation provided that employers could place their insurance in mutual companies. Up to that time, the law in the State of New York did not permit the organization of mutual companies to write casualty insurance. These companies were then organized pursuant to that law and because of the demands of employers to be allowed to insure in companies under their own management which could furnish insurance at actual cost. After twenty-one years of representing these companies, I am proud to stand before you and say that not a single claimant or employee of an employer insured in mutual companies has ever been deprived of one cent of compensation due to the failure of any mutual company doing compensation business in the State of New York."

Mr. Train offered much other evidence in support of a privately operated insurance system to provide workmen's compensation, and also filed a memorandum in which he pointed out, among other things, that mutual companies in New York had saved their policyholders $32 million through the payment of dividends.

Though the opponents of the monopolistic bill presented a strong case before the legislature, they recognized that the bill was nevertheless almost certain to pass unless they could furnish a concrete plan to ensure the payment of workmen's compensation in the event that any company should become insolvent. Working together, representatives of the mutual and stock companies devised a plan for setting up two funds —the Mutual Security Fund and the Stock Security Fund—totaling $3 million and made up by automatic, compulsory contributions from companies writing workmen's compensation in New York. The Security Funds would guarantee the payment of claims should any insurer, mutual or stock, become insolvent. A committee composed of mutual and stock representatives presented this proposed solution to Governor Lehman. He approved. The bill setting up the Security Funds was passed by the legislature and became law. The bill proposing the monopolistic state fund died in committee.

Thus ended the long struggle to prevent a state fund monopoly, a struggle in which the mutual companies had played a leading and decisive role. Since 1935, no mutual insurer authorized to write workmen's compensation insurance in New York has become insolvent, and the Mutual Security Fund has not had to be touched. The proud boast made by John L. Train in 1935—that no claimant or employee of an employer insured in mutual companies has ever been deprived of a single penny of compensation because of the failure of a mutual company—still holds true today.

With two exceptions, all the New York mutuals originally organized to write workmen's compensation exclusively have since branched out to include the writing of automobile and other casualty lines. In some companies, automobile premiums have come to exceed compensation premiums. In 1949, for example, the Utica Mutual wrote $9.2 million of automobile business and $7.2 million of workmen's compensation. The Bakers Mutual and the Utilities Mutual continue to specialize in their respective industries.

Through the years the ranks of New York mutual casualty

companies have increased. In the early twenties, three companies—the Amalgamated, Empire, and Service Mutuals—were founded to write insurance on taxicabs; of these, two now write additional lines. In the late twenties, owners of apartment houses in New York City, who had been charged prohibitively high rates by stock companies for owner's, landlord's, and tenant's liability insurance, organized three mutual companies—the Consolidated Taxpayers, the Greater New York Taxpayers, and the Security Mutuals—to specialize in this coverage; two of these have since extended their business to include workmen's compensation, automobile and other casualty lines.

Since 1935, only two mutual casualty companies (and one mutual fire insurance company) have been formed in the State of New York. Though many reasons account for the paucity of new mutual companies, the principal one stems from the stringent financial and other requirements imposed by the New York law. These requirements, in the opinion of the mutual companies already in the field, are excessively rigid. Far from favoring them, the existing mutuals have suggested legislation to relax the requirements sufficiently to encourage the formation of new companies.

The two New York casualty companies that have been founded in recent years were organized for particular purposes. The first, the Ideal Mutual Insurance Company, began business in 1944 with a surplus of $800,000 contributed by the National Dairy Products Corporation. Except for assigned risks, all the company's policies cover the interests of National Dairy and its various operating companies.

In 1945, the Atlantic Mutual Indemnity Company was organized by interests associated with the Atlantic Mutual Insurance Company in order to provide the parent organization with facilities for writing casualty lines. Following the enactment of multiple-line legislation in New York in 1949, Atlantic Indemnity merged with Atlantic Mutual, which is distinguished not only by the fact that it is the only ocean marine company operating on the mutual plan but also by the fact that it is one of the largest and most venerable ocean marine companies in the United States.

Founded in New York City in 1842, the Atlantic Mutual Insurance Company prospered from the start. One of its founders as well as its first president, Walter Restored Jones, and his successor and nephew, John Divine Jones, together directed the company's destinies during its first fifty-three years. Throughout this period, the Atlantic Mutual returned a dividend averaging more than 30 per cent in every year but one. That was in 1853, following a year in which maritime disasters were, according to a contemporary record, "greater than any previous year in the commercial history of the world." Since then, the company has never failed to declare a dividend. Up to the close of 1950, the Atlantic Mutual, upon completing its one hundred and eighth year of business, had returned to its policyholders dividends exceeding $136 million.

In its operations in the ocean marine field, the Atlantic Mutual has had to deal with special perils in war and peace. In 1863, its losses caused by the depredations of Confederate raiders amounted to $818,296; its total losses from this cause during the Civil War were slightly more than double that figure. Dividends throughout the war years nevertheless averaged 37 per cent.

A few years after the war, the Atlantic Mutual issued a policy for $3,400 on freight aboard the brigantine *Mary Celeste,* which sailed from New York on November 7, 1872, for Genoa, Italy, with a cargo consisting of 1,700 barrels of alcohol. The vessel was under the command of Captain Benjamin S. Briggs, who took with him on the voyage his wife and two-year-old daughter. On December 4, twenty-seven days after the *Mary Celeste* set sail, she was discovered at sea out of control and with not a soul on board. The disappearance of the entire ship's company, leaving not a single clue to their fate, is one of the most haunting of all the unfathomed mysteries of the sea.

Though most of the $5,556,820 of insurance on the *Titanic* was carried by European underwriters, the Atlantic Mutual had $100,000 of coverage on the ill-fated ship when it went down in 1912 with a loss of 1,517 lives. In 1950, the company had at least two rather unusual losses at sea. One of the ships it insured was dented by a shark; another was damaged when it ran into a whale.

Fifty years ago, the Atlantic Mutual's business was exclusively marine insurance, and its staff numbered sixty people. Today the company, with some 860 employees, writes almost all forms of insurance except life. Ocean marine continues to account for an impressive share of its business. The combined net premium writings of the Atlantic Mutual and its affiliate, the Centennial Insurance Company, reached $20.7 million in 1950; of the total, $8.9 million came from ocean marine. With assets of $40 million and a surplus of $4.5 million, the Atlantic Mutual has fulfilled the promise of its first president, Walter Restored Jones, who said in 1853 that it had been and would continue to be his desire "to conduct the company so as to satisfy the expectations of all reasonable men and so that all those friends who feel any particular interest in it may be proud of it."

At present, there are eighteen mutual casualty companies

domiciled in New York. Their combined assets in 1949 exceeded $120 million and their combined surplus stood at $28.7 million. That year, their combined premiums reached $65.1 million, and they paid dividends to their policyholders of $7.3 million.

Having survived ruthless competition, the perils of depression, and the threat of a state monopoly, mutual casualty insurance is today an indispensable fixture in the economy of New York. It has saved employers scores of millions of dollars. More intangible but even more praiseworthy has been the notable contribution of the New York mutuals in accident prevention and the promotion of industrial safety. The number of lives and limbs saved in industry through the work of their engineering departments and their safety programs cannot be calculated, but the actual reduction in the number of industrial fatalities is on the record. In New York, the fatality rate per 100,000 workers has dropped 50 per cent since 1924. By contrast, it has dropped only 30 per cent in Ohio. The mutual companies think it is significant that workmen's compensation insurance in Ohio is written by a monopolistic state fund.

CHAPTER XIX

Enter the Automobile

IN 1898, two hundred automobiles were manufactured in the United States. One of the noisy little contrivances was purchased by a physician in Buffalo, New York. The doctor, being adventurous but not reckless, applied to the Travelers Insurance Company for insurance to protect himself against liability for damage that might be done by his horseless carriage to the person or property of others. The Travelers obliged by issuing a policy on a teams' form, previously used to protect owners of horse-drawn vehicles. With the issuance of that policy—the first automobile policy written in the world—thc automobile entered the realm of underwriting.

Then in the experimental stage, the automobile made phenomenal advances during the next decade. In 1900, twelve manufacturing companies turned out 4,000 vehicles. Ten years later, there were sixty-nine firms engaged in making automobiles, and their combined annual output had soared to 181,000 cars. Meanwhile, advances were being made in automobile insurance. In addition to the liability coverage, fire insurance was now being offered on the machines themselves. Fire coverage was especially important in the early days because of the frequency with which the gas tanks blew up. Owners of early steam cars also frequently carried boiler insurance to protect themselves against the explosion hazard.

Theft insurance was of less importance. Because the early machines were such conspicuous commodities, they did not appeal to the light-fingered gentry. By 1919, however, cars were being stolen at the rate of thirty a month. That year, the Ford Motor Company, which had been started in 1903 with a capital of $28,000, turned out more than 800,000 units of the doughty Model T. In 1920, the eighty-four firms that then made up the automotive industry manufactured 1,906,000 cars. Their purchase was facilitated by the installment plan of buying, which had been introduced shortly after World War I, and their use was made increasingly attractive by a gigantic program of road improvement. A curiosity at the turn of the century, the automobile in twenty years had become a commonplace in American life.

So had automobile insurance. As early as 1907, a mutual company to provide fire and theft coverage on automobiles was founded in Providence, Rhode Island. Called the Automobile Mutual Insurance Company of America, it was organized by a group of Rhode Island businessmen and began operations by insuring only selected risks. At the end of its first year, the company returned a dividend of 25 per cent. The dividend rate was gradually increased until it had doubled by 1916, and it remains at 50 per cent today.

In 1921, the Automobile Mutual sponsored the organization of the Factory Mutual Liability Insurance Company of America as a companion carrier to write automobile liability coverage. Though residence, general liability, and burglary insurance were added in 1938, the company confines its operations mainly to the automobile field, in which it has been notably successful. Since its founding, it has annually paid dividends of not less than 25 per cent.

Both companies are under the same management and both have adhered strictly to the practice of insuring only preferred risks, such as business executives, lawyers, doctors, clergymen, and other persons who are regarded as especially desirable from the insurance standpoint. Business is obtained through direct writing–by mail–neither agents nor salesmen being employed. Losses and expenses have remained consistently low, and both companies have grown steadily. At the close of 1950, their combined assets totaled $31.1 million, and surplus had grown to $20.6 million. In that year, premium writings of the two companies amounted to $9.5 million, while dividends returned to policyholders exceeded $3 million.

By the close of 1921, Ford jokes had become established in American folklore and more than ten million cars of all kinds were on American roads. The general-writing mutual fire companies were doing a brisk business in providing fire and theft coverage on automobiles. The mutual casualty companies that had been formed to write workmen's compensation insurance were surveying the automobile field with keen interest, and many were preparing to revise their charters in order to provide liability coverage. In addition, several mutual casualty companies were brought into existence during this period to specialize in the automobile line. One of the first and most successful of these was the State Farm Mutual Automobile Insurance Company, of Bloomington, Illinois.

The story of the State Farm Mutual, which now writes the largest volume of full-coverage automobile insurance in the United States, is essentially the story of George Jacob

Mecherle, a farmer who became an underwriter in his middle age. The son of a German immigrant, Mecherle was born on a farm near Bloomington, Illinois, in 1877. He was the fifth of six children. His mother, who had been born in Ohio, had been a schoolteacher before her marriage. She began young George's education at home, after which he attended a public school near the farm. At the age of thirteen he passed an examination entitling him to a teacher's certificate. He taught school for a short time, studied for a term at Illinois State Normal College, and then returned to work on his father's farm. He was a big, strong young man, over six feet tall, a hard worker and ambitious.

In 1899, when he was twenty-two, Mecherle rented a farm of his own in the vicinity of Bloomington. Two years later, he was married and began raising a family. Mecherle was successful as a farmer. Within a few years he had bought and paid for his place and made many improvements on it. A gregarious young man and much respected by his neighbors, he was elected a member of the local school board as well as the township's road commissioner. He was also elected a director of the Old Town Mutual Fire Insurance Company.

After twenty years of farming, Mecherle retired. He was then forty-two and estimated to be worth a quarter of a million dollars. His decision to leave the farm was prompted by the illness of his wife, who had become afflicted with arthritis. At the suggestion of her doctors, the family moved to Florida. The climate failed to improve her health, and Mecherle, with no work to do, was restless. After about a year in Florida, they returned to Illinois and rented a house in a small town adjacent to Bloomington.

For a while Mecherle sold insurance for a small local company, and it quickly developed that he was a born salesman.

Brown Brothers

A DEATH TRAP IN NEW YORK CITY

n March 25, 1911, the Triangle Waist Company, which occupied the top three oors of this ten-story loft building, suffered a disastrous fire in which 147 employees, mostly women and girls, lost their lives. Almost no provision had been ade for fighting fire. Hole at bottom of shaft was made by bodies of employees ho hopelessly jumped to escape the blaze. The disaster not only brought about veeping reforms in building laws but sped the enactment of workmen's compention legislation in New York.

Brown Brother

GET A HORSE!

Sometimes owners of the newfangled contraptions had to follow the jeering advice. The photograph above was made near Saginaw, Michigan, in 1904. By that time about 75,000 cars were in operation in the United States, and the automobile had entered the realm of underwriting. The automotive industry, which was destined to change the life of the nation, had far-reaching effects on the insurance industry as well.

In one week he earned as much as $1,500 in commissions. The company, however, had a habit of haggling over every claim, and this practice irked Mecherle so much that he quit his job. He then went to work selling tractors. Within a year he had set a new sales record, his annual commissions amounting to $25,000.

As a tractor salesman, driving about the countryside in his Model T and calling on farmers, Mecherle conceived the idea of forming what he called a "different kind of insurance company" to provide farmers with automobile insurance at reasonable rates. The farmers he called upon had little or no automobile insurance. The larger stock companies were charging high premiums based on city experience, and these rates farmers could not and would not pay. Many of the smaller companies were unreliable. The time was 1921, when farm income and the prices of farmland had declined to severely low levels. In the preceding boom years, however, farmers had been among the large purchasers of automobiles, and the hard-road program in rural areas was rapidly developing. In Illinois, Mecherle's home state, a governor was elected on a platform that included the straightforward plank—"Pull the Farmer out of the Mud." The time was propitious, Mecherle believed, for forming an insurance organization to specialize in furnishing coverage on farm automobiles.

Mecherle's ideas for "a different kind of insurance company" were radical for those times. He visualized a company that would issue a so-called continuous policy—that is, one that would be written for the life of the risk, like a life insurance policy, and not have to be renewed every year or so. This scheme, Mecherle felt, would result in a twofold saving: first, it would do away with the annual expense of renewing the policy; second, it would eliminate the necessity of paying the agent a full commission, amounting to some 25 per cent of the premium, year after year. Agents, Mecherle believed, should spend their time mainly on producing new business.

The company that Mecherle conceived of would issue policies for a six months' term rather than a year. From the customer's point of view, this would make the insurance easier to pay for, half as much cash being required twice a year. From the company's point of view, the six months' term would give management the advantage of being able to review its experience semi-annually and to relate its premium rates to current costs.

Upon taking out a policy, according to Mecherle's plan, a policyholder would pay a membership fee, which would entitle him to insure an automobile at net cost thereafter, as long as the company wrote that kind of insurance and the policyholder remained a good risk. The membership fee would be paid but once.

To effect further economies, Mecherle planned that the writing of all policies, the making of all collections, and the handling of all correspondence would be done at a central office. This would relieve the agent of those duties, thus enabling him to keep down his overhead costs and to devote his time to selling.

Finally, Mecherle planned to offer a new kind of collision insurance. Instead of the orthodox collision coverage with a deductible clause requiring the policyholder to pay the first $50 or $100 of damage, Mecherle thought up the "80-20" collision policy. Under this scheme, the company would pay 80 per cent of all damage from the first dollar and the policyholder would pay 20 per cent. This co-insurance feature,

Mecherle believed, would encourage policyholders to keep repair costs at a minimum.

Fundamentally an idea man rather than an underwriter, Mecherle read up on insurance at the public library in an effort to work out the means for translating his scheme into practical form. He also talked about it incessantly to insurance men, farmers, businessmen in Bloomington, and just about anyone else who would listen. "George became sort of a pest in those days," one of his friends has recalled. "You couldn't get through a game of cards or a street-corner conversation without his bringing up this insurance idea. Why, it got so we used to duck around corners when we saw him coming."

Though his friends tried to discourage him, Mecherle could not be dissuaded. On February 1, 1922, he attended the state convention of the Illinois Association of Farm Mutual Insurance Companies in Streator, Illinois, and presented his plan to the delegates. He pointed out that since the farm mutual companies did not sell automobile insurance their agents could add to their income by taking on the additional line that would be offered by his projected company. The delegates approved of Mecherle's idea and gave it their unanimous endorsement.

With that encouragement, Mecherle decided to go ahead with organizational plans at once. He also decided that the time had come to seek some expert legal and technical advice. He accordingly went to Chicago to consult with the firm of Ekern, Meyers & Janisch, well-known insurance counselors. On his first visit, Mecherle talked with the head of the firm, Mr. Ekern, a former insurance commissioner of Wisconsin and one of the country's outstanding insurance lawyers. After listening for a while, Ekern, who was vastly unimpressed by

Mecherle's notions, eased him out of the office by suggesting that he give the matter more thought and come back at some later date.

Exactly one week later, Mecherle returned and again asked for Mr. Ekern. This time Ekern called in his associate, Mr. Meyers, and asked him, as Meyers has recalled, to please see "that downstate farmer with the crazy insurance scheme and get rid of him." Meyers decided that the best way to dismiss the persistent farmer once and for all would be to request a large retainer fee. Accordingly, after Mecherle had outlined his scheme, Meyers said that the firm would be pleased to study the matter, the initial fee for which would be one thousand dollars. Mecherle said that would be all right, wrote a check, and departed, promising to return in a week to see how they were doing. Astonished, Meyers called the Bloomington bank on which the check was drawn to see if it was good. From then on Meyers worked very closely with Mecherle, helping him to implement his ideas and to devise workable solutions to problems that arose in the ensuing years. He has remained in continuous and intimate association with the company. Mecherle's check, incidentally, was never cashed; it is still in the files of the firm.

On March 29, 1922, the articles of association of the State Farm Mutual Automobile Insurance Company were approved by the state authorities. The necessary incorporators had been obtained from the ranks of the county farm mutual organizations. As a sentimental gesture, Mecherle chose his forty-fifth birthday, June 7, 1922, as the date for the official launching of the company. On that day the first policy was issued to Henry B. Stubblefield of Bloomington, the owner of a 1919 six-cylinder Hudson sedan. The policy provided liability and property damage, fire and theft, and movable-objects collision coverage. On June 8, the incorporators held their first official meeting and elected a board of directors. They in turn negotiated a contract engaging Mecherle as general manager of the corporation and then elected him president. To provide the company with operating funds, Mecherle and one of the other incorporators loaned the firm $4,000 on a note.

Before the company was a month old, Mecherle found that he needed someone in Bloomington to handle the legal end of the business, and accordingly retained a young attorney named A. H. Rust. As time passed, Rust was drawn into many other phases of the company's affairs. In 1937, he was elected executive vice-president, and Mecherle thereafter gradually delegated to him more and more executive responsibility, limiting his own activities to major policy decisions. An officer of the company, describing the respective roles played by the triumvirate that shaped the State Farm Mutual, once said, "Mecherle supplied the genius, Meyers the know-how, and Rust the stabilizing influence."

During the first several months, Mecherle was not only the president and general manager but also the entire agency force, office force, and claims department. He operated out of a small office furnished with a secondhand desk and a converted packing case. Mecherle sold insurance the way he sold tractors, driving up and down the country roads, calling on farmers and converting them not only to insurance but to his kind of insurance. By the end of 1922, after having been in business for less than six months, the company had 1,300 policies in force. Net premiums and fees amounted to $23,734; the company had assets of $27,444 and a surplus of $7,758. Better offices were engaged, a girl was hired to keep books, and the first agent was put on the staff.

Practically all of the business written during the first year was personally handled by Mecherle, in some cases with the assistance of agents of the county mutual fire insurance companies. Mecherle enjoyed teaching the agents how to sell. One day, accompanied by an agent, he wheeled into a farmyard and, hearing sounds of activity coming from a hog pen, walked over to investigate. The farmer and his son were trying to ring a bunch of hogs. Mecherle leaned over the fence and offered some advice. "If you know so much about it, don't stand there and talk," the farmer said. "Get in here and lend a hand." Mecherle rolled up his sleeves, vaulted into the pen, and went to work. After finishing the job, he washed himself at the pump and sold the farmer a policy on his car.

"We went out that afternoon and we bowled them over," Mecherle once recalled in speaking of another day's work. "I put the pen in one fellow's hand four times before I got his signature. I had a nice fountain pen that this fellow had in his hand three times, and then he put it down on the application. I accidentally tipped the application and the pen rolled off, so he had to catch it. I said, 'Sign it now,' and he signed it. In about three weeks he had a loss, and I was certainly glad that I used quite a little pressure to get that signature."

In 1923, the State Farm Mutual's net premiums reached $95,000, and the following year $155,000. Up to that point, the company had operated only in Illinois. In 1925, the Indiana Farm Bureau Federation, seeking to represent State Farm Mutual in Indiana, asked the company to expand operations to their state. The matter was seriously debated by the directors. Mecherle was all for expansion, but some of the directors opposed the move. Those who disagreed with the majority decision resigned. In April 1925, State Farm was licensed in Indiana; later in the same year it was licensed in

Missouri and South Dakota. Within ten years it was operating in thirty-three states. Today the company does business in forty states, the District of Columbia, and the province of Ontario.

The growth of the State Farm Mutual has been continuous and remarkable. Assets doubled every year for the first seven years. With the exception of a slight dip in premiums in 1932, net premiums, assets, and surplus have moved steadily upward. Since 1934, annual premium volume has doubled every five years. And since 1941, the State Farm Mutual has written each year the largest volume of full-coverage automobile insurance of any company in the United States. In 1950, the company's net premiums amounted to $92.6 million, and membership fees to $5.3 million. Thus, the State Farm Mutual received in that year from its policyholders a total of $97.9 million.

After the automobile company had become well established, Mecherle organized two companion carriers—the State Farm Life Insurance Company and the State Farm Fire and Casualty Company. Except for directors' qualifying shares, the outstanding stock of both subsidiary companies ($300,000 in the life company and $1 million in the fire and casualty company) is wholly owned by the State Farm Mutual. In 1950, the life company's insurance in force amounted to $399.5 million; net premiums written that year by the fire and casualty company totaled $3.3 million.

With minor modifications, the State Farm Mutual's present method of operation is the same as that originally visualized by its founder. Today, as in the beginning, the company's business is limited almost exclusively to the insurance of automobiles. Of its 1950 premium volume, 98.8 per cent was derived from automobile insurance, 0.4 from general liability, and 0.8 from reinsurance from the fire and casualty company. Following the original scheme, most of the automobile insurance is written on family cars rather than on commercial vehicles, and the company still concentrates on rural rather than city business. Of its 1950 premium volume, 62 per cent was written in rural areas or in towns with a population of less than ten thousand.

Being "a different kind of insurance company," the State Farm Mutual has always compiled its own rate schedules, based on its own loss experience, and its policies have never paid dividends, except in the few states where rates are legally fixed. Dividends are "anticipated" by the State Farm Mutual in setting its premium rates, which tend to be lower than prevailing standard rates. A membership fee is collected when the policy is written, and all policy writing, correspondence, and renewals are handled by the central office. The State Farm Mutual's business is written entirely by agents, a force now numbering about 6,500, who represent only State Farm companies.

In March 1951, George J. Mecherle died at the age of seventy-four. He was then chairman of the board, a position he had occupied since 1937, when his eldest son, Raymond P. Mecherle, was elected president of the State Farm Mutual and another son, George E. Mecherle, was elected secretary of the company. The founder lived to see the novel idea that he had conceived three decades earlier develop into an outstanding insurance organization with assets of $148 million and a surplus exceeding $61 million. The day the State Farm Mutual issued its first policy, a friend asked Mecherle how many more he thought he could sell. "Well," Mecherle replied, "I guess if I can sell one policy I can sell a million." At the close of 1950, three months before Mecherle's death, the State Farm Mutual's policyholders numbered 1,810,794.

In 1925, at about the same time that the Indiana Farm Bureau Federation invited the State Farm Mutual to extend its operations into Indiana, the Ohio Farm Bureau Federation also requested Mecherle's company to begin writing in the Buckeye State. Mecherle was willing, but the Ohio insurance commissioner was not. As a result, the Ohio Farm Bureau Federation, determined to furnish its members with comparable low-cost automobile insurance, went ahead and organized its own company. Created in the image of its Illinois godparent, the Farm Bureau Mutual Automobile Insurance Company, of Columbus, Ohio, has been a spectacular success. It began business in 1926. Its net premiums in 1950 reached $55.8 million in addition to membership fees of $2.9 million.

The Farm Bureau Mutual was brought into being largely through the efforts of two dedicated men. One was an Ohio farmer known to practically everybody as Uncle George Cooley. The other was Murray D. Lincoln, who was born on a farm in Massachusetts and spent his early adult life working with farm organizations. Neither had had any training in insurance, but both had had plenty of experience in helping farmers solve problems through mutual undertakings. Uncle George has been described as a man who "combined vision with horse sense." Though he had worked at various times as a schoolteacher, a general contractor, and a federal highway engineer, his primary interest had always been farming. He organized the first farm bureau in Cuyahoga County, and when the Ohio Farm Bureau was organized in 1919, he was one of its original trustees.

During the Bureau's early days, Uncle George met Murray Lincoln, who had recently arrived in Cleveland. At the behest of Myron T. Herrick, a former governor of Ohio and for many years United States Ambassador to France, Lincoln had moved West to become an agricultural agent for the Society for Savings, a Cleveland bank of which Herrick was president. Lincoln was then twenty-five. After graduating from Massachusetts Agricultural College in 1914, he had become the first county agent in Connecticut and in 1916 had organized one of the first co-operative milk-distributing plants in New England. Three years after his arrival in Cleveland, he was invited by the directors of the new Ohio Farm Bureau Federation to become its executive secretary. He accepted, and the Federation began its development into one of the outstanding organizations of its kind in the country.

When toward the close of 1925 the Federation decided to sponsor the formation of an automobile insurance company, funds to pay its organizational expenses were advanced by the Federation, which also put up $35,000 to provide the new company with its initial assets. (This sum was returned with interest in 1930.) To secure a license, it was necessary to obtain one hundred pledged policies. To be on the safe side, the officers decided to obtain ten times the minimum number.

Leading farmers in each county bureau worked without pay to muster the thousand initial applications; this task was completed by the spring of 1926. Murray Lincoln was named secretary-treasurer of the new company, retaining his post as executive secretary of the Federation. (The latter position he continued to hold until 1948). On April 26, 1926, the Farm Bureau Mutual received its license, and two days later issued its first policy. Success was immediate. By December 31, 1926, the company had assets of $114,100.

Two years after commencing business, the company was

asked by farm bureaus or similar organizations in Vermont, Delaware, West Virginia, North Carolina, and Maryland to extend its operations into those states. In 1929, the company began writing in Pennsylvania and Virginia under similar sponsorship, later enlarging its territory to include New York, the District of Columbia, Connecticut, Rhode Island, and South Carolina. In seven of the twelve states in which it now operates, the Farm Bureau Mutual is the leading writer of automobile insurance. In Vermont, the company insures one car out of every five. Specializing during the first five years in the farm field, the company began in 1931 to write in towns and in 1934 in cities. At present, approximately 65 per cent of its business is written in urban areas. The company has not, however, lost its essentially grass-roots character. All but two of its present board of sixteen directors are farmers.

Now, as in the past, the Farm Bureau Mutual collects a membership fee at the beginning of the policy term ($12.50 for full coverage), issues policies for a six months' term, and performs many of the routine functions, such as the collection of renewal premiums, from the home office. Business is written by a force of some three thousand agents. The company is at present in the process of decentralizing its operations by setting up regional offices in various cities. By 1954, it expects to have established about eighteen regional headquarters, each of which is intended to be a virtually complete and self-sufficient unit for sales, customer accounting, and claims handling.

Though the charter of the Farm Bureau Mutual was revised in 1931 to permit the writing of almost all casualty lines, automobile insurance continues to provide the predominant share of the business. Of the company's $55.8 million premium income in 1950, approximately 90 per cent was derived from automobile coverage. The second largest line, accounting for $1.5 million in premiums, was workmen's compensation, written primarily in rural areas. After twenty-four years of remarkable and almost uninterrupted growth, the Farm Bureau Mutual, at the close of 1950, had assets of $58.8 million and a surplus exceeding $16 million.

When the company was presented with its first claim, in May 1926, reimbursement of $25 (to cover a tire, tube, and rim stolen from one Russell Fox) was made within twenty-four hours. That established the target at which the company still shoots. In 1950, 41 per cent of all automobile claims were paid within twenty-four hours after they were reported to the claims department. The company employs its own staff of some 450 field adjusters.

On the basis of its experience, the claims department holds the opinion that people are honest. Many cases have led it to this conclusion. One involved a policyholder whose automobile was damaged by a driver who was drunk. That, the company discovered, was the driver's usual state. Furthermore, he had no insurance, no credit, no resources. Since he proved uncollectible, the company reimbursed its policyholder for the damage, which amounted to $300. Ten years later, the company received a letter from the rascally driver, who said that he had given up drinking, joined the church, and was enclosing a check to pay the old debt. The check was for $600—$300 for damage caused by the accident, the letter explained, and $300 for compound interest. The company returned the interest and congratulated him on his redemption.

In addition to co-operating with local, state, and national safety councils, the Farm Bureau Mutual conducts its own safe-driving and accident-prevention program aimed at educating the younger age groups. Members of its Safety Department have delivered a series of lectures and, using specially rigged cars, given demonstrations in more than a thousand high schools in the Eastern part of the country. The company has also campaigned for the installation of driver-training programs in secondary schools. Since, as statistics show, the most dangerous drivers are those under twenty-five, the general practice among insurance companies is to charge higher rates for drivers under twenty-five. The Farm Bureau Mutual now offers insurance at adult rates, in states where permitted, to people under twenty-five, provided they have successfully completed a state-approved driver-training course.

To provide its policyholders with fire, windstorm, and crop-hail insurance, the company sponsored the organization in 1934 of the Farm Bureau Mutual Fire Insurance Company. It began business with a guaranty fund of $325,000 contributed by the parent company. The fire company has done well. Its net premiums increased from $2.1 million in 1945 to $7.3 million in 1950. Entering still another field, the automobile company bought controlling interest in the Life Insurance Company of America in 1936. Now known as the Farm Bureau Life Insurance Company, it has more than one third billion dollars of insurance in force, and its assets exceed $31 million.

Together, the three companies had 1,762,414 policies in force at the close of 1950. Their combined assets in 1950 totaled $99 million, while their annual premium volume reached $75 million. In the matter of office space alone, the three companies have had a hard time keeping up with their runaway growth. Having outgrown three office buildings by 1948, they decided that year to erect a new one, eight stories high and containing 341,000 square feet of floor space. The building was dedicated on the automobile company's twenty-fifth anniversary in April 1951. To celebrate, the companies tossed a barbecue for ten thousand people—employees, agents, policyholders, and friends. Based on their growth during the past fifteen years, the companies figure that by 1960 they will need two and a half times as much space as they have in the new building.

Except for corporate purposes, the three companies have almost no separate identity, being managed for the most part by the same officers and directors. Murray Lincoln is the president and general manager of each company and the dominant influence in the organization. (Uncle George Cooley was president of the automobile company from 1928 until his death in 1949.) A tall, vitally energetic man in his late fifties, Lincoln has had a lifetime, all-pervading interest in helping people to help themselves by banding together. In addition to his insurance posts, he is president of the Co-operative League of the U.S.A., president of the Cooperative for American Remittances to Europe (CARE), and a consultant to the United Nations Economic and Social Council. He has served as a member of presidential advisory groups on rural electrification, farm tenancy, and higher education, and he was appointed in 1950 one of the twelve members of the mobilization policy committee, popularly known as the Symington Committee.

Under Lincoln's direction, the Farm Bureau Companies have invested in several subsidiary corporations, which, the companies believe, provide "practical investment opportunities" in addition to serving a "human need." One of these projects is the Peoples Development Company, which was established in 1948 to provide low-cost housing, initially in Bellevue, Ohio, where the National Machinery Cooperative was adding new employees faster than houses could be found for them. The Peoples Development Company has since built in Bellevue a residential community called Amsden Heights, which consists of thirty-four individually designed homes, a large public park, and a playground. All the homes have been sold.

The Farm Bureau Companies also own two radio stations —WOL in Washington, D.C., and WRFD in Worthington, Ohio. On a 260-acre tract near Worthington, the companies are at present constructing a project known as WRFD Radio Farm. Patterned after a New England community, for which Lincoln has a pronounced nostalgia, WRFD Radio Farm will include a modern studio building, homes for members of the station's staff, an overnight inn, a town hall with village green and bandstand, a general store, church, restaurant, blacksmith shop, and another structure called a theater barn. When completed, all these facilities will be made available to members of the Grange, Farm Bureaus, 4-H Clubs, Future Farmers of America, and similar groups for meetings, square dances, and other business and recreational uses.

Along with these holdings, the Farm Bureau Companies own controlling interest in an Ohio company that originated a new kind of fire-resistant building material for use in prefabricated houses, and they are contemplating, among other things, organizing a mortgage company and an automobile finance company. Though unorthodox by some standards, the manifold activities of the Farm Bureau Companies are consonant with the original principles upon which the organization was established. As expressed by the founders, one of these principles observed: "People have within their own hands the tools to fashion their own destiny."

CHAPTER XX

Of Principles and People

THE morning of April 16, 1947, dawned bright and sunny in the Gulf port town of Texas City, Texas, known to its boosters as "The Port of Opportunity." It had grown big and prosperous during the war. Strung along its water front were one hundred and twenty-five million dollars' worth of oil refineries, tin smelters, and chemical plants, including the huge installation of the Monsanto Chemical Company. Docked some seven hundred feet from the Monsanto plant was the 7,000-ton freighter S.S. *Grandcamp*. Lying next to it was the S.S. *High Flyer*. Both were partly loaded with cargoes of fertilizer-grade ammonium nitrate and were about to be loaded with more. It was 7:50 A.M. The eight o'clock shift of longshoremen was due to go to work in a few minutes, and many were hanging around the dock. One of them noticed a wisp of smoke coming out of the number-four hold of the *Grandcamp*.

The ship's crew, having been alerted, investigated and found a fire burning briskly among the closely stacked bags of ammonium nitrate fertilizer. Aided by the longshoremen, they tried to put it out but with no success. By the time the city fire department had arrived on the scene, the hold of the *Grandcamp* was in flames. Efforts to extinguish the blaze with water proved fruitless. It was then decided to try an old naval trick of battening down the hatches and flooding the hold with live steam. In this case, with chemicals involved, the procedure was to prove disastrous. By nine o'clock, some two hundred curious onlookers, attracted by the billowing black smoke, had gathered at the dock. Concerned over the possibility of explosion, the fire fighters decided to move the ship out into Galveston Bay. It was too late.

At twelve minutes after nine the *Grandcamp* blew up in a thundering roar and vanished completely. Three-hundred-pound chunks of ship's steel were blown hundreds of feet into the air. A wall of oil-covered water deluged the docks. Bodies of the people who had been standing there were strewn for half a block. Then began a rapid series of deafening explosions. The Monsanto plant and most of the rest of the water front blew up. Refineries, gasoline and oil tanks shot up like rockets. In the business section of the city, a mile away, the force of the blast wreaked crazy havoc. Rows of houses were flattened; people were blown out of second-story windows; the gas, light, and water systems were knocked out. Roofs and walls of schools, theaters, and commercial buildings were blown out or puffed in. Out of the rubble of the Texas Terminal Railway Building emerged a bedraggled man carrying ten million dollars' worth of insurance policies tied up in a bed sheet. Meanwhile, down at the docks, an inferno raged. The water front, the police said, had become "pluperfect hell." In the Monsanto plant, buildings sagged slowly down on eight hundred workers. Trucks loaded with the dead and the dying began rumbling through the streets.

As soon as he could get a telephone line, the head of the Monsanto plant at Texas City put through a call to the president of the corporation in New York. He, in turn, telephoned the home office of the Liberty Mutual Insurance Company in Boston. Liberty Mutual, the largest writer of workmen's compensation insurance in the United States, carried the compensation on the Monsanto plant. Word of the disaster reached Liberty Mutual around noon. The office moved into high gear.

At one-thirty a meeting was held in the Boston office and a plan of operation drawn up. Three groups were to depart for Texas City immediately. One was to investigate all workmen's compensation claims. The second was to be in charge of all clerical and paper work, such as processing claims and issuing checks. The third, composed of members of the legal staff, was to conduct an investigation to determine the cause of the disaster. Arrangements were made to send quantities of supplies, including forms and blanks of every variety as well as all necessary records, by air. Reservations were made by phone for ample hotel accommodations in Houston, fifty miles from Texas City, and for the hiring of a fleet of cars to transport the staff from one place to the other. Within five hours after news of the disaster reached the Liberty office, the first group of Liberty employees was on its way to Texas City by plane.

While they were en route, tragedy visited Texas City the second time. Though heat from the unquenchable fires along the water front was blistering, firemen and squads of rescue workers wearing protective clothing and gas masks had moved into the area. They were obliterated when, at one-eleven on the morning of the seventeenth, the *Grandcamp's* sister ship, the *High Flyer,* which had caught fire, exploded. Blown to bits, the ship, as one witness said, "mushroomed like the Bikini bomb." The explosion, which was recorded on a seismograph in Denver, rocked and raked Texas City again.

Additional scores of people were killed and injured. Scarcely a single structure was left that was not ruined or badly damaged. Panic-stricken residents, desperate over the possibility of further catastrophe, began a wild evacuation of the city.

At the moment of the first explosion, a claimsman from Liberty's Houston office who was driving toward Texas City heard the news on his car radio. Racing to the scene, he was able to get into the roaring, devastated city before the police lines were closed. He went into action immediately and did a great deal of useful, grim work, such as identifying bodies.

Within forty-eight hours after the *Grandcamp* exploded, Liberty Mutual had assembled a staff of some four dozen people in Texas City. Besides the home office group, twenty-six claimsmen had been recruited from Liberty offices in New York, Chicago, Kansas City, Newark, and other cities. Clerical help was hired in Galveston and Houston. When the first Liberty man arrived, the city was still blazing. Fires lasted for three days. In all, 468 people were killed; 100 were missing; and 3,000 were injured. Property loss amounted to $67 million.

As soon as the embers had cooled, Liberty established headquarters in a section of the building that Monsanto had taken over as a temporary office. Liberty shared its space with representatives of Metropolitan Life, which carried Monsanto's Group Life insurance. Putting up in hotels in Houston, the Liberty men commuted daily to Texas City. Because eating facilities there were practically non-existent, they were obliged to travel to Galveston, twelve miles away, for lunch. On the average, members of the Liberty group worked eighteen hours a day.

During the first few days, Liberty claimsmen visited every hospital between Texas City and Houston to learn the names of all Texas City victims who had been admitted and whether they were insured by Liberty. This search produced some 260 persons who subsequently brought claims for injury against Liberty Mutual. In every case where it was possible to do so, the claimsmen visited the injured person and made sure that he was receiving proper care. As tactfully as possible Liberty had several of its patients moved from one hospital to another in order to secure the doctors best qualified to treat the particular kind of injury. Burns, fractures, and, particularly, piercing injuries caused by flying glass and steel were widespread. Some of the most tragic cases were those of attractive girls whose faces had been disfigured. Fortunately, the staff of the medical school of the University of Texas, located at Galveston, included many top-notch plastic and orthopedic specialists. Liberty saw to it that they ministered, in cases where needed, to Liberty's injured.

Some of the cases classified as injured posed complex problems in fixing a fair compensation. One man became psychopathically deaf. Though experts were unable to find any physical impairment of his hearing, he swore that he couldn't hear a sound. A tough woman foreman, who had been in charge of a group of Negro laborers, was discovered after the explosion running up and down the streets completely naked, chasing people with a blanket. She never recovered her mind. Another woman employee for weeks afterward suffered from uncontrollable fits of crying and habitually dived under a table at the slightest sudden sound, such as that made by a book dropping to the floor. However, within a year or so she was able to return to work, having flatly refused in the meantime to admit that she was a compensable case.

A source of gratification to the Liberty Mutual people was the eventual remarkable recovery of many of the physically injured. A claimsman who spent twelve weeks in Texas City recalls having visited in the hospital three Monsanto employees who were in a room together. They seemed then to be hopelessly disabled. One was an engineer named Bill, whose pelvis had been shattered into fifteen fragments. The second, a worker named Jerry who had an artificial leg, had had his other one broken in three places. He nearly drowned in the Monsanto plant (several people did), but somebody got to him, unstrapped his artificial leg, and lifted him to safety. The third patient, Al, had suffered several fractures and such severe injuries to one of his legs that amputation was necessary. Two years after the tragedy, the Liberty claimsman returned to Texas City. As he walked through the rebuilt Monsanto plant he was greeted not only by Bill, Jerry, and Al, who were all back at work, but also by a great many others among the badly injured, including one man who had been so terrified by the explosion that he had run a mile and a half on a broken ankle.

Besides claims brought by the injured, 147 claims were made against Liberty by survivors of those who were killed. Each death claim had to be thoroughly investigated. About twenty were disallowed. In handling the death claims, as in all other casualty matters, the problem was liability. Since the Texas law provides compensation for injury or death of an employee "in the course of his employment," it was necessary to determine who was and who was not actually employed at the time disaster struck. This was difficult. Fortunately, Monsanto's time-clock cards, punched by all employees from office boys to executives, were recovered; though all were badly charred, some could be read with the naked eye while markings on most of the others could be made out under ultra-violet rays.

As a working rule, it was decided that if a person had checked in on the day shift he or she was presumed to have been at work. However, that rule could not be applied to four or five employees who were members of the city's volunteer fire department and who left the plant when the fire on the *Grandcamp* got out of control. Their next of kin were eligible for compensation benefits under public employee coverage carried by the city. Owing to the chemical properties of the fertilizer on board the ship, the fire was unusually spectacular, and a great many people had come down to the water front to watch. This group included many members of Monsanto's night shift, but since their deaths did not occur in the course of their employment, their claims could not be paid. Their next of kin were, however, eligible for death benefits under Monsanto's Group Life policy. In another category was the case of the unfortunate boy who was sitting at the time of the tragedy in Monsanto's employment office waiting to hear whether or not he had been hired. Because he was not then on the pay roll, his next of kin were not eligible for benefits under the compensation law. However, his family as well as the next of kin of all the Texas City victims could, and did, bring suit on the grounds of negligence against the federal government.[1]

[1]Several test cases have been heard. Total suits pending run into the neighborhood of $350 million. The test case for the casualty group, which was prepared in part by Liberty's legal staff though not involving a Liberty claimant, was decided on April 13, 1950, by the presiding judge in favor of the plaintiff on the basis of findings of fact. At this writing, the case is before the Circuit Court of Appeals.

In his summary of the decision handed down on April 13, 1950, the judge observed: "This Record discloses blunders, mistakes and acts of negligence both of omission and commission on the part of the defendant [the United States Government], its agents, servants and employees in deciding to become the manufacturer of this inherently

Further complications in settling death claims were caused by the fact that in many instances it was impossible to recover or identify bodies. Under the law, if a man cannot be proved dead, he is assumed to be alive for seven years. Therefore, in the strictest legal sense, many of the next of kin of the Texas City victims could not have received compensation benefits until some time after 1954. Liberty Mutual took the position that this was absurd hairsplitting. Taking the lead in arranging for the settlement of this category of claims, Liberty brought a test case before the Texas Industrial Accident Board, which, like other state compensation boards, must in general approve the disposition of compensation cases. In the test case, the Liberty Mutual people showed that they had traced a certain Monsanto employee to his place of work, that he had been on the job within a matter of minutes before the explosion occurred, and that, even though his

---

dangerous fertilizer. And from the beginning of its manufacture on down to and after the day of the Texas City disaster, it discloses such disregard of, and lack of care for, the safety of the public and of persons manufacturing, handling, transporting and using such fertilizer as to shock one. When all the facts in this Record are considered, one is not surprised by the Texas City disaster, i.e., that men and women, boys and girls, in and around Texas City, going about their daily tasks in their homes, on the streets, in their places of employment, etc., were suddenly and without warning killed, maimed or wounded and vast property damage done. The surprising thing is that there were not more such disasters."

Five days after the Texas City disaster, one of Liberty Mutual's staff discovered an almost exactly similar situation in Galveston. A cargo of fertilizer-grade ammonium nitrate was being loaded on a freighter bound for the Netherlands. The cargo, which had been sitting in boxcars in Texas City or headed there, had apparently been quietly rerouted around the bay. In June 1947, a few weeks after the Texas City tragedy, a ship carrying a cargo of ammonium nitrate fertilizer exploded in the harbor at Brest, France.

body could not be found, he must be presumed dead. The Accident Board approved, and Liberty and other companies were accordingly enabled legally to settle many doubtful cases.

Other complexities were encountered in handling cases in which more than one widow appeared to claim compensation or in which a woman claimed that she was a common-law wife of one of the deceased. All such claims had to be painstakingly investigated and ironed out, the problem in some instances being further complicated by the presence of two sets of children. Some restless husbands, it was suspected, chose the turbulent time following the disaster as the propitious moment to light out in the general confusion, hoping that they would be considered dead. Liberty paid on these cases, doubtfully. To ease the financial burden on all survivors, the head of Liberty's Texas City contingent, Ashley St. Clair, encouraged the lawyers of Galveston, through their local bar association, to represent the Texas City victims at very low cost in performing the necessary legal procedures.

In what may be an all-time record, considering the enormity of the disaster, the Liberty Mutual staff completed the bulk of its work in Texas City in about one month. During that time, they had handled the largest single workmen's compensation loss in the history of the country. Liberty's total incurred losses from the Texas City catastrophe, up to the close of 1950, amounted to $1,311,200. Of that, Liberty had $1 million of reinsurance. The loss figure may rise further if medical payments on certain cases are extended beyond the period contemplated.

It was with considerable satisfaction that Liberty Mutual received the following letter from the Texas Industrial Accident Board: "The Board wishes to take this opportunity to commend your company for the splendid manner in which you have and are handling the claims of the unfortunate victims of the Texas City disaster. We doubt if there is any instance on record where the victims of disaster, accident, or catastrophe of the magnitude of this one were accorded the co-operation and their claims given the prompt attention that your company has given these unfortunate people."

The performance of Liberty Mutual in Texas City was gratifying but not surprising to S. Bruce Black, who has been associated with the company for the past thirty-five years, its president for the past twenty-eight. An outstanding figure in the insurance industry, he believes that any organization is only as strong, first, as its principles and, second, as its people. Directing his own organization in accordance with this precept, he has watched Liberty Mutual grow to the point at which it is today the largest mutual casualty insurance company in the country. It ranks second among all casualty carriers—mutual and stock. As previously noted, Liberty Mutual has the distinction of writing more workmen's compensation insurance than any other American company. Its companion corporation, the Liberty Mutual Fire Insurance Company, is the country's second largest writer of mutual fire insurance. All this has been accomplished in the space of forty years.

Like many other mutual casualty companies, Liberty was originally organized to write workmen's compensation insurance exclusively. The company was especially incorporated as a part of the Workmen's Compensation Act of Massachusetts, which became law in 1912, under the name of the Massachusetts Employees Insurance Association. As first contemplated in Massachusetts, the writing of workmen's compensation insurance was intended to be a state monopoly. However, as the concept evolved, it was decided, first, to allow competition and, second, to sanction the formation of a privately operated mutual company that would write compensation insurance at cost and thus provide a means of holding down the compensation rates of the existing casualty companies. From the beginning, the Massachusetts Employees Insurance Association (MEIA) provided a yardstick to measure the cost of compensation insurance.

Following the familiar pattern, the stock companies, of which there were then twenty-three operating in Massachusetts, did all they could to drive the newcomer out of business before it could get a toe hold. MEIA met the situation aggressively. It was the first company to get its compensation rates approved and it was also the first company in the state to establish a merit rating system. "Under this system," the company announced, "the assured will receive, through percentage reductions in his premium rate, the advantage to which he is fairly entitled by reason of the superior physical condition of his plant." As a further means of meeting competition, MEIA paid dividends at the end of its first six months. These amounted to 20 per cent in heavy industry and 30 per cent in light industry.

Because competitive methods of the stock companies were becoming increasingly reckless, a recess commission of the Massachusetts legislature was appointed in 1914 to investigate "rates and practices of insurance companies and whether monopoly exists." It did, according to the findings of the commission. "It is clear," the commission's report stated, "that many of the stock companies entered into an improper agreement, giving one man full authority to change compensation rates in Massachusetts alone for competitive purposes—a situation which is indefensible." One result of the investigation was the establishment in 1915 of a compensation rating bureau, in which both the mutual and stock companies had equal representation.

At every turn MEIA made it plain that it intended to give the stock companies a very brisk and interesting contest, under whatever rules they chose to play. It never missed an opportunity to publicize a comparison between its rates and those of the stock companies and to point out that, while MEIA's costs were going steadily down, stock company costs were going steadily up. For example, on the ratio of expenses to earned premium, MEIA boasted 22.5 per cent for 1913, 16.5 per cent for 1914, and 14.8 per cent for 1915. This compared with 36.3 per cent for the stock companies during that period. The wide difference lay in acquisition costs. From the beginning, MEIA (and Liberty) has been a direct selling company.

All in all, the company's first five years showed steady progress. Premium writings in 1917 amounted to $2,434,027—a fourfold increase in five years. The company's charter had been amended to allow it to write coverages other than compensation (and thus break into the burgeoning automobile liability field) and to do business outside of Massachusetts. Branch offices had been opened in New York City, Pittsburgh, Philadelphia, and other cities. The company had made reinsurance agreements with Lloyds, enabling it to write large risks. Its loss ratio during the 1912–17 period averaged 48 per cent, compared with 70 per cent for the stock companies. In 1917, the company had 106 employees. Its name, now outgrown, was changed that year to Liberty Mutual. And at the end of its first five years, the company was the largest writer of compensation insurance in Massachusetts.

At the root of the company's success, then as now, lay its devotion to the principle of loss prevention. Liberty's activities in this field will be treated later. In addition to the company's principles, there were its people. The first president of the company was Wallace Donham, who was then vice-president of the Old Colony Trust Company, of Boston, and later for many years dean of the Harvard Business School. He served as president until 1914, when he became chairman of the board, a post he held for many years. His successor as president was Walter S. Bucklin, who, as executive vice-president, had from the start been the active chief executive officer of the company.

A talented organizer, Bucklin pushed the expansion of the company into new territories and new lines. Immaculately turned out, he was known among his subordinates as a man with a passion for neatness and detail, personally as well as professionally. He made it a rule that no office employee could wear a mustache, though that adornment was then popular, and he issued a general memorandum, followed by frequent reminders, that no one could have anything on his desk except the blotter, pen and ink, and the work immediately at hand. He had great enthusiasm for the company, was extremely ambitious for it, and drove hard for business. He once arranged for all the men in the office, including himself, to write a sales letter to interest new prospects. Each man was to send his own letter to a certain number of prospective clients, and the letter pulling the most responses, Bucklin said, would be adopted for general use by the company. He spent several days composing his own entry. After results of the test mailings were in, Bucklin was somewhat dismayed to find that his and all the other letters had been outpulled more than two to one by a brisk communication written by one of the younger staff members. The winning letter read in full: "Dear Sir: Would you be willing to tell us when your workmen's compensation policy expires, so that we can come out and try to sell you some insurance?"

Above all, Bucklin displayed the ability to surround himself with able young men. Most of the original staff were in their twenties. Thirty was considered old. One of the senior vice-presidents today went to work for the company in 1912, another in 1913. Seven other men hired in the early years became vice-presidents. Bucklin's talent for recruiting bright young men resulted in building an organization composed of people who were scrappy as a unit and competitive against each other. It also often resulted in the company's writing more daringly, though actually more cannily, than some of the older companies. Liberty, for example, went in more heavily for writing compensation in the New York subway field than any other company. It came through successfully because it put permanent safety engineers on the job, a notion that would have occurred to few other insurance companies of that day.

One of the young men hired by Bucklin in the early years was S. Bruce Black, a rising Boston insurance executive. Born in Fort Atkinson, Wisconsin, Black attended Ripon College before transferring to the University of Wisconsin, where he took his degree. After graduating, he passed a civil service examination for a job with the State Industrial Commission, and was hired as an assistant statistician. The head of the Commission was Dr. E. H. Downey, who was known as the greatest expert in the country in the workmen's compensation field.

In the summer of 1915, Dr. Downey was asked by Charles Edward Hodges, president of the American Mutual, of Boston, to recommend a suitable man to strengthen American's compensation department. Dr. Downey presented the opportunity to Black and to another young member of the Commission's staff, W. E. Burhop, who was, and is, Black's close friend. Burhop, who is now executive vice-president of Employers Mutual, decided to remain in Wisconsin. Black went East. He remained at American Mutual until the summer of 1917, when Walter S. Bucklin invited him over to Liberty's offices one afternoon and offered him the position of treasurer. Black accepted, became vice-president two years later, and general manager in 1923. The following year, Bucklin resigned to join the National Shawmut Bank of Boston, of which he is now president, and Black was elected to the presidency of Liberty Mutual.

In the following years the company expanded with tremendous rapidity. It began writing general liability insurance in 1924. A fidelity department was established in 1925. In 1926, Liberty took over the business of the Gopher Mutual Casualty Company of St. Paul, Minnesota, thereby acquiring considerable compensation business in that area. Automobile premiums meanwhile kept pace. By 1927, they accounted for 21 per cent of Liberty's total premiums. By 1928, the company had forty-two branch offices. In 1930, Liberty's total premium writings amounted to more than $18 million.

Then came the depression. In 1932, the company's premium writings dropped to slightly more than $15 million. All companies writing compensation insurance suffered during that period; Liberty's method of dealing with the situation differed from that of most. Whereas the general tendency was to pull out of compensation or to cut down on it sharply, Liberty went out and sold all the compensation it could, figuring that pay rolls sooner or later were bound to pick up. By the late thirties, when the depression was over, Liberty's position in relation to other casualty companies had changed enormously. In 1928, Liberty had ranked sixth among all companies, both stock and mutual, in the writing of compensation insurance; in 1936, Liberty ranked first. In the writing of all casualty lines, Liberty had ranked eighteenth among all companies in 1928; in 1936, Liberty ranked third. Its total premium writings that year amounted to $34 million, nearly double the volume for 1928. And it has not stopped growing since.

In 1950, Liberty's total premium writings exceeded $137 million. Workmen's compensation accounted for $71 million, and automobile for $41 million. Of the five general casualty lines, workmen's compensation was one and a half times all the others put together. The largest proportionate gain in recent years has been in the writing of accident and health insurance. In the three-year period beginning with 1948, Liberty's accident and health premiums more than doubled. This coverage in 1950 produced $9.3 million in premiums.

One reason for the general boom in accident and health insurance is that the benefits it provides are increasingly being tied into union contracts. Because of its extensive cultivation of the industrial field through its compensation writings, Liberty Mutual is in a convenient position to handle this new business. Experience in the accident and health line is not, however, all beer and skittles. Not long ago Liberty received a claim under a policy that had been in force for little more than a month. It covered a man, his wife and seven children, all of whom had had their tonsils out on the same day.

Back of Liberty's underwriting is its research department, launched many years ago by S. Bruce Black and developed since into a unique unit whose work underlies both the company's current operations and future plans. The research department conducts a continuing study of insurance in general and of Liberty Mutual in particular. Among the department's many functions is the collection and analysis of statistics bearing on all aspects of casualty underwriting. It may, for example, set itself to discover where loss ratios are higher than they should be. It may find that loss experience, compensation-wise, in hotels is good (Liberty salesmen should therefore go after that kind of business), or it may discover that rates in this or that category are not adequate. In addition, the department constantly studies where Liberty is being crowded by competitors and in what lines Liberty is crowding its competition. The purpose of this intensive self-analysis, one of the company's executives has said, "is to show where management stands, and why." Under the heading of pure research the department prepares studies of disability and compensation schemes in effect in various parts of the world and also develops long-range general business forecasts with particular emphasis on the probable effect that developing economic and social trends will have on the insurance industry in the years ahead.

To keep the company abreast of present conditions and to assist in its top-level planning, operations, and decisions, Liberty maintains a large group of Advisory Boards, composed of leading industrial figures. The first Advisory Board was formed in 1919 in Pennsylvania. There are now nineteen of them, located in states from Massachusetts to California; in addition to the state boards, there is one industry board—the Motor Transport Advisory Board. Each of the twenty boards, whose members are all Liberty Mutual policyholders, performs the consultative functions of a board of directors. They meet at regular intervals, are paid directors' fees, and discuss the conduct of Liberty's affairs in their respective

Wide World

MONSANTO CHEMICAL PLANT AT TEXAS CITY

On April 16, 1947, a cargo of fertilizer-grade ammonium nitrate in the hold of the freighter *Grandcamp* exploded at the docks at Texas City, Texas. In the resulting holocaust at the Monsanto works, which was an innocent bystander, 147 employees were killed and 260 injured. Within forty-eight hours after the explosion, the Liberty Mutual Insurance Company, which carries Monsanto's workmen's compensation insurance, had assembled a large staff at Texas City to secure medical aid for the injured and to make financial compensation to the survivors of those who were killed. The Texas City disaster resulted in the largest single workmen's compensation loss in the history of the country.

FRANKLIN THE FIREMAN

The first volunteer fire-fighting organization in Philadelphia, the Union Fire Company, was founded by Benjamin Franklin in 1736. After his death the Union commemorated its founder by decorating its hand pumper with the above likeness. The original is in the collection of the Insurance Company of North America and is reprinted with the North America's kind permission.

states or regions. Among other things, they check on Liberty service, including the handling of claims and the performance of loss-prevention activities, keep a watch on the insurance situation in the local legislatures, and, when possible, steer business Liberty's way. Being in close touch with local conditions, they often are aware of new situations developing on the horizon before they become generally visible.

The Advisory Boards, to which Liberty assigns great importance, are under the general management of Clark E. Woodward, a senior vice-president who went to work for the company as a bookkeeper in 1912. He had previously been employed by General Electric and went to work for Liberty at a 50 per cent increase in salary, or from $8 to $12 a week. He has had a notably wide range of experience during his forty years with the company. Liberty's other senior vice-president, Oscar Simmons, joined the company in 1913. A financial expert during business hours, Simmons is a military historian during his leisure. He has the third largest collection of lead soldiers in the world. (The largest belongs to an English peer, the second to an elderly gentleman in Maine.) Simmons's collection of the armies of the world, by regiment, is nearly complete. His particular interest is the Napoleonic era, and he has the troops to fight the Battle of Waterloo on the living-room rug.

In its claims work, as the Texas City episode demonstrated, Liberty Mutual is second to none. At the outset, the company recognized that the proper handling of claims would be of the first importance. Unlike many companies, which delegated their claims work to independent adjusters whose ethics were sometimes questionable, Liberty immediately organized its own staff of salaried claimsmen. The department was formed in 1912 by a lawyer named John Cronin, who came to the company from the legal staff of the Boston Elevated. He headed the department for five years, after which he became the company's general counsel, a post he held until his death in 1943.

After Cronin moved up, the claims department was taken over and built into its present form by Colonel Percy H. Titus, a military figure of the Kentucky variety. A horse lover and a dog breeder and fancier, Titus took over the claims department in 1917, was made a vice-president ten years later and rendered the company yeoman service until his death in 1947. Titus operated on the principle that the way to get a good claimsman is to catch him young and treat him rough. He did all the hiring himself and habitually opened the interview by announcing cordially, "I hire only one man out of fifty." Titus had a strong preference for college graduates. Since 1919, Liberty has employed in its claims department, which today numbers more than 1,000 technical personnel, only young men fresh out of college.

As a means of developing incentive and spirit, Titus initiated the practice, still in effect, of making promotions only from within the department. He asked a great deal of his men. "If the Colonel called you in on Friday afternoon and said, 'I want you to start work Monday morning in Atlanta,' you did—and you got your wife and children down there later if need be," a Liberty claimsman who worked under Titus for many years has recalled.

The Colonel felt that he had a right to expect peak performance from his men because he originated the practice, still followed, of paying them well. The reason for this was ethics. Titus was well aware that the path of the claimsman is strewed with temptation, that opportunities to add to his income by becoming a party to dubious deals are seldom lacking. Titus was a bear for honesty and fair dealing. Partly because of the philosophy he implanted, no man in Liberty has ever got a raise for settling a $1,000 claim for $150.

The settlement of claims in the casualty field is a highly complicated business. By comparison, casualty men feel, the settlement of fire losses is mere child's play. Casualty claims are rendered intricate because of the third-party aspects and the difficulty of determining who is ultimately responsible for the damage or injury incurred. For example, a workman unloading a flatcar of telegraph poles in Iowa was killed when the binding around them broke. Liberty did not carry workmen's compensation on the workman, but it did carry the public liability insurance on the lumber mill in Mississippi that made and shipped the poles. The company carrying the compensation paid the benefits due the workman's family but was able to prove that the poles had been improperly loaded. It was thus able to recover its loss from Liberty, whose policyholder was shown to have been negligent and therefore ultimately liable.

On a New York construction job, a plumber insured by Liberty got hit on the head by a brick dropped by a workman insured by another company. Liberty paid compensation benefits to the plumber, and then by subrogation went after the company that insured the workman who dropped the brick, their grounds being that his negligence caused the accident. The other company refused to make what Liberty considered a reasonable offer. Liberty accordingly took the case to court and won considerably more than it had originally asked. A driver for a parcel-delivery company, whose public liability Liberty insures, once, upon finding nobody at home to receive a package, decided to leave it in the garage. There was a dog in the garage, and it happened to be a thoroughbred bitch in season. When the driver opened the door, the dog got away. Liberty paid the difference between the value of a litter of thoroughbreds and a litter of mongrels.

The life of a Liberty claimsman, by no means all routine in peacetime, can become both exciting and dangerous in wartime. In World War I, though then a small company with, as one of the executives has remarked, "more nerve than britches to cover its backside," Liberty participated in writing workmen's compensation in the Hog Island shipbuilding venture. In World War II, Liberty did more defense business, with one possible exception, than any other casualty company. With no possible exceptions, Liberty did more overseas business. During the war, the government engaged private contractors to construct bases and other installations in all parts of the world—North Africa, Eritrea, Somaliland, Ethiopia, and throughout the Pacific. Liberty carried the workmen's compensation insurance on a great many of these projects.

Since injuries on such jobs are inevitable, the construction company's crews were accompanied by a Liberty claimsman and usually by one or more loss-prevention engineers, who lived on the job. One Liberty claimsman was captured with the marines on Wake Island, and two of the company's engineers were captured in the Philippines. After the Japanese had taken some twelve hundred men off Wake Island, the government asked Liberty to settle the various cases and decide to whom indemnity should be paid. This did not prove easy, mainly because so many of the men were blessed with several wives scattered around the country. Trying to get at the truth called for wisdom that might have taxed even King

Solomon, that venerable pioneer in the art of handling a harem.

"Your Directors have from the beginning recognized that the prevention of industrial accidents is more important than any other phase of the work upon which they are engaged." So stated the first annual report issued by Liberty Mutual, in 1912. Ever since, the prevention of loss has continued to be Liberty Mutual's primary concern.

Today the Loss Prevention Department, which is under the direction of Vice-President William H. Seymour, has a total technical force of 360. In addition to 154 regular service engineers, the personnel includes 30 construction engineers, 18 elevator inspectors, 16 motor transport engineers, 16 fleet engineers, 8 industrial hygienists, 4 doctors and 20 nurses, 18 men who specialize in servicing small plants, and more than six dozen supervisors and members of the home office force.

Organizationally, the department is decentralized. Attached to each of the company's division offices, of which there are seven, is a division manager in charge of loss prevention. His staff consists of a group of supervisors and a force of engineers. In addition, the home office force of the department has a staff of consultants, headed by four assistant vice-presidents, who handle special research problems and other projects requiring extensive facilities and sustained study. In its organization and in the scope of its operation, the department is unique in the casualty insurance world.

As an over-all term to describe its loss-prevention program, Liberty has coined the word "Humanics," which the company defines in general terms as "the science of saving through safeguarding human values." In specific terms, Humanics is a co-ordinated program of five branches—industrial engineering, industrial hygiene, industrial preventive medicine, claims medical service, and rehabilitation. Together, they make up a rounded effort to keep people from being hurt, to help them return to work if they are injured, and to restore them to usefulness if they are seriously crippled.

Industrial engineering is the oldest, best-known, and most widely practiced activity in the prevention of loss. It has many sides. Guarding machines and establishing safe operating methods are two of the most important. For example, a company that manufactures textile machinery was plagued by a dangerous operation that required an operator's hand, in the performance of a single process, to pass eight times in close proximity to an unguarded circular saw. Injuries were frequent. A Liberty field engineer studied the problem and sent a detailed description of the operation, together with a series of photographs, to the home office. Within ten days, Liberty engineers designed and sent to the plant the model for a jig, or holding fixture, the use of which simplified the process, eliminated bringing the operator's hand close to the saw, and made the operation safe.

Industrial engineering also includes arranging machinery in the safest possible pattern, setting up standards for maintenance and good housekeeping, and cutting down the physical effort required to handle materials. If a man is fatigued by his job, the chances of his being injured increase. It frequently develops that an easier and safer method of doing a job is also a more efficient way. For a plant in Arkansas a Liberty field engineer was able to design a piece of machinery called a mechanical feed and double-end trim saw, which not only increased the safety factor but also enabled the operator to perform in two hours a volume of work that had formerly taken eight.

Since the early twenties, Liberty Mutual has been a leader

in writing compensation on big-scale construction projects and has consequently made many contributions to industrial engineering in that field. At present, the company is writing compensation insurance on the workmen constructing a twenty-seven-mile-long tunnel that is being blasted through graywacke stone to extend the New York City water system. To prevent accidents on this job, Liberty built an engineering laboratory on the construction site. Using a variety of instruments, some of which are set in the tunnel roof, Liberty engineers keep a constant check on the forces developing in the rock and are thus able to determine what sections might fall. To protect the workers from other hazards, rock-dust samples and samples of gas present in the tunnel after blasting are regularly analyzed. All these activities are designed not only to safeguard the workmen on this particular project but also to add to Liberty's accumulated lore on tunnel construction —and ultimately to reduce insurance costs for contractors.

The same principle underlies Liberty's approach to industrial hygiene, the second branch of Humanics. The aim of industrial hygiene is to create a safe, comfortable place to work. Originally, the emphasis was primarily on safety. Liberty's first major undertaking in the field of industrial hygiene, begun some twenty years ago, was directed toward detecting and reducing the exposures that bring on silicosis. Turning to other respiratory ailments caused by occupational conditions, the company extended its research into the effects of exposure to lead, benzol, and carbon tetrachloride. Investigation was also launched into substances causing skin poisonings. These inquiries were spurred by the increasing use of chemicals in industry, and by the fact that compensation laws were being steadily widened in the early thirties to include benefits for occupational diseases. To keep pace with technical developments, Liberty Mutual established in the home office a fully staffed laboratory devoted exclusively to research in the chemical aspects of industrial hygiene.

The ascendancy of labor in recent years has been accompanied by demands for improvements in environmental working conditions, such as the reduction of noise and the elimination of disagreeable odors. Satisfying these demands is a relatively new aspect of industrial hygiene, which promises to absorb an increasing share of attention in the years immediately ahead.

Fitting the right man to the job, or adjusting the job to the man, is the goal of industrial preventive medicine—the third, and newest, branch of Humanics. Liberty Mutual works to reach this goal by helping plants to develop or improve their own medical departments, staffed by full-time or part-time doctors and nurses. Many plants, especially the larger ones, already have such facilities. But as a rule they have concentrated their efforts on dealing with the injury *after* it has happened. Liberty believes that a properly organized and well-run plant medical department can prevent the injury altogether.

Liberty Mutual's industrial preventive medicine program was started in 1943, under a special unit within the Loss Prevention Department. At present, the medical unit consists of seven full-time and four part-time doctors, in addition to twenty nurses. Their function is to survey a policyholder's plant and to assist in the installation or improvement of its medical facilities. Depending on individual circumstances, a plant medical department may range in size from a small installation employing a part-time nurse to a fully equipped clinic staffed by several nurses and a full-time doctor. In many cases, absenteeism has dropped as much as 50 per cent after the introduction of good medical programs, and lost time because of accidents has been reduced as much as 80 per cent.

As in all other aspects of loss prevention, Liberty Mutual has had to demonstrate the value of industrial preventive medicine in dollars and cents. It has many such exhibits. For example, a small plant in Massachusetts hired a nurse to spend two hours a day as a health consultant, at an annual cost of $1,000. During the first year that this modest program was in effect, the plant's compensation losses were $4,700 less than the year before, a reduction that brought a substantial saving in the cost of the company's insurance. In Maine, a textile plant with a force of 3,200 employees installed a medical department, staffed by a doctor and Liberty-trained nurses, at an annual cost of $27,000. In its retrospective rating credits, the plant has made a saving of $55,000.

Unfortunately, in spite of all enlightened loss-prevention activities, people still get hurt at work. When a worker insured by Liberty Mutual is injured, the company's claims medical service—the fourth branch of Humanics—goes into operation. How that service is performed has been seen in part in connection with the Texas City disaster. In ordinary circumstances, injured employees insured by Liberty are treated by doctors of their own choice. In addition, the company has developed a unique medical adviser system, composed of thirty-three eminent specialists in thirty-two of the country's principal industrial cities. These specialists are available for consultation on all cases that do not respond readily to treatment. Frequently they recommend specialized surgery or treatment. In one instance, a man had suffered a broken leg, and because it failed to knit, amputation seemed necessary. However, the case was referred to two of Liberty's medical advisers, one in Chicago, the other in Boston. Both recommended a difficult bone-grafting operation. It was successful, and the man's leg was saved.

The fifth and final branch of Humanics is rehabilitation. A comparatively new concept, rehabilitation is the process of restoring an injured person to self-reliance and to a useful place in the world. Until recent times, workers covered by compensation insurance who suffered severe injuries, such as a broken back or an amputation, received expert medical care and economic support, but little or nothing more. As a consequence, such persons usually remained invalids for life. During World War II, great progress was made in devising treatment and techniques to help the badly injured overcome the effects of their injury and readjust to society. It was Liberty Mutual's belief that many of the company's serious cases could be improved, and some sufficiently restored to be able to resume work, if facilities were developed for giving them proper treatment. After considerable research, Liberty decided to set up such an establishment. That decision bore fruit in 1943 with the opening, in Boston, of the Rehabilitation Center—the first tangible acknowledgment of a newly glimpsed social responsibility.

Occupying three floors of an office building, the Center has a full-time staff of sixteen and a consulting staff of four physicians, all of whom are specialists. Space and facilities permit the treatment of between fifty and sixty patients at a time, and the establishment is generally in use to its full capacity. In the beginning, only so-called general injury cases, such as fractures, were treated. Encouraged by its initial success, the Center began admitting patients who had suffered amputations. Up to 1950, it had provided treatment to 152 amputees. Of these, 75 per cent returned to work.

Since 1947, Liberty has undertaken the rehabilitation of paraplegic patients at the Center. Thirty paraplegics have so far been treated. Of these, fourteen have been sufficiently restored to be able to resume work. Many of the remaining sixteen have been improved to the point where they are relatively self-sufficient and are able to live at home without attendants.

Up to the close of 1950, the Center had provided treatment to 1,912 cases, of which 85 per cent were improved thereby. Two thirds of the patients thus benefited have returned to work. Decidedly encouraged by these results, Liberty Mutual recently opened a second Rehabilitation Center. The new one is in Chicago.

Since its founding nearly forty years ago, Liberty Mutual has hewed continuously to one fundamental and dynamic principle: to reduce the cost of insurance through the prevention of loss. One measure of its success in carrying that principle into practice can be found in a single set of statistics. Between 1936 and 1951, Liberty's average of fatalities per 100,000 workers was lower than the national average by an over-all figure of 14.6 per cent.

In the light of newly developed techniques and knowledge, Liberty sees no limit to the potentialities of reducing accidents. It scoffs at suggestions that the reduction of industrial accidents may have reached a plateau and that the current rate of injury and death must be accepted with a degree of resignation. In common with other mutual companies, Liberty is dedicated to the proposition that accidents in practically every category can be prevented. Liberty Mutual has no time for fatalism.

CHAPTER XXI

After Two Centuries

BACK in 1773, Benjamin Franklin, the founder of American insurance, expressed a wish. "Having a very ardent desire to see and observe the state of America a hundred years hence," he wrote, "I should prefer, to any ordinary death, the being immersed in a cask of Madeira wine, with a few friends, till that time to be recalled to life by the solar warmth of my dear country."

Franklin, who was nothing if not practical, had the earthly materials needed to make this wish come true. His wine cellar at that time inventoried 1,040 bottles, including a goodly share of his favorite Madeira. He had another quality that would have served him well had he been able to arrange for his recall to life in the nineteenth century or in the twentieth. To a most uncommon degree, Franklin possessed the happy faculty of being at home in any society. Were he to set himself down anywhere in America today, he would feel at home. And, with his insatiable curiosity, he would be interested, among other things, to see and observe the state of mutual insurance.

Two centuries have now passed since Franklin and some of his public-spirited friends established the first successful insurance company in America—the Philadelphia Contributionship for the Insurance of Houses from Loss by Fire. Its principal founder would be gratified to see how it has prospered. The Contributionship has not only remained continuously in business for two hundred years—an extraordinary achievement in itself—but it is today one of the strongest insurance institutions in the world.

During Franklin's lifetime, America's second insurance organization, the Mutual Assurance Company for Insuring Houses from Loss by Fire, was founded in Philadelphia. Beginning business 168 years ago, the Mutual Assurance Company has also become one of the sturdiest and most venerable insurance organizations anywhere.

Besides the original pioneers, scores of other companies have demonstrated, through their remarkable longevity, the enduring vitality of the mutual idea. At present, there are 108 mutual fire insurance companies that have been in business for more than a century.

As a thorough believer in the mutual principle, in all aspects of human endeavor, Franklin would be pleased to see that mutual insurance has become an integral part of American life. Infinitely adaptable, the mutual idea has been steadily extended during the past two hundred years to provide protection not only to householders but also to factory owners, farmers, grain dealers, and to every other branch of the business and industrial community. More often than not, mutual insurance was the pioneer, furnishing security to areas in which lack of insurance at reasonable cost was a bar to progress.

Even Franklin, whose faith in what could be accomplished by co-operative effort was practically unlimited, could scarcely fail to be impressed by the mammoth structure that has been built on the groundwork he laid down two centuries ago. In the United States today, 2,410 mutual fire insurance companies are doing business. In 1950, their total insurance in force reached the staggering figure of $142 billion.

Though mutual fire insurance has grown steadily since 1752, its expansion in the twentieth century has been phenomenal. In 1900, the total premiums of all mutual fire insurance companies amounted to $19 million. In 1950, they exceeded $502 million. That year, the combined assets of mutual fire insurance companies were in excess of $1 billion, and their surplus was $562 million. The savings they returned to policyholders in dividends amounted to more than $88 million.

The growth of mutual casualty insurance since the turn of the century has been even more phenomenal. In 1900, mutual casualty premiums stood at $403,000. In 1950, they exceeded $907 million. The 204 mutual casualty companies doing business in 1950 had combined assets that year of $1.3 billion and a combined surplus of $352 million. Their 1950 dividends to policyholders amounted to $93.7 million. An additional saving of a great many more millions of dollars was returned to policyholders of mutual fire and casualty companies that "anticipate" dividends in setting their rates, which are therefore lower than so-called standard rates.

Mutual insurance, which was successfully in operation twenty-four years before Franklin affixed his signature to the Declaration of Independence, has prospered because it is founded on the principle that positive and aggressive action can prevent losses. The dynamic application of that principle has brought about far-reaching changes in the philosophy and conduct of the entire insurance industry. The result has been not only to provide policyholders in mutual companies with insurance at cost but also, through the effects of competition, to reduce costs for all buyers of insurance.

Like the nation it serves, mutual insurance began with an idea. The growth of one has been the growth of the other. After two centuries, they stand on the threshold of a new era that is as promising as it is challenging. They can face it with confidence, for all their past acclaims their future.

Index